RELIGION AND THE SOCIAL SCIENCES

Program in Judaic Studies
Brown University
BROWN STUDIES IN RELGION
Edited by
JACOB NEUSNER,
ERNEST S. FRERICHS
CALVIN GOLDSCHEIDER
WILLIAM SCOTT GREEN
Consulting Editors

M. David Eckel, Harvard University (Buddhism)
John L. Esposito, College of the Holy Cross (Islam)
Ernest S. Frerichs, Brown University (Ancient Israel; Ancient Near East)
Karen E. Fields, University of Rochester (Sociology of Religion; Religion in Africa)
Elizabeth Fox-Genovese, Emory University (Feminist Study of Religion)
Calvin Goldscheider, Brown University (Social Study of Religion)
Jacob Neusner, Brown University (Judaism)
William Scott Green, University of Rochester (Judaism; Theory of Religion)
Ray L. Hart, University of Montana (Philosophy of Religion; Theology)
Hans H. Penner, Dartmouth College (Theory of Religion; Hinduism)
Jonathan Z. Smith, University of Chicago (Theory of Religion; Religion in the
Greco-Roman World)
Leonard I. Sweet, United Methodist Seminary (Religion in America;
History of Christianity)
Mark C. Taylor, Williams College (Theory of Interpretation)

The new series will publish monographs on the academic study of religion in the
areas represented by the editors. Proposals for submission should go to the senior
editors, c/o Program in Judaic Studies, Brown University, Providence, RI 02912-
1826.

Number 03
RELIGION AND THE SOCIAL SCIENCES

by
Robert A. Segal

RELIGION AND THE SOCIAL SCIENCES
Essays on the Confrontation

by
Robert A. Segal

Scholars Press
Atlanta, Georgia

RELIGION AND THE SOCIAL SCIENCES
Essays on the Confrontation

© 1989
Brown University

Library of Congress Cataloging in Publication Data

Segal, Robert Alan
  Religion and the social sciences : essays on the confrontation / by
Robert A. Segal.
  p. cm. -- (Brown studies in religion ; no.3)
  Reprint of essays originally published in various journals from
1976-1987.
Includes index.
ISBN 1-55540-295-X (alk. paper)
1. Religion--Study and teaching. 2. Social sciences--Religious
aspects. 3. Religion and sociology. I. Title. II. Series.
BL41.S42 1989
291.1'75--dc19   88-31162
                                                          CIP

Printed in the United States of America
on acid-free paper

To Alice

Contents

Introduction

The title of this book is somewhat misleading. The confrontation that, I contend, exists is not between *religion* and the social sciences. It is between *religious studies* and the social sciences. Indeed, the chief objection lodged in the book is to the identification of religion with religious studies. By "religion" I mean the object of study. By "religious studies" I mean the study of religion by persons in both departments of religious studies and seminaries – persons I call "religionists." By "religious studies" I most certainly do not mean the entire study of religion. On the contrary, the assertion that social scientists study psychology, sociology, or anthropology *rather than* religion evinces the dogmatism I oppose.

Religious studies, I contend, continues to be dominated, though not quite monopolized, by persons committed to the defense of religion. Against philosophy and the natural sciences religionists defend the *truth* of religion. Against the social sciences religionists likewise defend the truth but more distinctively defend the *religiosity* of religion: they defend an irreducibly religious analysis of the origin, the function, and by some definitions the meaning of religion.

The religionist rejoinder to the social scientific challenge takes disparate, not always consistent, forms: the denial that the social sciences deal at all with religion; the denial that the social sciences deal with the heart of religion; the denial that religion can be explained; the claim that religion can only be interpreted; the claim, or assumption, that an interpretation of religion is necessarily irreducibly religious; the claim that the social sciences have come round either to explaining religion the way religionists do or else to interpreting rather than explaining religion; and the claim that the issue of truth is beyond the social scientific ken.

In a few of the essays I consider some of these responses, none of which I find compelling. I consider more of them in forthcoming reviews of J. Samuel Preus' *Explaining Religion* (New Haven, Conn.: Yale University Press, 1987) in *Religion* and *Religious Studies Review*. In the present book I focus instead on the challenge itself posed by the social sciences. Some of the essays simply present cases of the social scientific approach. Others contrast that approach to the religionist one. Still others argue for the social scientific one.

The elucidation of actual religions is doubtless the ultimate payoff of social scientific theories, but the analysis of theories ought not be limited to their applicability. False theories may work remarkably well when applied, sometimes even better than true theories. Among other criteria, the presuppositions and implications of theories must also be assessed.

For example, to apply Carl Jung's theory to a myth is to commit oneself not only to a psychological reading of a text – what in one sense of the term gets called an "interpretation" – but also to a whole psychology – what at times gets labeled an "explanation." It is to claim not merely that archetypal patterns are present in the myth but, more, that they are present in the myth because they are present in the mind. The justification for that bold claim is, or should be, more than that the myth makes admirable sense *when* Jungian tenets are assumed. Lamentably, few religionists evaluate theories beyond their applicability.

Similarly, few religionists evaluate at all the ramifications of theories. If one accepts Jung's theory, then religion, on at least its empirical side, becomes an entirely psychological enterprise. Religion may be a most beneficial psychological phenomenon, but a psychological phenomenon it nevertheless is. I am amazed at religionists who fancy that because Jung praises religion, he is not reducing it to psychology, to which I, for my part, scarcely object.

All thirteen of the essays collected here were originally published in journals in religious studies. I have revamped all of them. The first three essays consider the views of Mircea Eliade, whom I deem the epitome of religionists. Admittedly, by no means all religionists are as uncompromisingly committed to the irreducibility of religion as he, but his insistence that religion is more or even other than an amalgam of secular dimensions garners the support of most religionists. In these three essays I make two claims: that Eliade systematically fails to prove that the origin, function, and meaning of religion are irreducibly religious, and that his theory presupposes the reality of the sacred.

In the fourth essay I argue that, contrary to the optimism of many religionists, the social sciences have not at long last adopted the religionist point of view. Even those social scientists most enamored of religion – Peter Berger, Clifford Geertz, Robert Bellah, Mary Douglas, Victor Turner, and Erik Erikson – still regard it as merely an efficacious means to a secular end. In the fifth essay I argue the same about the ambiguous Erikson in particular.

In the sixth essay, as in several forthcoming essays, I consider the most fundamental issue in the social sciences: whether the social sciences parallel the natural sciences or the humanities. Are the social sciences explanatory or interpretive? is the way the question is often put. I note the stake religionists have in the answer.

In the seventh essay I argue that, contrary to typical religionist and even social scientific opinion, social scientific findings about the origin of religion may bear on the truth of religion. One cannot breezily dismiss the relevance of the social sciences to the issue of truth by invocation of the genetic fallacy. In the eighth essay I consider the same issue in the case of Jungian psychology but reach a more mixed conclusion.

In the ninth essay I assert that Fustel de Coulanges was the pioneering modern sociologist of religion. In the tenth essay I assert that the sociological study of religion has become less sociological: contemporary sociologists see religion as a more independent of society, and so of sociology, than classical ones did, though religion for "contemporaries" is never so autonomous as it is for religionists like Eliade.

In the eleventh essay I focus on the theory of Victor Turner. In the twelfth essay I widen my focus to the movement of which Turner was a leading member: symbolic anthropology. In addition to Turner I discuss Clifford Geertz, Mary Douglas, and Claude Lévi-Strauss.

In the thirteenth and final essay I discuss two issues related to the autonomy of religion: the issues of relativism and of rationality. Concentrating on Lucien Lévy-Bruhl, I summarize the reactions of social scientists to his views of primitive thought, of which primitive religion is for him the prime expression.

The essays are reprinted with permission from the following journals:

1. "In Defense of Reductionism": *Journal of the American Academy of Religion* 51 (March 1983):97-124.

2. "Are Historians of Religions Necessarily Believers?": *Religious Traditions* 10 (July 1983):71-76.

3. "Eliade's Theory of Millenarianism": *Religious Studies* 14 (June 1978): 159-73.

4. "Have the Social Sciences Been Converted?": *Journal for the Scientific Study of Religion* 24 (September 1985):321-24.

5. Review of Donald Capps, Walter H. Capps, and M. Gerald Bradford, eds., *Encounter with Erikson: Religious Studies* 17 (March 1981):121-23.

6. "Response to Blasi and Nelson": *Journal for the Scientific Study of Religion* 25 (September 1986):369-72.

7. "The Social Sciences and the Truth of Religious Belief": *Journal of the American Academy of Religion* 48 (September 1980):403-13.

8. "A Jungian View of Evil": *Zygon* 20 (March 1985):83-89.

9. "The First Sociologist of Religion: Fustel de Coulanges": *Journal for the Scientific Study of Religion* 15 (December 1976):365-68.

10. "The 'De-Sociologizing' of the Sociology of Religion": *Scottish Journal of Religious Studies* 7 (Spring 1986):5-28.

11. "Victor Turner's Theory of Ritual": *Zygon* 18 (September 1983):327-35.

12. "The Application of Symbolic Anthropology to Religions of the Greco-Roman World": *Religious Studies Review* 10 (July 1984):216-23.

13. "Relativism and Rationality in the Social Sciences": *Journal of Religion* 67 (July 1987):353-62.

For their help in revising one or more of the essays I want to thank Richard Gale, Timothy Hatcher, E. Thomas Lawson, Edwin Wallace, and Don Wiebe.

I also want to thank both Dean David Harned of the College of Arts and Sciences, Louisiana State University, and Jacob Neusner, Co-Director of the Brown University Program in Judaic Studies, for generous financial assistance in the publication of this book.

Chapter One

In Defense of Reductionism

However crude the generalization, twentieth-century analyses of cultural phenomena often differ sharply from nineteenth-century ones. Far more than their predecessors, twentieth-century anthropologists, sociologists, psychologists, historians, and philosophers seek to understand those phenomena in the participant's own terms.[1] Whether earlier scholars were less tolerant of the participant's point of view or simply less interested in it, they were not the least reluctant to analyze human beliefs and actions in their own terms rather than the participant's. Indeed, they were not averse to pronouncing those beliefs and actions harmful or false. What contemporary sociologist J. D. Y. Peel says of his nineteenth-century counterparts holds for other disciplines as well: "Early attempts to understand social phenomena were so tied to the peculiar interests of the social world of the sociologist himself, that he only tried to understand what seemed odd, deluded, perverse or unusual; and his understanding consisted in showing how the odd, deluded, etc., came to be believed, in contrast to the true and usual – what his own society believed" (Peel, 70).

By contrast, contemporary scholars typically strive to overcome their own professed biases and to accept the participant's point of view. What Mircea Eliade says of myth applies to culture generally: "For the past fifty years at least, Western scholars have approached the study of myth from a viewpoint markedly different from, let us say, that of the nineteenth century. Unlike their predecessors, who treated myth in the usual meaning of the word, that is, as 'fable,' 'invention,' 'fiction,' *they have accepted it as it was understood in the archaic societies,* where, on the contrary, 'myth' means a 'true story' and, beyond

---

[1]Some examples are symbolic anthropologists, cognitive anthropologists, symbolic interactionists, ethnomethodologists, existential and humanistic psychologists, historians of "mentalities," and Wittgensteinian philosophers. Admittedly, the generalization is crude. On the one hand behaviorism and structuralism, for example, are twentieth-century movements which conspicuously spurn grasping human phenomena in participants' own terms. On the other hand romanticism and nationalism, for example, were nineteenth-century movements which equally clearly sought to grasp human phenomena in participants' own terms.

that, a story that is a most precious possession because it is sacred, exemplary, significant" (Eliade 1968a:1 [italics added]).

It is surely not coincidental that Eliade is widely regarded as at once the leading contemporary scholar of religion and the leading defender of its irreducibility. For by its irreducibility he means the inability to analyze religion from other than the standpoint of believers themselves. According to Eliade, religion is analyzable in only religious rather than, say, psychological or sociological terms because for believers it is.[2] To be sure, not all of those who seek the believer's point of view deem it irreducibly religious. In fact, I argue elsewhere that the contemporary social scientists often considered kindred souls of Eliade because they, too, seek the participant's point of view nevertheless analyze religion nonreligiously.[3] Still, Eliade's popularity surely reflects in part the popularity of the quest for the participant's point of view.

The Believer's Point of View

By the believer's point of view Eliade seemingly means a believer's conscious, or professed, view of the origin, function, or meaning of religion. Yet actually Eliade goes beyond the believer's conscious view, which is more the concern of Wilfred Cantwell Smith.[4] To begin with, Eliade does not hesitate to discuss dead religions, whose adherents are scarcely available for consultation. Moreover, his chief source of information for living and dead religions alike is not informants themselves but their sacred texts.

More important, Eliade exceeds and even violates the conscious views of many believers: in regarding the sacred phenomena of all religions as manifestations of an impersonal sacred realm over and above all gods; in deeming the exclusive aim of all religions proximity to that realm; and in considering the specific sacred phenomena of individual religions mere instances of universal religious categories – for example, seeing a specific tree as a sheer case of the Cosmic Tree.[5] Surely many believers postulate no impersonal sacred realm beyond all gods, deem the aim of religion more or other than proximity to the sacred, and stress the distinctiveness of their particular religion.[6]

Still, in the broader sense of deeming the referent of religion transcendent, Eliade might be said to be dealing with the conscious view of believers. Against

---

[2]Since writing this essay I have come to realize that Eliade is *not* identifying the irreducibility of religion with its irreducibility for believers, in whom Eliade is in fact interested only secondarily. Eliade is primarily interested in the irreducibility of religion in and of itself: see Segal (n. d.).
[3]See Segal (1985a).
[4]See above all Smith (1963a; 1963b; 1975; 1979).
[5]Eliade so characterizes religion in all his writings: see esp. Eliade (1959a; 1963; 1968a; 1968b).
[6]For other criticisms of Eliade's analysis of the believer's conscious view of religion see Saliba (ch. 4) and Allen (1978:208-12).

the argument that many believers have no formulated notion of the origin, function, or even meaning of their religion, so that there is often no believer's point of view, Eliade could maintain that at least for all believers the referent of their religion is transcendent, or irreducible to human or natural terms. Against the argument that formulated views differ from believer to believer, so that there is no one believer's point of view, Eliade could maintain, again, that all believers agree on at least the transcendent referent of their religion.

Yet Eliade explicitly ventures beyond the believer's *conscious* point of view. Of religious symbols, for example, he says that "we do not have the right to conclude that the message of the symbols is confined to the meanings of which a certain number of individuals are fully conscious, even when we learn from a rigorous investigation of these individuals what they think of such and such a symbol belonging to their own tradition. Depth psychology has taught us that the symbol delivers its message and fulfils its function even when its meaning escapes awareness" (Eliade 1959b:106-7).

Furthermore, Eliade asserts that despite the widespread overt atheism of moderns, virtually all humanity is religious: "For, as we said before, nonreligious man in the pure state is a comparatively rare phenomenon, even in the most [consciously] desacralized of modern societies. The majority of the 'irreligious' still behave religiously, even though they are not aware of the fact.... [T]he modern man who feels and claims that he is nonreligious still retains a large stock of camouflaged myths and degenerated rituals" (Eliade 1968b:204-5). Eliade outright bars any exceptions: "... even the most avowedly nonreligious man still, in his deeper being, shares in a religiously oriented behavior" (Eliade 1968b:211). When, then, Eliade imputes to professed atheists a religiosity of which they are not just partly but wholly unconscious and which not just exceeds but contradicts their own conscious one, his equation of the actor's point of view with an irreducibly religious one becomes entirely arbitrary. In fact, it becomes hard to see why his analysis of the actor's point of view is any less reductive than the analyses which he opposes as reductive, though, to be sure, he ignores the nonbeliever's viewpoint rather than, in the strict sense of reduction, translates it into a religious one.[7]

An Irreducibly Religious Analysis of Religion

An irreducibly religious analysis of religion may refer to the origin, the function, or the meaning of religion. Although Eliade often asserts the irreducible religiosity of the origin and function of religion, which thus arises to satisfy a panhuman need for the sacred, he concentrates on the meaning. Of, again, religious symbols he says: "What is the meaning of this symbol? What does it *reveal*, what does it *show* as a religious symbol?" (Eliade 1959b:93). More generally, he says that "like it or not, the scholar has not finished his work

---

[7]Fenton (esp. 69-71) labels Eliade reductive on these same loose grounds.

when he has reconstructed the history of a religious form .... In addition, he must understand its meaning ..." (Eliade 1969:2). Eliade even faults past scholars for their preoccupation with the origin *rather than* the meaning of religion: "... we must not confuse the historical circumstances which make a human existence what it actually is with the fact that there is such a thing as a human existence. For the historian of religions the fact that a myth or a ritual is always historically conditioned does not explain the very existence of such a myth or ritual. In other words, the historicity of a religious experience does not tell us what a religious experience ultimately *is*" (Eliade 1969:53).[8] Contrary to his insistence elsewhere on an irreducibly religious origin, Eliade here seems to be equating the origin of religion with something nonreligious!

The difference between the meaning and the function of religion is more elusive than that between the meaning and the origin. When Eliade implores fellow religionists to focus on "what a religious experience ultimately *is*," he is referring to the irreducible religiosity of the experience. A need for the sacred may be *necessary* for an experience to be irreducibly religious, but the experience is religious only when the need gets fulfilled by the presence of the sacred. The irreducible religiosity of religious experience, for Eliade the heart of religion, thus refers to the reality of the object of religious experience: the sacred. Where, then, the *function* of religion is to enable one to experience the sacred, the *meaning* of religion is the reality of the sacred itself.

Insofar as Eliade is primarily interested less in why believers believe than in what their believing means to them,[9] he circumvents the debate over explanation and interpretation. For in the strict sense of those terms that debate is over why believers believe. It is over the origin and function of religion.[10] Because Eliade, like many others, more loosely equates explanation per se with origin and function and equates interpretation with meaning, his usage will be followed.

Eliade's Endorsement of the Believer's Point of View

Assume, for convenience sake, that Eliade is concerned with only professed believers. Assume as well that he is concerned with only the meaning, not the origin or function, of religion. Assume, too, that he is concerned with only the believer's *conscious* view of the meaning of religion: equate "the believer's point of view" with the believer's *conscious* point of view. Assume above all that the believer's point of view is irreducibly religious. Assume, that is, that if only in deeming the object of religion transcendent, Eliade's interpretation of religion captures the believer's point of view. For the central issue is less whether Eliade

---

[8]On the quest for the origin of religion see also Eliade (1969:ch. 3).
[9]Again, I now realize that Eliade is chiefly concerned with the meaning of religion in itself, not with its meaning for believers: again, see Segal (n. d.).
[10]See Segal (1986; forthcoming₁; forthcoming₂).

accurately captures the believer's point of view than whether, if he does, he is merely presenting or actually endorsing that point of view.

On the one hand Eliade usually restricts himself to *presenting* the believer's conscious view of the meaning of religion: "A sacred stone remains a stone; apparently (or, more precisely, from the profane point of view), nothing distinguishes it from all other stones. *But for those to whom a stone reveals itself as sacred,* its immediate reality is transmuted into a supernatural reality. In other words, *for those who have a religious experience* all nature is capable of revealing itself as cosmic sacrality" (Eliade 1968b:12 [italics added]). Interpreting religion religiously thus means merely describing, or transcribing, the believer's conscious view of its irreducibly religious meaning.

On the other hand Eliade sometimes suggests strongly that in interpreting religion religiously he is presenting the *true* meaning of religion, not just the believer's conscious view of its meaning. Insofar as the believer's conscious view of the meaning of religion is irreducibly religious, Eliade is not merely describing but outright endorsing that view: "... a religious phenomenon will only be recognized as such if it is grasped at its own level, that is to say, if it is studied *as* something religious. To try to grasp the essence of such a phenomenon by means of physiology, psychology, sociology, economics, linguistics, art or any other study is false; it misses the one unique and irreducible element in it – the element of the sacred" (Eliade 1963:xiii).[11]

On the one hand Eliade continually implies that, as a historian of religions, he is only conveying, not evaluating, the believer's point of view: "The *ultimate* aim of the historian of religions is to *understand,* and to make understandable to others, religious man's behavior and mental universe" (1968b:162 [italics added]). In contrast to the theologian, from whom he repeatedly distinguishes himself, Eliade the historian relies on empirical evidence, not revelation, for his explication: "The procedure of the historian of religions is just as different from that of the theologian. All theology implies a systematic reflection on the content of religious experience, aiming at a deeper and clearer understanding of the relationships between God-Creator and man-creature. But the historian of religions uses an empirical method of approach. He is concerned with religio-historical facts which he seeks to understand and to make intelligible to others" (1959b:88).[12] The facts on which the historian relies include interpretations by believers themselves.

---

[11]See also Eliade (1960:13-20).

[12]As Ricketts, one of Eliade's self-proclaimed defenders, states: "Eliade has misled some readers by his definition of the sacred as the 'real.' Some have thought that this means that Eliade himself regards the sacred as Reality: that is, that he is making a theological statement. Eliade would deny this. All he means here is that *for the believer,* that which is sacred *for him* is the Real, the True, the meaningful in an ultimate sense. As for what the Real 'really' is, Eliade never ventures an answer: such a question lies beyond the methodology of the history of religions.

On the other hand Eliade far more regularly pits his interpretation of religion against all reductive ones, as his objection to those who "try to grasp the essence" of religion "by means of physiology, psychology, sociology," and so on evinces. If he intends to be only presenting the believer's point of view, he should logically have no objection to those who intend to do more. Not only would his antagonists surely agree that the believer's conscious view of the meaning of religion is irreducibly religious, but they themselves would surely distinguish between the believer's *conscious* view of the meaning and the believer's *actual,* or deepest, view of it. Freud, for example, hardly denies that the manifest meaning of religion for believers is scrupulously religious. He simply denies that the latent meaning is. He invokes the unconscious, latent level to *account for* the manifest one, not to *deny* the manifest one. For Eliade to be countering real opponents, he must, then, be claiming that the believer's conscious view is also the believer's actual one. He must be claiming that the believer's actual, not merely conscious, view of the meaning of religion is irreducibly religious. He must, then, be endorsing, not merely reporting, the believer's point of view. Against Freud and other reductionists, he must be claiming that the believer correctly grasps the actual meaning of religion for the believer. Whatever Eliade says he is doing, his argument commits him to much more.[13]

Admittedly, Eliade sometimes takes reductionists to be denying even the manifest level of religion: "It would be useless, because ineffectual, to appeal to some reductionist principle and to demystify the behavior and ideologies of *homo religiosus* by showing, for example, that it is a matter of projections of the unconscious, or of screens raised for social, economic, political, or other reasons" (Eliade 1969:68). It would be useless because the conscious meaning of religion for the believer is religious rather than psychological, social, economic, or political. As Eliade illustrates: "In a number of traditional archaic cultures the village, temple, or house is considered to be located at the 'Center of the World.' There is no sense in trying to 'demystify' such a belief by drawing the attention of the reader to the fact that there exists no Center of the World and that, in any case, the multiplicity of such centers is an absurd notion because it is self-contradictory" (Eliade 1969:69). No reductionist, however, denies that to the

---

To answer that question one must go beyond the limits of the history of religions – and speak as philosopher, theologian or perhaps psychologist" (Ricketts, 28).

[13]Proudfoot, I have since discovered, likewise faults Eliade for failing to distinguish between a "description," which must be in the believer's own, irreducibly religious terms, and an "explanation," which need not be. In proceeding to fault Eliade for appealing to his description as justification for either his explanation or his interpretation, I say the same. But Proudfoot is wrong to argue that the description must be nonreductive. The *putative* description must be, but the final, underlying one need not be. Freud, for example, is not merely accounting for religion psychologically but also redescribing it psychologically.

believer the village, temple, or house is the center of the world. On the contrary, the reductionist wants to know why the believer considers that place the center of the world. Either, then, Eliade is attacking straw men, or, as I think, he is really arguing that the true, not merely conscious, meaning of religion for the believer is irreducibly religious.

Any distinction between the true meaning of religion for believers and the true meaning of religion itself, as if Eliade might be restricting himself to only the true meaning of religion for believers, is fallacious.[14] The true meaning of religion *is* its true meaning for believers. For whose meaning can religion be save that for believers? The issue is whether believers are aware of the true meaning of religion, which means at once its true one for them and its true one in itself. For Eliade, they largely are. At the same time Eliade's willingness to exceed and indeed violate even professed believers' views of the *specific* meaning of religion demonstrates that he is concerned with the meaning of religion in itself as well as with their view of the meaning of religion.

Put another way, Eliade means to be either a humanist or a social scientist. If he means to be a humanist, he is seeking only to present the believer's point of view. If he means to be a social scientist, he is seeking to assess that point of view: he is seeking to determine the believer's actual, not just conscious, view of the meaning of religion and so is necessarily evaluating, as correct or incorrect, the believer's conscious view. As a social scientist, Eliade can be either nonreductive or reductive: the believer's actual view can as readily tally as break with the believer's conscious one. The point is that a humanist and even a reductive social scientist run askew, not contrary, to each other: in seeking only to capture the believer's conscious view, the humanist is not asserting that that view is necessarily the actual one, and in seeking to determine the believer's actual view, the reductive social scientist is not denying that the believer's conscious view is irreducibly religious. In order, then, for Eliade to be confronting real antagonists, he must be "operating" as a social scientist – of a nonreductive variety. He must be seeking the believer's actual, not merely professed, view.

Seemingly, Eliade is dismissing nonreligious interpretations altogether. Seemingly, he is maintaining that secular interpretations, which come above all from the social sciences, are wholly irrelevant. Thus he warns his fellow historians of religions against continuing "to submit to the audacious and irrelevant interpretations of religious realities made by psychologists, sociologists, or devotees of various reductionist ideologies" (Eliade 1969:70).

Yet occasionally Eliade grants the social sciences a secondary role. They can, he sometimes says, delineate the *background* to religion, though still not illuminate religion itself: "In sum, a religious phenomenon cannot be understood outside of its 'history,' that is, outside of its cultural and socioeconomic

---

[14]Once again, I failed to see that Eliade is in fact drawing this distinction.

contexts. There is no such thing outside of history as a 'pure' religious datum....
But admitting the historicity of religious experiences does not imply that they
are reducible to nonreligious forms of behavior. Stating that a religious datum is
always a historical datum does not mean that it is reducible to a nonreligious
history – for example, to an economic, social, or political history" (Eliade
1968c:250-51). As he illustrates: "Few religious phenomena are more directly
and more obviously connected with sociopolitical circumstances than the modern
messianic and millenarian movements among colonial peoples (cargo-cults,
etc.). Yet identifying and analyzing the conditions that [merely] *prepared and
made possible* [italics added] such messianic movements form only a part of the
work of the historian of religions. For these movements are equally creations of
the human spirit, in the sense that they have become what they *are* [italics added]
– *religious movements*, and not merely gestures of protest and revolt – through a
creative act of the spirit" (Eliade 1969:6).[15] It is not clear whether the secular
"conditions" antedating millenarianism are for Eliade identical with its origin. If
they are, he would still be equating origin with reductionism.

Because Eliade considers only earlier social scientific analyses of religion,
his rejection or curtailed acceptance of them is not inconsistent with the trend
within the social sciences toward nonreductionism. In fact, it is doubtful that
Eliade recognizes this trend. The trend toward a nonreductive approach to myth
which, as quoted, he notes probably refers to the increased study of myth by
historians of religions rather than to any change in the study of it by social
scientists, who for him likely remain incorrigibly reductive.[16]

Eliade's Defense of Nonreductionism

Eliade does not merely announce his nonreductive stance but attempts to
prove it. He attempts to prove that the believer's conscious view of less the
origin or the function than the meaning of religion is the true one. He appeals to
what he considers the evidence: the irreducibly religious importance of religion
for the believer. Religion, he argues, *functions* to provide both knowledge of the
sacred and, even more, entrée to it. Myth in particular reveals not only the
existence of the sacred but also the origin of the profane by it. The knowledge

---

[15]For further examples see Allen (1978:134-35).
[16]To my knowledge Eliade's sole acknowledgment of this trend is a one-sentence
qualification in his otherwise uncompromising indictment of anthropologists for
ignoring the actor's point of view: "Indeed, as it is well known, the main interest
of the western scholars has been the study of material cultures and the analysis of
family structure, social organization, tribal law, and so on. These are problems,
one may say, important and even urgent for western scholarship, but of secondary
importance for the understanding of the *meaning of a particular culture,* as it was
understood and assumed *by its own members* (Broader, sympathetic and intelligent
studies like those of Marcel Griaulle, E. G. *[sic]* Evans-Pritchard or R. G.
Lienhardt, and a few other cultural anthropologists are rather exceptional)" (Eliade
1967:502-3 [italics in original]). See also Eliade (1969:ch. 2).

that a sacred reality underlies the everyday one is itself comforting. But myths, together with rituals, also enable humans to encounter that reality. The *meaning* of religion is the reality of that encounter.

The issue at hand is not whether Eliade's interpretation of the believer's view of the meaning of religion is the believer's own, conscious one. That it is it has been assumed. The issue is whether that meaning is the *true* meaning of religion for the believer. The issue is not whether the true meaning of religion for the believer is the true meaning of religion itself. That it is it has been explained.[17] The issue is whether the conscious meaning of religion for the believer is the true meaning of religion both for the believer and in itself.

Eliade systematically fails to prove that it is. All he does is continually assert, as cited, that reductive interpretations of religion are either irrelevant or secondary because they skirt the believer's own view of the irreducibly religious meaning of religion. But he thereby begs, not answers, the key question: whether the believer's own view of the meaning of religion *is* the true meaning of religion both for the believer and in itself. In the light of discoveries by modern psychology, sociology, anthropology, and other disciplines, Eliade can hardly contend that human beings know all the possible meanings of any of their beliefs and actions, not just of their religious ones. He can contend only that participants know the primary or relevant ones. That contention, however, is precisely what is at issue. In the absence of any noncircular justification for a nonreductive interpretation alone, a reductive one proves no less proper.

Other Defenses of Nonreductionism

Eliade's failure to provide a sturdy defense of nonreductionism does not, of course, mean that none exists. At least three possible defenses have commonly been offered: the comparative method, the process of *Verstehen,* and the phenomenological approach. Eliade himself indirectly invokes one or two of them.

When Eliade says that "it is impossible to understand the meaning of the Cosmic Tree by considering only one or some of its variants" and that "it is only by the analysis of a considerable number of examples that the structure of a symbol can be completely deciphered" (Eliade 1959b:94), he is presenting the standard comparativist argument: that only a comparison of many instances of any phenomenon, religious or nonreligious, discloses its true nature.[18] At first glance this assertion might seem self-evident, but it is in fact tenuous.

In the first place it is not clear that a survey of the instances of a phenomenon provides a unique source of even hypotheses about the phenomenon. The meticulous scrutiny of a single instance might well prove as

[17]Once again, I err.
[18]See Segal (1987b:95-96).

revealing "heuristically" as an inevitably more cursory scrutiny of many instances. Moreover, if one does not understand a single instance, on what basis can one understand other instances? What is objectionable is not the claim that the comparative method may be *useful* in generating hypotheses but the claim that it is *indispensable* to doing so.

In the second place it is certainly not the case that, even if the comparative method were an indispensable *source* of hypotheses, those hypotheses would be *self-validating*. The objection here is to the tacit claim that the comparative method provides not merely a unique source of hypotheses but also an automatic validation of them. Surely the hypotheses derived from comparative study, like those derived from any other source, must be tested in turn – by the application of them to as many further instances as possible. Surely even hypotheses derived from the study of all instances of a phenomenon would not automatically be correct.

In the third place it is hardly the case that even if the comparative method yielded both unique and self-validating hypotheses, those hypotheses would necessarily be nonreductive. For all theorists of religion, like all theorists of other classes of phenomena, are by definition comparativists: they seek the universal origin, function, or meaning of a phenomenon. Reductive theorists of religion use the comparative method as fully as Eliade, in which case he can scarcely appeal to it to support his approach. In short, the comparative method yields no defense of nonreductionism.

The concept of *Verstehen,* or "understanding," offers a weightier possible defense of nonreductionism. The understanding sought is the meaning of phenomena for participants themselves. Underlying the concept is the conviction that humans are different in kind from natural phenomena and that the brand of understanding sought by the humanities and the social sciences, both of which study humans exclusively, must therefore be different in kind from that sought by the natural sciences, which study humans as part of nature.

Where, it is said, the behavior of natural objects is caused, much of human behavior is intended. Where natural objects behave in response to a cause, humans often behave for a purpose. To analyze human behavior is thus necessarily to analyze the purposes, motives, or reasons behind it – the differences among purposes, motives, reasons, and other kinds of intentions aside. A causal analysis gets called an "explanation"; an intentional one, an "interpretation."

Proponents of *Verstehen* characterize intent in different ways. For most social scientific practitioners – Talcott Parsons, Robert Bellah, Peter Berger, and in actuality both Max Weber and Clifford Geertz – an intent is simply a mental rather than physical cause. Because these proponents assume that causes can be only physical, they label would-be mental causes meanings rather than causes, but the sole difference for them between meanings and causes is that meanings are mental and causes physical. By contrast, for philosophical proponents of

Verstehen like Alfred Schutz, R. G. Collingwood, William Dray, and Peter Winch, an intent is no cause at all, mental or physical. For it is not separate from the behavior it produces, in which case that behavior is the expression rather than the effect of the intent and the intent truly the meaning rather than the cause of the behavior.[19]

What unites both groups of practitioners of *Verstehen* is their association of meaning with intent rather than, like Eliade, with significance. Contrary to the usage employed elsewhere in this essay, to interpret religion is, for them, to *account for* it. Because Eliade is primarily concerned not with why believers believe but with what religion signifies to believers, this brand of *Verstehen* is of scant aid. There are, however, advocates of *Verstehen* who, like Eliade, concentrate on what human behavior signifies. The grandest figure is Wilhelm Dilthey. But in especially his later writings he is chiefly interested in what culture signifies *about* the actor, not signifies *to* the actor.[20]

In any case the practice of *Verstehen,* like the comparative method, poses various problems in its own right.[21] In the first place it is not clear that the distinction between interpretation and explanation is genuine.[22] Against those who define intentions as meanings rather than physical causes, critics say that explanation allows for mental as well as physical causes.[23] Against those who define intentions as meanings rather than causes per se, critics say that meanings must also be causes in order to be meanings.[24]

In the second place it is not clear that even if one distinguishes interpretation from explanation, it is *necessary* to analyze human behavior in terms of intentions rather than either physical causes or causes per se. Admittedly, advocates of *Verstehen* never claim that *all* human behavior must be analyzed "intentionally," but they do claim that much of it must be. Critics deny that much or even any of it must be.[25]

In the third place it is not clear that even if it is necessary to analyze human behavior in terms of intentions rather than either physical causes or causes per se, it is *sufficient.* Admittedly, few advocates of *Verstehen* claim that all human

---

[19]See Segal (1986; forthcoming$_1$; forthcoming$_2$).

[20]Eliade, I now realize, is primarily interested in the same: yet again, see Segal (n. d.).

[21]On the practice of *Verstehen* generally see, pro, Dilthey, Weber (1947:87-157; 1949), Schutz, MacIver, Hayek, Wax. See, con, Abel, Nagel (1961:473-85; 1963:200-6), Hempel (1963b:218-19; 1965:335-76, 447-87), Davidson. See, both pro and con, Brodbeck (part I), Natanson (part III), Dallmayr and McCarthy (parts I-II).

[22]See Segal (1986; forthcoming$_1$).

[23]See Hempel (1965:463-87; 1962:25-31), Nagel (1961:476-80), Grünbaum (69-94), Spiro (271-73).

[24]See Davidson.

[25]See Nagel (1961:475), Hempel (1962:29-30; 1965:483-86).

behavior analyzed "intentionally" can be analyzed only "intentionally," but most do claim that much of it can be. Critics, again, deny that much or even any of it can be.[26]

In the fourth place even if it were both necessary and sufficient to analyze humans in terms of intentions, the act of *Verstehen* would at most provide only a source of hypotheses about humans. Those hypotheses would still have to be tested. For how can one be sure that one has discovered the actor's true intentions unless one sees them borne out by the actor's behavior, which goes beyond the act of *Verstehen* itself?[27] Admittedly, many of those who consider intentions mental causes concur – notably, Weber.[28] Even those who consider intentions meanings rather than causes of any kind grant that meanings are testable to a point.[29]

In the fifth place it is uncertain whether *Verstehen* is even meant to be a *method* of analyzing humans and not simply the *aim* of analysis. Admittedly, many advocates of *Verstehen* agree.[30] But in that event not only would the aim still have to be justified; a method for practicing it would still be needed.

In the sixth place it is by no means the case that even if *Verstehen* provided an incontestable aim and method for analyzing humans, it, any more than the comparative method, would offer support for nonreductionism. For to say that the intentions which alone make sense of an actor's behavior are the actor's own is not, for advocates of *Verstehen,* to say that they must be conscious. The alternative to conscious intentions need not be either physical causes or causes per se. It can be unconscious intentions.

Certainly in the fields of history,[31] sociology,[32] and anthropology,[33] where the practice of *Verstehen* has been most pervasive, the actor's intentions have not been restricted to conscious ones. Among proponents of *Verstehen* in history, Dray grants that "not all high-grade actions are performed deliberately in the sense that they are undertaken with a plan consciously preformulated" (Dray 1957:123).[34] Collingwood says that the historian "can even discover what, until

---

[26]See Nagel (1961:475-76).
[27]See Nagel (1961:482-83), Hempel (1963b:218-19).
[28]See Weber (1947:96ff.).
[29]See Schutz (51-52, 65-66), Winch (1958:91-94, 82-83; but see also 113-16).
[30]See Winch (1958:136).
[31]On the practice of *Verstehen* in history see, pro, Collingwood (introduction; pt. V), Dray (1957; 1959; 1963; 1964:chs. 2-4). See, con, Hempel (1942; 1962; 1963a; 1965:335-76, 447-87), Gardiner (1952). See, pro and con, Gardiner (1959:344-475), Hooke (pts. III, IV).
[32]On the practice of *Verstehen* in sociology see, pro, Blumer, Goffman, Garfinkel, Turner, Sudnow, Douglas, Berger, Bellah (1970:esp. pt. III). See, con, Gellner (1975b), Denzin, Coser. See, pro and con, Dallmayr and McCarthy (pt. IV).
[33]On the practice of *Verstehen* in anthropology see, pro, Tyler, Geertz. See, con, Radcliffe-Brown, Harris, Spiro.
[34]See also Dray (1963:111).

he discovered it, no one ever knew to have happened at all" (Collingwood, 238). Among advocates of *Verstehen* in sociology and anthropology, Winch permits even entirely unconscious, Freudian interpretations of the actor's intentions.[35]

In the seventh and final place Weber, Geertz, Bellah, Berger, and other practitioners of *Verstehen* who focus on religion attribute it not, like Eliade, to an irreducibly religious intent but to an entirely secular, typically unconscious one, which religion merely fulfills. They attribute religion to a need for meaningfulness, not for the sacred. Even if for some practitioners religion is the best and possibly even sole means to that end, the end itself remains secular.[36] The need for meaningfulness doubtless comes closer to the actor's point of view than the needs postulated by earlier social scientists and historians, so that the increasing popularity of this approach to religion does, then, spell a move toward nonreductionism. But in reducing Eliade's irreducibly religious need to merely a means to a secular one, the approach nevertheless stops short – and thereby offers no support for nonreductionism.

Where proponents of *Verstehen* in history and the social sciences assert only that human behavior must be seen from the actor's point of view, Wittgensteinian proponents of *Verstehen* assert that the actor's point of view is true.[37] Dubbed "fideists," Wittgensteinians maintain not merely that humans know the true reasons for which they act but also that their reasons – more precisely, the beliefs underlying those reasons – are true, cognitive, or rational. Since a believer's reasons for being religious involve beliefs about the world, the Wittgensteinian approach seemingly supports Eliade's.

In actuality, it does not, and only partly because the Wittgensteinians, like their counterparts in history and the social sciences, do not equate the actor's reasons and even beliefs with the actor's conscious ones. More important is the fact that many, though scarcely all, Wittgensteinians are relativists. Among Wittgensteinian relativists who focus on religion, the best known are Winch and D. Z. Phillips.[38] Truth, cognitivity, and rationality are for them determined either solely or largely internally.

By contrast, Eliade's endorsement of the believer's point of view is not relativistic. Eliade is not, like the Wittgensteinians, appealing to the distinctiveness of the religious "game" to justify its truths. He is not saying relativistically that whatever believers deem the meaning of religion must therefore be correct but rather that believers get right the true meaning of

---

[35]See Winch (1958:46-49).

[36]See Segal (1985a).

[37]On the Wittgensteinian practice of *Verstehen* see, pro, Winch, Louch, Phillips, Braithwaite, Wisdom. See, con, Nielsen, MacIntyre, Gellner (1962; 1968; 1975a), Jarvie (1972:ch. 2; 1984:pt. 3), Richards. See, in between, Alston. See, pro and con, Borger and Cioffi (231-69), Dallmayr and McCarthy (pt. III).

[38]By contrast, Braithwaite and Wisdom are not relativists. The part-Wittgensteinian Alston is half-relativist, half-absolutist.

religion, which, again, means the true meaning of religion both for them and in itself. For Eliade, the difference between overt believers and overt nonbelievers is that overt believers get right the true meaning of religion for *both*. To be sure, Wittgensteinians appeal to the nature of the religious game itself, not to its analysis by "players." But the game for them is in order because it is played.

Eliade can take small solace from not only the relativism but also the "noncognitivism" of many, though again not all, Wittgensteinians. The most prominent Wittgensteinians here are Phillips, R. B. Braithwaite, and at times Winch.[39] The religious game for them is in order as it stands not because its cognitive claims are assessible only internally but because it makes none. Rather than, like science, a set of assertions, religion is either the expression of an attitude – Braithwaite and Winch – or the disposition to behave a certain way – Phillips. Clearly, noncognitivists provide no succor to anyone for whom religiosity involves the beliefs that the sacred exists and that humans encounter it. Religion for Eliade may primarily be experiential, but the believers whose views he endorses make cognitive claims about the content of their experiences.

The utility of the Wittgensteinian position aside, there are many objections to it, just as there are to the concept of *Verstehen* in general. Put summarily, it has been argued that the actor's beliefs are in fact subject, not impervious, to external criteria and that those beliefs are subject to being judged false, noncognitive, or, in the case of practices as well, irrational. Whether or not valid, these criticisms must surely be met before Wittgensteinian fideism can be used to bolster Eliade's stance.

The third and final appeal which Eliade might make in defense of nonreductionism is to the phenomenology of religion.[40] Although phenomenologists of religion can also, like Eliade himself, be historians of religions, by definition phenomenologists deal with religions collectively rather than, like historians, individually: they are comparativists rather than particularists.

The goal of the phenomenology of religion is ambiguous.[41] Minimally, the aim is sheer description: an accurate recording of the believer's point of view. As W. Brede Kristensen, a leading phenomenologist, says: "History of Religion and Phenomenology do not have as their object the formulation of our conception of the essence of religious data. This is the task of the philosopher. They must, on the contrary, investigate what religious value the believers ... attached to their faith, what religion meant for them" (Kristensen, 13). To the extent that the goal of the phenomenology of religion is mere description, it

---

[39]By contrast, Wisdom and Alston are cognitivists.
[40]For a most helpful summary of the phenomenology of religion see Allen (1987).
[41]On the ambiguity of the phenomenologists' goal see Saliba (30-31), Smart (19-21), Allen (1978:57-96; 1987:279-84).

offers no help to Eliade, who, again, is committed to defending, not merely describing, the believer's point of view.

Maximally, however, the aim is the same as Eliade's. As C. Jouco Bleeker, another prominent phenomenologist, asserts: "From the studies of its [i.e., phenomenology of religion's] adherents it appears that nobody is any longer content with a pure description of the religious facts. People want to understand their significance and structure.... The scholars ... wanted to penetrate deeper into their object than is possible with a simple description. They aimed at the understanding of the spirit, the *essence,* the structure of the religions which they treated" (Bleeker, 101 [italics added]).

By the "essence" of religion phenomenologists do not mean the ultimate nature of religion. They rigidly distinguish themselves from metaphysicians. They equally rigidly distinguish themselves from those who seek the origin and function of religion. Phenomenologists seek the *meaning* of religion. Insofar as the phenomenology of religion is merely descriptive, the meaning sought is merely the conscious meaning of religion for the believer. Insofar as the phenomenology of religion is more than descriptive, the meaning sought is, as for Eliade, the *true* meaning of religion for the believer.

To justify their claim that the true meaning of religion for the believer is irreducibly religious, phenomenologists would doubtless appeal to the three procedures they employ: the comparative method, the *epoché,* and the "eidetic vision." All three procedures are, however, moot. The comparative method, which is so tightly tied to phenomenology that the term "comparative religion" is often used synonymously with the phenomenology of religion, has already been discussed. The *epoché,* according to Bleeker, means "the suspension of judgment. In using the *epoché* one puts oneself into the position of the listener, who does not judge according to preconceived notions" (Bleeker, 98). But then the *epoché,* as the bracketing of judgment, secures only a description, not an endorsement, of the conscious meaning of religion for the believer.

Even if the *epoché* is intended to reveal the *true* meaning of religion for the believer, phenomenologists of religion invariably neglect to explain how to practice it. To *prescribe* the suspension of biases is one thing. To *achieve* it is another. Until the actual means of ridding oneself of all biases gets explained, the *epoché* must remain only a forlorn ideal.

The "eidetic vision," according to Bleeker, "has as its aim the search of the eidos, that is the essentials of religious phenomena" (Bleeker, 99). Even if the phenomenological goal here is undeniably to decipher the true meaning of religion for the believer, the secondary objection to the *epoché* proves the primary one here: the absence of a means. Just as phenomenologists of religion fail to explain how to exorcise biases, so they fail to explain how to grasp intuitively the true meaning of religion for the believer. Is it by will? Is it by training? If so, of what kind? How does one know when one has succeeded? Can one validate one's vision? If not, then, as Willard Oxtoby concludes: "There is nothing outside one's intuitive grasp of a pattern which validates that pattern. The phenomenologist is obliged simply to set forth his understanding as a whole, trusting that his reader will enter into it. But there is no procedure stated by which he can compel a second phenomenologist to agree with the adequacy and incontrovertibility of his analysis, unless the second phenomenologist's eidetic vision happens to be the same as the first's. For this reason phenomenological expositions of religion are in fact very personal appreciations of it, akin more to certain forms of literary and aesthetic criticism than to the natural or even the social sciences" (Oxtoby, 597). But where, then, is the dividing line between the neutral vision itself and the very judgment which phenomenologists strive to expunge?

In seeking both the true and the irreducibly religious meaning of religion for the believer, the phenomenological method may, in sum, provide more support for Eliade's ends than either the comparative method or the practice of *Verstehen*, but it proves at least as tenuous as they.[42]

The Impossibility of Reductionism for Nonbelievers

In the wake of the failure of any of these arguments to justify an exclusively nonreductive analysis of religion, a reductive one proves no less proper. Yet in addition a reductive analysis is the only one possible for nonbelieving scholars. If Eliade fails to prove that a nonreductive analysis is alone proper, he also fails to prove that, for nonbelievers, it is even possible. Indeed, he does not even try. He simply assumes that it is. Like his assumption of the *propriety* of only nonreductive analyses, his assumption of their *possibility* for nonbelievers is typical of "religionists."[43]

In another essay I argue that Eliade's view of the *function* of religion bars nonbelievers from accepting a nonreductive analysis of religion.[44] Here I will focus anew on his view of the meaning. I will revert to using "interpretation" for the meaning *rather than* the origin and function of religion.

The issue is not whether a nonbeliever can accept a believer's interpretation of religion as the *nonbeliever's* own. By definition a nonbeliever cannot. The issue is whether a nonbeliever can accept a believer's interpretation of religion as even the *believer's* own. "Nonbeliever" here means not simply atheist but also agnostic. It means anyone who refrains from espousing the reality of the sacred.

---

[42]Whether or not as a phenomenologist of religion, Eliade gets faulted on the same basic grounds as one: see Saliba (ch. 4), Baird (74-91), Dudley (chs. 3-4). In defense of Eliade see Allen (1978:ch. 7).

[43]For a refreshing, if narrow, challenge to this happy assumption see Robbins, Anthony, and Curtis. See, in reply, Bellah (1974) and, in counterreply, Anthony, Robbins, and Curtis.

[44]See Segal (1987a).

Because the meaning of religion *is* the reality of the sacred, nonbelievers cannot accept that meaning.

The issue is not whether nonbelievers can accept the reality of the sacred as the *conscious* meaning of religion for the believer. The issue is whether nonbelievers can accept the reality of the sacred as the *true* meaning of religion for the believer. The issue is not whether nonbelievers can *describe* the believer's view of the meaning – or origin or function – of religion. The issue is whether nonbelievers can *accept* that view as the *true* meaning, origin, or function of religion for the believer.

Take the conventional statement that nonbelievers can accept, as the true meaning of religion for the believer, the reality of the sacred. How can nonbelievers accept the reality of the sacred for even the believer when they themselves refuse to accept the reality of it? Of course, nonbelievers can *profess* to accept the believer's point of view – as, that is, the believer's *true* view. They can profess to "respect" the believer's point of view. But such respect is self-deceptive. One cannot respect what one denies. One cannot will respect or grant it blindly. The purported respect would be doubly self-deceptive. For one would be left not only with a meaning that one could not accept as the believer's real one but also with a meaning that one probably could accept as the believer's real one – for example, a psychological or sociological meaning. Nonbelievers would be left with a meaning that they not only would *have* to reject but would *want* to reject, yet would be prohibited from rejecting by their espousal of nonreductionism. They would be left not with an indecipherable phenomenon but with a phenomenon which they had barred themselves from deciphering. They would be left not agape but gagged.

In arguing that the acceptance of science keeps moderns from accepting the Bible literally, Rudolf Bultmann best describes the self-deception that any attempt at literalism involves: "Can Christian preaching expect modern man to *accept the mythical [=literal] view of the world as true?* To do so would be both senseless and impossible. It would be senseless, because there is nothing specifically Christian in the mythical view of the world as such. It is simply the cosmology of a pre-scientific age. Again, it would be impossible, because no man can adopt a view of the world by his own volition – it is already determined for him by his place in history.... [I]t is impossible to revive an obsolete view of the world by a mere fiat, and certainly not by a mythical view. For all our thinking to-day is shaped irrevocably by modern science. A blind acceptance of the New Testament mythology would be arbitrary, and to press for its acceptance as an article of faith would be to reduce faith to works.... It would involve a sacrifice of the intellect which could have only one result – a curious form of schizophrenia and insincerity. It would mean accepting a view of the world in our faith and religion which we should deny in our everyday life" (Bultmann, 3-4).

Whether Bultmann and others like him[45] are correct is not the point. Whether Eliade, who interprets all religions and all religious texts almost literally, must confront the difficulties posed by modern science and, more, modern culture is. Yet he considers none of them. He never questions whether acceptance of the believer's point of view requires more than open-mindedness on the interpreter's part. Even among social scientific and philosophical relativists, few deny that a considerable sharing of concepts is prerequisite to accepting, not just grasping, the views of others, which, again, means accepting those views *as* the views of others.

Nonbelievers seeking to accept, say, the economy of another society might well disapprove of it. But the acceptance required would be of only the utility of the economy, not of its existence. One might prefer one's own economy as more efficient but surely not as alone real. By contrast, nonbelievers seeking to accept the believer's point of view must accept the reality of the sacred – a reality that by definition they do not accept. The difference between a nonbeliever's acceptance of other phenomena and a nonbeliever's acceptance of religion is exactly that the acceptance of other phenomena does, or need, not challenge the nonbeliever's beliefs about the world.

Still, suppose that nonbelievers *sought* to accept the believer's point of view. How would they secure that point of view? The most direct way would be to ask a believer. A less direct way would be to observe a believer or, in the case of dead religions, to scrutinize extant texts. But immediately the prior problem recurs: how would nonbelievers be able to accept the believer's point of view? How, directly or indirectly, could a believer say what the sacred meant when by definition nonbelievers could not accept that the sacred meant what a believer said it meant? Nonbelievers would not question the believer's sincerity. They would not doubt that the believer was sure that the sacred is real. They would simply doubt that the sacred is in fact real and so would translate the sacred into other terms. They could not suspend what would be literally their disbelief.

Yet suppose that nonbelievers still sought to accept the believer's point of view. Again, how would they be able to accept that point of view? The common answer is: through "empathy."[46] Certainly empathy need not construed as a magical intuition of the actor's stream-of-consciousness – a caricature of the process. Collingwood, Weber, Schutz, and even Dilthey, the most psychological of "empathizers," see empathy as the careful inference to the actor's thoughts.[47] Yet even as what historians of science call rational reconstruction empathy

---

[45]See, notably, Ricoeur (3-24, 151-57, 161-74, 347-57).
[46]To be sure, anthropologically inclined advocates of *Verstehen* like Geertz, Winch, and all cognitive anthropologists recommend fieldwork in place of empathy, which is utilized by more historically minded advocates like Dilthey, Collingwood, and Weber.
[47]See, for example, Collingwood (171-74, 205, 296, 302, 305). See also Rickman (309).

appears doomed – if one spurns as delusory, not merely neutral, uncertain, or even objectionable, that with which one seeks to empathize. *How* to "empathize" with that which one denies the reality of is the question – the original one.

The means typically offered are open-mindedness, sincerity, and will power. Unfortunately, they are of little help. They are psychological solutions to a logical problem: how to accept that which one does not accept. Open-mindedness, sincerity, and will power may be *necessary* to accepting the believer's point of view, but they are not *sufficient*. Were the problem one of persuading nonbelievers to *want* to accept the believer's point of view, they might be helpful, but it is taken for granted that nonbelievers want to accept the believer's point of view. The problem is that they logically, rather than psychologically, cannot, and all the determination they can muster is therefore to no avail.

If, then, no means exist by which nonbelievers can accept the believer's point of view, accepting that point of view proves a forlorn goal – unless one is a believer. Doubtless many believers would agree,[48] but few academic interpreters of religion, including Eliade, do. If they did, not only would they thereby be saying that nonbelieving interpreters themselves cannot accept the believer's point of view. They would be saying that no interpreter can make nonbelievers accept that point of view in turn. Contemporary academic interpreters may argue that religion is only acceptable *from* the believer's point of view, but they rarely assume that that point of view is only acceptable *to* believers. If in fact believers alone can accept the believer's point of view, then many academic interpreters and their audiences cannot. Eliade's assertion that *all* humans are at heart believers does not help – both because believers are in this essay defined as *conscious* devotees and, more, because the issue is over the *conscious* meaning of religion for nonbelievers, who are necessarily religious only unconsciously.

Not everyone, however, seeks to accept the believer's view of the meaning – or origin or function – of religion. Most earlier scholars did not. It is largely only contemporary ones who do. The reason may lie in the alienness of the phenomenon which nonbelieving scholars encounter and in their subsequent desire to surmount that alienness by viewing the phenomenon exclusively from the believer's standpoint. Since, however, their predecessors encountered the same phenomenon, the alienness of it cannot alone account for the kind of analysis they espouse. Yet it can perhaps account for the extreme character of the analysis contemporary nonbelievers espouse and the equally extreme character of the analysis often espoused by their predecessors: the resolve of contemporary

---

[48]To be sure, many believers would demand that one be not just a believer of any kind but a believer in the particular religion one wants to accept the practitioner's view of.

scholars to approach religion from only the believer's point of view and the wholesale dismissal by their predecessors of that point of view.

For the phenomenon which nonbelieving scholars confront is not merely mildly alien but radically alien, so radically alien that it permits no compromise. To approach it in nonreligious terms is to approach it in ruthlessly other terms, and to approach it in its own terms is to approach it in solely its own terms, lest the barest admission of other terms admit ruthlessly other ones. Scholars must make an either/or choice, and contemporary ones, in rejecting the choice of their predecessors, are left with its opposite.

If it is in the effort to overcome the alien nature of religion that contemporary scholars strive to approach it in its own terms, it is exactly the refusal of nonbelieving contemporaries to dispense with those terms that makes religion all the more inscrutable and therefore all the more alien. Contemporary scholars perceive that to reduce religion to something nonreligious terms is in that respect to keep it alien. What they overlook is that to refuse to do so is, for nonbelievers, to keep it much more alien.

Doubtless no reductive analysis of religion to date has proved adequate. Doubtless all have failed to make sense of some, if not much, of religion. But then they have failed not, as Eliade would say, because they have ignored the believer's point of view but because they have not reduced that point of view to another one. They have failed not because they have been reductive at all but because they have not been reductive enough. Their failure, moreover, is that of individual analyses. It is not, like that of nonreductive analyses for nonbelievers, the failure of the approach itself. Where all nonreductive analyses are doomed for nonbelievers, future reductive ones may succeed.

There are several issues which it is not the purpose of this essay to consider. First, it is not the purpose here to consider whether reductive analyses of religion are adequate. The purpose is to argue only that their adequacy is an open rather than closed question, an empirical rather than *a priori* one. Whether or not reductive analyses ultimately prove adequate, they are not, it has been argued, inadequate *a priori*.

Second, it is not the purpose of this essay to consider whether nonbelievers can become believers or vice versa. To deny that nonbelievers can accept the believer's view of religion because they do not accept the reality of the sacred is not to deny that they can change their minds. Indeed, it is not even to deny that they can change their minds upon deciding that all reductive analyses of religion are likely inadequate. The purpose here is to argue only that as long as nonbelievers are nonbelievers they cannot accept the believer's point of view. Conversion is prerequisite to acceptance.

Third, it is most certainly not the purpose of this essay to argue that believers alone can analyze religion. On the contrary, it is the purpose of the first part of this essay to argue that believers, like other humans, have no automatic, privileged, incorrigible entrée to the true nature of their behavior. The fact that they are the subject of their behavior is almost coincidental. It scarcely entails that they are the best, let alone sole, judge of that behavior. Their own view may prove correct, but not merely because it is theirs. John Fenton puts it well: "Autobiography is not necessarily more reliable than biography" (Fenton, 70).

The purpose of the second part of this essay is to argue that, in the case of religion in particular and not of human behavior in general, believers alone can accept their own analyses of it. If their own analyses were the only permissible ones, all analyses of religion would be confessional. Because analyses askew and even contrary to theirs are permissible as well, analyses of religion can be social scientific as well.

If Eliade is wrong to oppose reductive analyses of religion on the grounds that they misconstrue religion, he is right to oppose them on the grounds that they threaten it. For what underlies, if hardly justifies, his abhorrence of reductive analyses is his fear that they reduce religion to a delusion. Eliade insists on a nonreductive analysis of religion in order to preserve the reality of religion.[49]

His effort might, however, appear to be unnecessary. For, according to most philosophers of science, a scientific explanation of a phenomenon does not dissolve the phenomenon but only accounts for it. A neurological explanation of pain specifies the neurological conditions under which pain occurs but does not reduce pain to the stimulation of nerve endings. The stimulation may cause the pain but is not the pain itself. Indeed, a neurological explanation must presuppose the reality of pain in order to have something to explain. As Carl Hempel illustrates: "The kinetic theory of gases plainly does not show that there are no such things as macroscopic bodies of different gases that change volumes under changing pressure, diffuse through porous walls at characteristic rates, etc., and that there 'really' are only swarms of randomly buzzing molecules. On the contrary, the theory takes for granted that there are those macroscopic events and uniformities, and it seeks to account for them in terms of the microstructure of the gases and the microprocesses involved in their various changes" (Hempel 1966:78).[50] A scientific explanation challenges not the phenomenon being explained but only alternative explanations of it. If, for example, chemistry were able to account for all aspects of pain presently accounted for biologically, it would reduce the biological terms to chemical ones – without dissolving the pain itself.

---

[49]I have since come to recognize that Eliade is seeking to preserve the religiosity of less the *object* than the *source*, not to mention the meaning, of religion: an irreducibly religious need for the sacred.
[50]See also Nagel (1961:364-66).

This distinction between the reducibility of one theory to another and the irreducibility of one phenomenon to another has been invoked by Hans Penner and Edward Yonan against Eliade.[51] They argue that he, together with other nonreductionists, needlessly fears that reductive analyses reduce religion to a delusion. Were he to realize that reductive analyses challenge only nonreductive analyses, not religion itself, he would have no reason to oppose them: "As we have shown, reduction is an operation concerned with theories or systems of statements, not with phenomena, data, or the properties of the phenomena.... None of the scholars we have examined ... states that reduction wipes out, levels, or demeans the phenomena or data being explained. On the contrary, reduction in the sciences implies an *explanation* of one *theory* by the use of another in the same discipline (or, different disciplines)" (Penner and Yonan, 130-31). Put another way, reduction is methodological rather than, as Eliade assumes, ontological.

Surprisingly, Penner and Yonan never say what aspect of religion nonreductionists consider threatened: origin, function, meaning, or object. Since they mention only the sacred itself, they likely have in mind the object, which might well seem the most readily threatened aspect. Eliade himself, however, seeks to defend less the object than the origin, function, and especially meaning of religion.

More surprisingly, Penner and Yonan cite nothing to support their claim that Eliade fears the reduction of religion itself. In actuality, he, like other nonreductionists, fears the reduction of a nonreductive *analysis* of religion. He wants to preserve the reality of the theoretical entities he postulates to explain and interpret religion: an innate need for the sacred, the transconscious, and the sacred itself. Even though Eliade is still more interested in the meaning than in the origin and function of religion, the meaning for him depends on the origin and function: a reductive explanation of religion undermines a nonreductive interpretation of it. The function depends in turn on the object of religion: religion cannot serve to make contact with the sacred unless the sacred exists. The sacred is not, like pain, a reality to be explained and interpreted but is rather, like atoms, an explanation and interpretation itself of reality – here of both the function and the object of religion. The physical world, society, and the psyche are among the entities offered by Eliade's reductive nemeses. Those entities, as rivals to the sacred, do challenge the reality of the sacred, so that Eliade is justified in fearing them, even if not justified in rejecting them.[52]

---

[51]See Penner and Yonan (117-22, 130-31).

[52]Pals (24-25) rightly criticizes Penner and Yonan on this count. Where Penner and Yonan seek a reconciliation between religion and the social sciences on the grounds that the social sciences cannot reduce religion itself to a delusion, Saliba (ch. 5) and Fenton (passim) seek reconciliation on the grounds that the social sciences are incomplete. If Saliba and Fenton are contending that all present social scientific explanations are incomplete, few would disagree. But if they are

ADDENDUM

I am aware of two responses to this essay. In neither case would the journal in which the response appeared let me respond in turn. I summarize here the issues and my rejoinder.

Donald Wiebe (1984) partly misconstrues my claims:

(1) I never claim, at least in this essay, that reductive analyses are superior *intellectually* to nonreductive ones. I claim only that they are superior *practically:* one does not have to be a believer to accept them.

(2) I never claim that nonbelievers alone can accept reductive analyses of the *origin, function,* or *meaning* of religion. At the end I claim only that nonbelievers alone can accept reductive analyses of the *object* of religion. I would be most surprised if Wiebe himself thought otherwise. If he did, how, save by the noncognitivist tactics of Braithwaite and Phillips, would he distinguish nonbelievers from believers? At the same time I have since come to recognize that some reductive analyses *presuppose* the falsity of religion in their analyses of above all the function of religion (see Segal 1985b). Nonbelievers alone, I now concede, can accept *those* reductive analyses, but all others are open to believers as well as nonbelievers.

(3) I am fully aware that, to spawn the open competition between nonreductive and reductive analyses envisioned by Wiebe, I need argue for only the *possibility,* not the *necessity,* of reductive analyses. I simply intend to be claiming more. I mean to claim that reductive analyses are not only permissible for anyone but also, for nonbelievers, ineluctable.

(4) I never claim that religion is false and so am not guilty of failing to justify that claim. At the end I claim only that reductive analyses of just the *object* of religion assume the falsity of religion. Who would demur?

(5) In the original version of the essay I most lamentably used the vague "appreciation," which Wiebe understandably takes to mean "grasp" rather than, as I state at least once, "explain" – or, in the terms I employ in the present version for the meaning of religion, "interpret." Equating "appreciate" with "describe," Wiebe rightly says that nonbelievers can scarcely espouse reductive analyses if they cannot even grasp the phenomenon being analyzed. Despite my unfortunate use of "appreciate," I never claim that nonbelievers cannot *grasp* the believer's point of view. I claim only that they cannot *accept* it.

(6) I never claim on behalf of reductive analyses what Eliade claims on behalf of nonreductive ones: that they alone are proper. I claim only that they are not improper.

---

maintaining that all social scientific explanations are *necessarily* incomplete, and incomplete because they cannot reduce what is irreducibly religious, they are begging the same fundamental question as Eliade: whether what is putatively religious is in fact religious.

(7) I never deny that nonbelievers can become believers and vice versa. I even say that nonbelievers can do so on the basis of their assessment of reductive analyses. I claim only that as long as nonbelievers are nonbelievers reductive analyses are the sole ones possible for them. Wiebe himself apparently concurs.

(8) I hardly claim that reductive analyses to date are adequate. I therefore never claim – or deny – that the reductive approach constitutes what Imre Lakatos would call a progressive research program. Like Wiebe himself, I claim only that a reductive approach is not inherently inadequate.

Daniel Pals (1986) partly misconstrues my claims and partly offers unconvincing responses:

(1) I never deny that a nonbelieving interpreter can accept some of the believer's point of view. Indeed, in the original version I stated that "undeniably, a nonbeliever can appreciate [i.e., accept] some aspects of a believer's point of view" (109). I claimed only that "the decisive issue is whether [the nonbeliever] can appreciate [i.e., accept] the *reality* of [the object of] religion for the believer" (109).

(2) I never deny that Eliade *professes* to offer a convincing irreducibly religious analysis, explanatory or interpretive, of religion. I claim only that he offers no justification for his analysis. Just like Eliade himself, Pals confuses the cogency of Eliade's *description* of the data with its cogency as an *analysis* of the data. As I state explicitly, not even the most uncompromising reductionist denies the putatively religious origin, function, and meaning of religion. No less than Eliade does the reductionist *start* at the irreducibly religious level, and the reductionist can even thank Eliade for organizing the putatively religious data so well. Unlike Eliade, the reductionist does not stop at the surface level. Moreover, the reductionist sees no reason to do so save for Eliade's question-begging one: that to go beyond that level would be to go beyond the believer's point of view.

(3) I never deny that the most convincing analysis of religion may turn out to be the irreducibly religious one. I claim only that its cogency must be demonstrated empirically rather than declared dogmatically. I oppose Eliade's denial *a priori* that a cogent analysis can be nonreligious. In addition, I would maintain that even if the most cogent analysis is religious, nonbelievers, while nonbelievers, still cannot accept it.

(4) Far from failing to see that the relationship between nonbeliever and believer parallels that between believer in one religion and believer in another, I myself note the parallel (see present footnote 48). At the outset of the essay I even stress the believer's likely insistence on the uniqueness of the believer's own religion.

(5) Only at the end of the essay do I turn to the believer's view of the object of religion and so to the issue of the truth of religion. I do not, then, concentrate on the nonbeliever's obvious inability to accept the truth of religion. I concentrate on the nonbeliever's rather less obvious inability to accept an

irreducibly religious origin, function, and above all meaning of religion. Agreeing with me that nonbelievers cannot accept the truth of religion, Pals argues that they can nevertheless accept an irreducibly religious origin, function, and meaning of religion – as if I were oblivious to the very aspects of religion on which I focus. *How* nonbelievers can do so – the very issue I raise – Pals never sees the need to consider. Instead, he says only that nonbelievers need not accept reductive analyses – as if nonbelievers were somehow not thereby left by default with the nonreductive ones I argue they cannot accept.

REFERENCES

ABEL, THEODORE

1948   "The Operation Called *Verstehen*." *American Journal of Sociology* 54 (November):211-18.

1967   "A Reply to Professor Wax." *Sociology and Social Research* 51 (April):334-36.

ALLEN, DOUGLAS

1978   *Structure and Creativity in Religion*. Religion and Reason Series, No. 14. The Hague: Mouton.

1987   "Phenomenology of Religion." In *Encyclopedia of Religion* 11:272-85.

ALSTON, WILLIAM P.

1981   "The Christian Language-Game." In *The Autonomy of Religious Belief*, ed. Frederick J. Crosson, pp. 128-62. Notre Dame, Ind.: University of Notre Dame Press.

ANTHONY, DICK, THOMAS ROBBINS, AND THOMAS E. CURTIS

1974   "Reply to Bellah." *Journal for the Scientific Study of Religion* 13 (December):491-95.

BAIRD, ROBERT D.

1971   *Category Formation and the History of Religions*. Religion and Reason Series, No. 1. The Hague: Mouton.

BELLAH, ROBERT N.

1970   *Beyond Belief.* New York: Harper.

1974   "Comment on 'The Limits of Symbolic Realism'." *Journal for the Scientific Study of Religion* 13 (December):487-89.

BERGER, PETER L.

1969   *The Sacred Canopy*. Garden City, N.Y.: Doubleday Anchor Books. Original publ.: Garden City, N.Y.: Doubleday, 1967.

BLEEKER, C. JOUCO

1959   "The Phenomenological Method." *Numen* 6 (December):96-111.

BLUMER, HERBERT
1969   *Symbolic Interactionism.* Englewood Cliffs, N.J.: Prentice-Hall.

BORGER, ROBERT, AND FRANK CIOFFI, EDS.
1970   *Explanation in the Behavioural Sciences.* Cambridge, Eng.: Cambridge University Press.

BRAITHWAITE, R. B.
1955   *An Empiricist's View of the Nature of Religious Belief.* Cambridge, Eng.: Cambridge University Press.

BRODBECK, MAY, ED.
1968   *Readings in the Philosophy of the Social Sciences.* New York: Macmillan.

BULTMANN, RUDOLF
1961   "New Testament and Mythology." In *Kerygma and Myth,* ed. Hans Werner Bartsch and tr. Reginald H. Fuller, pp. 1-44. New York: Harper Torchbooks.

COLLINGWOOD, R. G.
1946   *The Idea of History.* Ed. T. M. Knox. New York: Oxford University Press.

COSER, LEWIS
1975   "Presidential Address: Two Methods in Search of a Substance." *American Sociological Review* 40 (December):691-700.

DALLMAYR, FRED R., AND THOMAS A. MCCARTHY, EDS.
1977   *Understanding and Social Inquiry.* Notre Dame, Ind.: University of Notre Dame Press.

DAVIDSON, DONALD
1963   "Actions, Reasons, and Causes." *Journal of Philosophy* 40 (November):685-700.

DENZIN, NORMAN K.
1969   "Symbolic Interactionism and Ethnomethodology." *American Sociological Review* 34 (December):922-34.

DILTHEY, WILHELM
1961   *Pattern and Meaning in History.* Ed. and tr. H. P. Rickman. London: Allen & Unwin.

1976   *Selected Writings.* Ed. and tr. H. P. Rickman. Cambridge, Eng.: Cambridge University Press.

DOUGLAS, JACK D., ED.
1970   *Understanding Everyday Life.* Chicago: Aldine.

DRAY, WILLIAM H.
1957   *Laws and Explanation in History.* Oxford: Clarendon Press.

1959   "Explaining 'What' in History." In Gardiner (1959:402-8).

1963   "The Historical Explanation of Actions Reconsidered." In Hook (105-35).

1964   *Philosophy of History*. Foundations of Philosophy Series. Englewood Cliffs, N.J.: Prentice-Hall.

DUDLEY, GUILFORD, III
1977   *Religion on Trial*. Philadelphia: Temple University Press.

ELIADE, MIRCEA
1959a   *Cosmos and History*. Tr. Willard R. Trask. Bollingen Series XLVI. New York: Harper Torchbooks. Original publ. of tr.: *The Myth of the Eternal Return:* New York: Pantheon, 1954.

1959b   "Methodological Remarks on the Study of Religious Symbolism." In *The History of Religions,* eds. Eliade and Joseph M. Kitagawa, pp. 86-107. Chicago: University of Chicago Press.

1960   *Myths, Dreams and Mysteries*. Tr. Philip Mairet. New York: Harper.

1963   *Patterns in Comparative Religion*. Tr. Rosemary Sheed. Cleveland: Meridian Books. Original publ. of tr.: New York: Sheed & Ward, 1958.

1967   "On Understanding Primitive Religions." In *Glaube/Geist/Geschichte,* eds. Gerhard Müller and Winfried Zeller, pp. 498-505. Leiden: Brill.

1968a   *Myth and Reality*. Tr. Willard R. Trask. New York: Harper Torchbooks. Original publ. of tr.: New York: Harper, 1963.

1968b   *The Sacred and the Profane*. Tr. Willard R. Trask. New York. Harvest Books. Original publ. of tr.: New York: Harcourt, Brace, 1959.

1968c   "Comparative Religion: Its Past and Future." In *Knowledge and the Future of Man,* ed. Walter J. Ong, pp. 245-54. New York: Holt, Rinehart.

1969   *The Quest*. Chicago: University of Chicago Press.

FENTON, JOHN Y.
1970   "Reductionism in the Study of Religions." *Soundings* 53 (Spring):61-76.

GARDINER, PATRICK
1952   *The Nature of Historical Explanation*. Oxford: Clarendon Press.

GARDINER, PATRICK, ED.
1959   *Theories of History*. New York: Free Press.

GARFINKEL, HAROLD
1967   *Studies in Ethnomethodology*. Englewood Cliffs, N.J.: Prentice-Hall.

GEERTZ, CLIFFORD
1973   *The Interpretation of Cultures*. New York: Basic Books.

1983   *Local Knowledge.* New York: Basic Books.

1984   "Anti Anti-Relativism." *American Anthropologist* 86 (June):263-78.

GELLNER, ERNEST

1962   "Concepts and Society." In *Transactions of the Fifth World Congress of Sociology,* vol. I, pp. 153-83. Louvain, Belgium: International Sociological Association.

1968   "The New Idealism – Cause and Meaning in the Social Sciences." In *Problems in the Philosophy of Science,* eds. Imre Lakatos and Alan Musgrave, pp. 377-406. Proceedings of the International Colloquium in the Philosophy of Science, London, 1965. Vol. 3. Amsterdam: North-Holland.

1975a   "A Wittgensteinian Philosophy of (or against) the Social Sciences." *Philosophy of the Social Sciences* 5 (June):173-99.

1975b   "Ethnomethodology: The Re-Enchantment Industry, or The California Way of Subjectivity." *Philosophy of the Social Sciences* 5 (December):431-50.

GOFFMAN, ERVING

1959   *The Presentation of Self in Everyday Life.* Garden City, N.Y.: Doubleday Anchor Books.

1961   *Asylums.* Garden City, N.Y.: Doubleday Anchor Books.

GRÜNBAUM, ADOLF

1984   *The Foundations of Psychoanalysis.* Berkeley: University of California Press.

HARRIS, MARVIN

1968   *The Rise of Anthropological Theory.* New York: Crowell.

1979   *Cultural Materialism.* New York: Random House.

HAYEK, F. A.

1952   *The Counter-Revolution of Science.* Glencoe, Ill.: Free Press.

HEMPEL, CARL G.

1942   "The Function of General Laws in History." *Journal of Philosophy* 39 (January 15):35-48.

1962   "Explanation in Science and in History." In *Frontiers of Science and Philosophy,* ed. Robert G. Colodny, pp. 7-33. Pittsburgh: University of Pittsburgh Press.

1963a   "Reasons and Covering Laws in Historical Explanation." In Hook (143-63).

1963b   "Typological Methods in the Social Sciences." In Natanson (210-30).

1965   *Aspects of Scientific Explanation and other Essays in the Philosophy of Science.* New York: Free Press.

1966   *Philosophy of Natural Science.* Foundations of Philosophy Series.
           Englewood Cliffs, N.J.: Prentice-Hall.

1969   "Reduction: Ontological and Linguistic Facets." In *Philosophy, Science,
           and Method,* eds. Sidney Morgenbesser, Patrick Suppes, and Morton
           White, pp. 179-99. New York: St. Martin's Press.

HOOK, SIDNEY, ED.
1963   *Philosophy and History.* Fifth Annual New York University Institute of
           Philosophy. New York: New York University Press.

JARVIE, I. C.
1972   *Concepts and Society.* London and Boston: Routledge & Kegan Paul.

1984   *Rationality and Relativism.* London and Boston: Routledge & Kegan
           Paul.

KRISTENSEN, W. BREDE
1960   *The Meaning of Religion.* Tr. John B. Carman. The Hague: Martinus
           Nijhoff.

LOUCH, A. R.
1966   *Explanation and Human Action.* Oxford: Blackwell.

MACINTYRE, ALASDAIR
1964   "Is Understanding Religion Compatible with Believing?" In *Faith and
           the Philosophers,* ed. John Hick, pp. 115-33. New York: St. Martin's
           Press.

1967   "The Idea of a Social Science." *Aristotelian Society Supplementary
           Volume* 41:95-114.

1971   *Against the Self-Images of the Age.* New York: Schocken Books.

MACIVER, R. M.
1942   *Social Causation.* Boston: Ginn.

NAGEL, ERNEST
1961   *The Structure of Science.* New York: Harcourt, Brace.

1963   "Problems of Concept and Theory Formation in the Social Sciences." In
           Natanson (189-209).

NATANSON, MAURICE, ED.
1963   *Philosophy of the Social Sciences.* New York: Random House.

NIELSEN, KAI
1967   "Wittgensteinian Fideism." *Philosophy* 42 (July):191-209.

1971   *Contemporary Critiques of Religion.* New York: Herder & Herder.

OXTOBY, WILLARD G.
1968   "*Religionswissenschaft* Revisited." In *Religions in Antiquity,* ed. Jacob
           Neusner, pp. 590-608. Supplements to *Numen,* No. 14. Leiden: Brill.

PALS, DANIEL
1986   "Reductionism and Belief: An Appraisal of Recent Attacks on the
          Doctrine of Irreducible Religion." *Journal of Religion* 66 (January):18-
          36.

PEEL, J. D. Y.
1969   "Understanding alien belief-systems." *British Journal of Sociology* 20
          (March):69-84.

PENNER, HANS H., AND EDWARD A. YONAN
1972   "Is a Science of Religion Possible?" *Journal of Religion* 52 (April):
          107-33.

PHILLIPS, D. Z.
1965   *The Concept of Prayer.* London: Routledge & Kegan Paul.

1967   "Faith, Skepticism and Religious Understanding." In *Religion and
          Understanding,* ed. Phillips, pp. 63-79. New York: Macmillan.

1970   *Faith and Philosophical Enquiry.* London: Routledge & Kegan Paul.

1976   *Religion without Explanation.* Oxford: Blackwell.

PROUDFOOT, WAYNE
1981-82   "Religion and Reduction." *Union Seminary Quarterly Review* 37 (Fall-
          Winter):13-25.

RADCLIFFE-BROWN, A. R.
1922   *The Andaman Islanders.* Cambridge, Eng.: Cambridge University Press.

1952   *Structure and Function in Primitive Society.* Glencoe, Ill.: Free Press.

1958   *Methods in Social Anthropology.* Ed. M. N. Srinivas. Chicago:
          University of Chicago Press.

RICHARDS, GLYN
1978   "A Wittgensteinian Approach to the Philosophy of Religion: A Critical
          Evaluation of D. Z. Phillips." *Journal of Religion* 58 (July):288-302.

RICKETTS, MAC LINSCOTT
1973   "In Defence of Eliade." *Religion* 3 (Spring):13-34.

RICKMAN, H. P.
1960   "The Reaction against Positivism and Dilthey's Concept of
          Understanding." *British Journal of Sociology* 11 (December):307-18.

RICOEUR, PAUL
1969   *The Symbolism of Evil.* Tr. Emerson Buchanan. Boston: Beacon Press.

ROBBINS, THOMAS, DICK ANTHONY, AND THOMAS E. CURTIS
1973   "The Limits of Symbolic Realism: Problems of Empathetic Field
          Observation in a Sectarian Context." *Journal for the Scientific Study of
          Religion* 12 (September):259-71.

SALIBA, JOHN A.
1976   *'Homo Religiosus' in Mircea Eliade.* Supplementa ad *Numen,* Altera
            Series V. Leiden: Brill.

SCHUTZ, ALFRED
1962   "Concept and Theory Formation in the Social Sciences." In his
            Collected Papers, ed. Maurice Natanson, vol. 1, pp. 48-66. The Hague:
            Martinus Nijhoff.

SEGAL, ROBERT A.
1985a   "Have the Social Sciences Been Converted?" *Journal for the Scientific
            Study of Religion* 24 (September):321-24. Reprinted in revised form in
            the present book as ch. 4.

1985b   "A Jungian View of Evil: A Review Essay of John Sanford's *Evil.*"
            Zygon 20 (March):83-89. Reprinted in revised form in the present book
            as ch. 8.

1986   "Response to Blasi and Nelson." *Journal for the Scientific Study of
            Religion* 24 (September):369-72. Reprinted in revised form in the
            present book as ch. 6.

1987a   "Are Historians of Religions Necessarily Believers?" *Religious
            Traditions* 10 (July):71-76. Reprinted in revised form in the present
            book as ch. 2.

1987b   *Joseph Campbell: An Introduction.* New York: Garland Publishing.

forth-   "Comment on Steven Kepnes' 'Bridging the Gap Between Understanding
coming1   and Explanation Approaches to the Study of Religion'." *Journal for the
            Scientific Study of Religion.*

forth-   "Interpreting and Explaining Religion: Geertz and Durkheim."
coming2   *Soundings.*

n. d.   "How Historical Is the History of Religions?"

SMART, NINIAN
1977   *The Science of Religion and the Sociology of Knowledge.* Princeton,
            N.J.: Princeton University Press.

SMITH, WILFRED C.
1963a   *The Meaning and End of Religion.* New York: Macmillan.

1963b   *The Faith of Other Men.* New York: Mentor Books.

1975   "Methodology and the Study of Religion: Some Misgivings." In
            Methodological Issues in Religious Studies, ed. Robert D. Baird, pp. 1-
            30. Chico, Calif.: New Horizons Press.

1979   *Faith and Belief.* Princeton, N.J.: Princeton University Press.

SPIRO, MELFORD E.
1986   "Cultural Relativism and the Future of Anthropology." *Cultural
            Anthropology* 1 (August):259-86.

SUDNOW, DAVID, ED.
1972   *Studies in Social Interaction.* New York: Free Press.

TURNER, ROY, ED.
1970   *Ethnomethodology.* Harmondsworth, Eng.: Penguin Books.

TYLER, STEPHEN A., ED.
1969   *Cognitive Anthropology.* New York Holt, Rinehart.

WAX, MURRAY L.
1967   "On Understanding *Verstehen:* A Reply to Abel." *Sociology and Social Research* 51 (April):323-33.

WEBER, MAX
1947   *The Theory of Social and Economic Organization.* Ed. Talcott Parsons. Trs. A. M. Henderson and Parsons. Glencoe, Ill.: Free Press.

1949   "'Objectivity' in Social Science and Social Policy." In his *The Methodology of the Social Sciences*, eds. and trs. Edward A. Shils and Henry A. Finch, pp. 49-112. New York: Free Press.

WIEBE, DONALD
1984   "Beyond the Sceptic and the Devotee: Reductionism in the Scientific Study of Religion." *Journal of the American Academy of Religion* 52 (March):157-65.

WILSON, BRYAN, ED.
1970   *Rationality.* Oxford: Blackwell.

WIMSATT, WILLIAM C.
1979   "Reduction and Reductionism." In *Current Research in Philosophy of Science*, eds. Peter D. Asquith and Henry E. Kyburg, pp. 352-77. Proceedings of the P. S. A. Critical Research Problems Conference. East Lansing, Mich.: Philosophy of Science Association.

WINCH, PETER
1958   *The Idea of a Social Science and Its Relation to Philosophy.* London: Routledge & Kegan Paul.

1964   "Understanding a Primitive Society." *American Philosophical Quarterly* 1 (October):307-24.

WISDOM, JOHN
1953   "Gods." In his *Philosophy and Psycho-Analysis*, pp. 149-68. Oxford: Blackwell.

1965   "The Logic of God" and "Religious Belief." In his *Paradox and Discovery*, pp. 1-22 and 43-56. Oxford: Blackwell.

Chapter Two

Are Historians of Religions Necessarily Believers?

As defined by leading practitioners like Mircea Eliade, the history of religions purports only to present, not to endorse, the believer's view of the origin, function, and meaning of religion. I argue that historians in fact commit themselves to endorsing the believer's view.

Take, as representative, the position of Eliade. According to him, religion originates and functions to link believers to the "sacred" – an impersonal realm over and above individual gods. Believers seek to encounter the sacred both temporally and spatially. They long to experience both the places where the sacred has manifested itself – for example, a particular stone or tree – and the pre-fallen, Edenic epoch when the gods, who are agents of the sacred, were near: "... since religious man cannot live except in an atmosphere impregnated with the sacred, we must expect to find a large number of techniques for consecrating space" (Eliade 1968b:28). "It is easy to understand why the memory of that marvelous time haunted religious man, why he periodically sought to return to it. *In illo tempore* the gods had displayed their greatest powers. The cosmogony is the supreme divine manifestation, the paradigmatic act of strength, superabundance, and creativity. Religious man ... seeks to reside at the very source of primordial reality, when the world was *in statu nascendi*" (Eliade 1968b:80).

Believers, says Eliade, yearn to experience the sacred not as the means to an end but as the end itself. They seek the sacred because they seek the sacred, not because they seek something else through it. Security and peace of mind are among the many happy consequences of contact with the sacred, but contact itself remains the end. Believers not merely want but need contact with the sacred: "... religious man can live only in a sacred world, because it is only in such a world that he participates in being, that he has a real existence. This religious need expresses an unquenchable ontological thirst. Religious man thirsts for being" (Eliade 1968b:64).

In saying that religion serves to reach the sacred, Eliade invariably professes to be merely presenting the believer's own view of religion: "A sacred stone remains a stone; apparently (or, more precisely, from the profane point of view), nothing distinguishes it from all other stones. *But for those to whom a stone reveals itself as sacred,* its immediate reality is transmuted into a supernatural reality. In other words, *for those who have a religious experience* all nature is capable of revealing itself as cosmic sacrality" (Eliade 1968b:12 [italics added]). Eliade laments, for example, that "the main interest" of Westerners who study primitives "has been the study of material cultures and the analysis of family structure, social organization, tribal law, and so on. These are problems, one may say, important and even urgent for western scholarship, but of secondary importance for the understanding of the *meaning of a particular culture,* as it was understood and assumed *by its own members*" (Eliade 1967:502-3 [italics in original]). Contrasting himself to the theologian, Eliade says that "the *ultimate* aim of the historian of religions is [merely] to *understand,* and to make understandable to others, religious man's behavior and mental universe" (Eliade 1968b:162 [italics added]).

The issue at hand is not whether Eliade accurately depicts the believer's point of view.[1] Assume that he does. The issue is whether he is merely depicting or outright endorsing that point of view.

I argue that Eliade outright endorses the believer's view.[2] To begin with, Eliade maintains that believers are often unconscious of the full meaning of religion for them. As he says of religious symbols in particular: " ... we do not have the right to conclude that the message of the symbols is confined to the meanings of which a certain number of individuals are fully conscious .... Depth psychology has taught us that the symbol delivers its message and fulfils its function even when its meaning escapes awareness" (Eliade 1959:106-7). In imputing to believers a meaning of which they are considerably unconscious, Eliade is surely going beyond the believer's point of view. So far, however, he is saying only that the true meaning of religion for believers is partly unconscious, not that it is irreducibly religious.

More striking, then, is Eliade assertion that *nonbelievers,* whom he equates with moderns, are unconsciously religious: "The majority of the 'irreligious' still behave religiously, even though they are not aware of the fact.... [T]he modern man who feels and claims that he is nonreligious still retains a large stock of camouflaged myths and degenerated rituals" (Eliade 1968b:204-5). Eliade goes so far as to say that "even the most avowedly nonreligious man still, in his deeper being, shares in a religiously oriented behavior" (Eliade 1968b:211). In attributing to nonbelievers a religiosity of which they are not just partly but wholly unconscious and which not just exceeds but contradicts their professed atheism, Eliade is surely venturing far beyond the actor's point of view.

---

[1]See Segal (1983:98-99).
[2]I have taken the next few arguments from Segal (1983:98-102). In Segal (n. d.) I argue the opposite: that Eliade is in fact interested only secondarily in the believer's point of view.

Eliade is here saying that the true meaning of religion for *nonbelievers* is not only unconscious but also irreducibly religious: it is the encounter with the sacred in overtly secular activities. Surely, then, the true meaning of religion for *believers* must also be irreducibly religious. Because the *conscious* meaning of religion for believers is, according to Eliade, irreducibly religious as well, Eliade is thus endorsing, not merely presenting, the believer's conscious view. He is saying that believers correctly grasp the meaning of religion for them. So tightly connected is the meaning of religion to the origin and function of religion that Eliade is surely endorsing the believer's conscious view of the origin and function as well: the view that religion arises and serves to provide contact with the sacred.

If Eliade is endorsing the believer's view of the origin and function of religion, he is claiming to know why believers really are religious, not merely why they think they are. He is therefore claiming to be accounting for religion, not merely to be recording the believer's own account.

Indeed, Eliade pits his account against the accounts of social scientists, whom he faults for accounting for religion reductively: "... a religious phenomenon will only be recognized as such if it is grasped at its own level, that is to say, if it is studied *as* something religious. To try to grasp the essence of such a phenomenon by means of physiology, psychology, sociology, economics, linguistics, or any other study is false; it misses the one unique and irreducible element in it – the element of the sacred" (Eliade 1963:xiii).

The social sciences ordinarily seek only the origin, function, and meaning of religion, not its object. They seek to determine why believers believe and what their beliefs mean to them, not whether what believers believe is true. In opposing the social sciences, Eliade is thus committed to an irreducibly religious view – the believer's presumed one – of only the origin, function, and meaning of religion.

I argue that Eliade is in fact thereby committed to the believer's view of the object, or referent, of religion as well. I argue that he is committed to the reality of the sacred itself, not merely of the human quest for it. In an earlier essay I argued that Eliade's endorsement of the believer's view of the *meaning* of religion commits him to the reality of the sacred.[3] For the heart of the meaning of religion for believers *is* the reality of the sacred. Now I want to argue, more concretely, that Eliade's endorsement of the believer's view of the *function* of religion also commits him to the reality of the sacred. The *origin* of religion – a need for the sacred – does not entail the existence of the sacred, but the function – the fulfillment of that need – does.

In saying that the function of religion for believers is to reach the sacred, Eliade may, to be sure, be saying only that religion is *intended* to reach the

---

[3]See Segal (1983:109-15).

sacred, not that it necessarily does. Only if he is saying that religion actually *manages* to reach the sacred is he committed to the reality of the sacred.

The proof that religion for Eliade actually manages to reach the sacred stems not only from Eliade's endorsement of the believer's presumed view. It stems as well from Eliade's own relentless praise of religion. Why else would he laud it so effusively? Since the need for the sacred that he ascribes to all humans is for him both innate and, except for moderns, conscious, he cannot be crediting religion with either implanting that need or, insofar as the need remains unconscious in moderns, even awakening it. He must, then, be crediting religion with fulfilling it.

Indeed, Eliade declares outright that religion accomplishes its function. As he says of myth in particular: "He who recites or performs the origin myth is thereby steeped in the sacred atmosphere in which these miraculous events took place.... As a summary formula we might say that by 'living' the myths one emerges from profane, chronological time and enters a time that is of a different quality, a 'sacred' Time at once primordial and indefinitely recoverable" (Eliade 1968a:18).

Furthermore, Eliade says that even modern, seemingly secular myths, which he considers less potent than earlier, explicitly religious ones, work: "A whole volume could well be written on the myths of modern man, on the mythologies camouflaged in the plays that he enjoys, in the books that he reads.... Even reading includes a mythological function ... because, through reading, the modern man *succeeds in obtaining* an 'escape from time' comparable to the 'emergence from time' effected by [earlier] myths. Whether modern man 'kills' time with a detective story or enters such a foreign temporal universe as is represented by any novel, reading projects him into other rhythms, makes him live in another 'history'" (Eliade 1968b:205 [italics added]). Surely Eliade is saying here that modern myths work in fact, not just in the minds of moderns.

To be sure, Eliade is committed to the reality of the sacred only if he is committed to the reality of the need for it as well as of the fulfillment of that need. If Eliade is saying not that believers really need the sacred but only that they think they do, religion could succeed not by actually linking them to the sacred but only by convincing them that it had. Eliade could even be saying that the need religion fulfills is the need to *think* that one has reached the sacred, in which case religion could jauntily serve its function even in the face of the nonexistence of the sacred.

Nowhere, however, does Eliade characterize the need religion fulfills as less than a need actually to reach the sacred. Hence he writes, as quoted, of "religious man's desire to live in the sacred" (Eliade 1968b:28), not of his desire merely to think that he has.

What is true of Eliade is, I believe, true of other historians of religions as well. They profess to be only conveying the believer's point of view, but in actuality they are endorsing it. They are therefore necessarily believers themselves.[4]

REFERENCES

ELIADE, MIRCEA

1959   "Methodological Remarks on the Study of Religious Symbolism." In *The History of Religions,* eds. Eliade and Joseph M. Kitagawa, pp. 86-107. Chicago: University of Chicago Press.

1967   "On Understanding Primitive Religions." In *Glaube/Geist/Geschichte,* eds. Gerhard Müller and Winfried Zeller, pp. 498-505. Leiden: Brill.

1963   *Patterns in Comparative Religion.* Tr. Rosemary Sheed. Cleveland: Meridian Books. Original publ. of tr.: New York: Sheed & Ward, 1958.

1968a   *Myth and Reality.* Tr. Willard R. Trask. New York: Harper Torchbooks. Original publ. of tr.: New York: Harper, 1963.

1968b   *The Sacred and the Profane.* Tr. Willard R. Trask. New York: Harvest Books. Original publ. of tr.: New York: Harcourt, Brace, 1959.

SEGAL, ROBERT A.

1983   "In Defense of Reductionism." *Journal of the American Academy of Religion* 51 (March):97-124. Reprinted in revised form in the present book as ch. 1.

n. d.   "How Historical Is the History of Religions?"

forth-   "A Response to Eric J. Sharpe." *Religious Traditions.*
coming

SHARPE, ERIC J.

forth-   "History and 'Belief': A Response to Robert A. Segal." *Religious*
coming   *Traditions.*

---

[4]For a forthcoming response and counterresponse to this essay see Sharpe and Segal (forthcoming).

Chapter Three

Mircea Eliade's Theory of Millenarianism

Mircea Eliade classifies himself as a historian of religions, but by "history" he means more the significance than the origin or function of religion. Where the origin and function of religion say why believers are religious, the significance, or "meaning," says what their religiosity either means *to* them or reveals *about* them.[1] Eliade applies to the case of millenarianism[2] his interpretation of the meaning of religion generally. Yet presupposed in his interpretation of the meaning of millenarianism is an explanation, or theory, of its origin and function. That theory not only elucidates Eliade's theory of religion as a whole but also provides an atypical and possibly even unique theory of millenarianism in its own right.

Most, perhaps all other, theorists of millenarianism view it as an abnormal phenomenon, which only extraordinary circumstances can explain. By contrast, Eliade sees millenarianism as merely the realization of a normal, in fact inherent, eschatological desire in all human beings: a desire to abolish history, which is profane time, and return to primordial time, which is sacred. Humans desire to abolish history not annually, as in New Year festivals, or temporarily, as in mysticism, but once and forever. They desire to do so because they find history meaningless and because it stands between them and primordial time, where alone meaningfulness lies. Eliade's theory, then, is that, given the meaninglessness which humans find in history and the meaningfulness, or existential meaning, which they find in primordial time, all seek instinctively to abolish history and return to primordial time.[3] Millenarianism is but the fulfillment of that instinct.

Eliade's claim that the cause of millenarianism is an inherent desire in humans to break with history and return to primordial time rests on a prior claim: that millenarianism, whatever its cause, actually expresses a desire to break with history and return to primordial time. Both claims are testable. The second claim can prove false without the first one's being false, but the truth of the second depends on the truth of the first: if millenarianism does not represent

---

[1] See Segal.
[2] See esp. Eliade (1969a). See also Eliade (1959; 1968a).
[3] For an excellent assessment of Eliade's view of history see Allen.

a desire to break with history and return to primordial time, an innate human desire to do so can hardly be its cause. At the same time the truth of the first claim does not establish the truth of the second.

How, then, does Eliade proceed to prove his case? Rather than taking each claim in turn, first showing that millenarianism constitutes a desire to break with history and return to primordial time and then showing that the desire for millenarianism is universal and therefore somehow innate, he takes the truth of the second claim for granted and on the basis of it interprets every millenarian movement as a desire to break with history and return to primordial time. Having interpreted every millenarian movement as a desire to break with history and return to primordial time, he vaunts his effort as proof that there is a universal and therefore for him innate desire to break with history and return to primordial time.

Nowhere does Eliade quite spell out this procedure. One must reconstruct it from his analysis of millenarianism in particular and of religion in general.

For Eliade, all humans find themselves in the profane world yet seek the sacred one. They seek the sacred both spatially and temporally. Spatially, they seek the places and objects where the sacred has chosen to manifest itself – for example, the site of the burning bush. Temporally, they seek the period when the gods, who are agents of the sacred, were most fully present among humans – usually the pristine time just after creation, when, for example, God walked in the Garden of Eden. For Eliade, myths describe this sacred time. To read, hear, or re-enact a myth is literally to relive it and thereby to return magically to sacred, or primordial, time. To return is to abolish the ordinary, profane time that has come in between. That profane time is history. Millenarianism is therefore nothing other than the realization of the desire to abolish history and return to the time just after creation, and its cause is the innate human desire to do so.

Mythic and Historical Humans

If for Eliade all humans seek instinctively to abolish history, why are all not millenarian? Why have all not yet abolished history? To begin with, Eliade distinguishes between primitive, "anhistorical," mythic humans and modern, historical ones. Historical humans, he admits, do not seek – consciously – to abolish history. On the contrary, they are content with historical time, which they find meaningful. Mythic humans, by contrast, do seek to abolish history, which, as a series of "events that derive from no archetype," they find "intolerable" (Eliade 1959:75). The mythic individual "tends to set himself in opposition, by every means in his power, to history ..." (Eliade 1959:95). The difference between the meaning that historical humans find in history and the meaninglessness that mythic humans find is "the crucial difference" between the one group of humans and the other (Eliade 1959:154).

Far from explaining why, if humans naturally desire to abolish history, they have yet to do so, the distinction between mythic and historical humans seemingly only aggravates the difficulty. If mythic humans really seek to abolish history, why are they not all millenarian? If historical humans do not even seek to abolish history, how can Eliade claim that all humans strive to abolish it?

Eliade explains that as much as mythic humans do try to abolish history, they are unable to do so. For they are unable to avoid the experience of irreversibility, which Eliade equates with the experience of history. Mythic humans experience irreversibility through both memory and suffering. Their "memory is capable (though doubtless far less intensely than that of a modern man) of revealing the irreversibility of events, that is, of recording history" (Eliade 1959:75), and they are "powerless against cosmic catastrophes, military disasters, social injustices bound up with the very structure of society, personal misfortunes, and so forth" (Eliade 1959:95) – in short, suffering, which they doubtless experience as distinctly real.

Though mythic humans cannot exorcise history, they do learn to "tolerate" it. They tolerate history in two ways: "... either by periodically abolishing it through repetition of the cosmogony and a periodic regeneration of time or by giving historical events a metahistorical meaning ..." (Eliade 1959:142). Mythic humans periodically abolish history through ritual. They confer meaning on history by "fitting" events "into a well-consolidated system in which the cosmos and man's existence [has] each its *raison d'être*" (Eliade 1959:142). Suffering in particular gets explained by a theodicy.[4]

The difficulty which led Eliade to postulate the conferring of meaning on history by mythic humans was the apparent contradiction between his assertion that mythic humans seek to abolish history and his acknowledgment that they have yet to abolish it. His claim that mythic humans confer meaning on history as an antidote to their inability to abolish it leads, however, to an even keener difficulty: the seeming contradiction between that claim and his prior claim that mythic humans find history meaningless. This difficulty is identical with the one posed by his characterization of historical humans: the fact that historical humans find history meaningful yet, as humans, should not.

The resolution which Eliade provides in the case of mythic humans is surely the one which he would provide in the case of historical humans as well. Indeed, by ascribing to mythic humans the conferring of meaning on history he has effaced the distinction between mythic and historical humans: insofar as mythic

---

[4]See Eliade (1959:95-102). Eliade lists other means of rationalizing suffering, but these strategies – "suffering [it is said] proceeds from the magical action of an enemy, from breaking a taboo, from entering a baneful zone, from the anger of a god ..." (1959:97) – have nothing to do with the bestowal of metahistorical meaning on history.

humans find history meaningful, they are no different from historical humans. Eliade's resolution of the contradiction his interpretation of mythic humans poses must therefore apply to the contradiction his interpretation of historical humans poses.

That resolution is twofold. First, Eliade asserts that the bestowal of meaning on history by mythic humans is only a psychological antidote to its intrinsic meaninglessness. The bestowal of meaning is simply a means of "tolerating" history, and the meaning bestowed is merely "consoling" (Eliade 1959:142). Second, Eliade deems that meaning not historical but "metahistorical," or "transhistorical." History itself thereby remains meaningless: "Whether he abolishes it periodically, whether he devaluates it by perpetually finding *transhistorical* models and archetypes for it, whether, finally, he gives it a *metahistorical* meaning (cyclical theory, eschatological significations, and so on), the man of the traditional civilizations accord[s] the historical event no value in itself ..." (Eliade 1959:141 [italics added]).

Even though Eliade would surely explain the meaningfulness of history for historical humans in the same way, he must still explain why historical humans are reluctant to abolish history in the first place. Mythic humans, he argues, try to abolish history but because of their experience of irreversibility cannot do so. Historical humans, however, do not even try to abolish history. Rather than explaining why they do not try, Eliade assumes only that the meaningfulness that they, like their mythic counterparts, find is merely an artificial means of tolerating history, which remains intrinsically meaningless.

This happy resolution of the seeming contradiction between humanity's finding history meaningful and its finding history meaningless is, however, problematic, though not contradictory, in turn. How, first of all, does Eliade know that the meaning found in history is but a rationalization for its true meaninglessness rather than its native significance? He doesn't. He assumes rather than proves this key point. What should be his conclusion is really his premise, and what should be a falsifiable claim becomes a dogmatic assertion. The claim that humanity finds history meaningless and seeks its extinction is itself falsifiable. Eliade's interpretation of the evidence is what makes the claim nonfalsifiable: meaningless history automatically bolsters his claim, and meaningful history automatically becomes only a rationalization for its actual meaninglessness. His claim is thus beyond disproof.

But there *is* untampered evidence for the inherent meaninglessness of history, Eliade would retort, and he would proceed to invoke the other part of his explanation of humanity's finding history meaningful: his claim that the meaning found is not historical but "metahistorical." A "metahistorical" meaning not only transcends history but in so doing confirms the meaninglessness of history. For that meaning both exceeds a single historical event and is fulfilled in the abolition of history. Calling a meaning which exceeds a single event metahistorical rather than historical is, however, arbitrary.

For any meaning that history possesses would, as the meaning of all history, exceed the bounds of a single event. Labeling metahistorical a meaning which finds fruition in the abolition of history would seem a more persuasive argument.

The Millenarianism of Cargo Cults

Undeniably, the millenarian eschatologies of many, perhaps most, peoples are interpretable as breaking with history and therefore abolishing it, so sparse is the value conferred on events preceding the end. For example, in the Melanesian cargo cults, as Eliade describes them,[5] events do not lead naturally to the return of the ancestors and the realization of the millennium. On the contrary, each of the two stages of the millenarian movement constitutes a rupture, and an unanticipated rupture, with the present. When the whites come to Melanesia, they come unexpectedly, and the natives greet them as the dead ancestors not because the natives have been predicting their return but because the whites look and act like the ancestors. They have white skins, have obviously come from far away, sail in magnificent ships, and bear goods of plenty.[6] Only *with* their arrival, not before, is the millennium proclaimed.

Once the whites establish themselves, however, they "behave as masters, despise the natives, compel them to work very hard and try to convert them to Christianity" (Eliade 1969a:130). Above all, the whites refuse to share their cargo with the natives. Certain as the natives are that this situation cannot constitute the millennium yet that the cargo represents the abundance intended for them, they accuse the whites of stealing the cargo from the real ancestors and prophesy the whites' imminent downfall at the hands of those ancestors. In the new millennium now announced not only are the traditional promises of abundance and immortality to be realized, but so, then, is a previously unimagined yearning: for the ouster of the whites. The fulfillment of both ends marks a sharp severance with the present, which therefore scarcely leads to the millennium. As the restoration of prelapsarian abundance and immortality, the millennium represents a return to primordial time and therefore the abolition of history.

The Millenarianism of Ancient Israel

Perhaps only Eliade's interpretation of the seeming value placed on history by avowedly historical religions like Judaism and Christianity and by secular ideologies like Marxism reveals the tendentiousness of his view. His interpretation of the Israelite notion of history provides the best illustration.

---

[5]See Eliade (1969a:125-40).
[6]See Eliade (1969a:128).

In the Hebrew Bible history is the sphere in which God acts, and it is by his actions in history that he is defined. Rather than an abstract being, God is the God of Abraham, Isaac, and Jacob, with each of whom he makes or renews a covenant. God is he who leads Israel out of slavery in Egypt, he who gives Israel the Law at Sinai, he who gives the people the land of Canaan, and he who establishes the monarchy.

Yet history remains the province of humans. God has no history of his own. He is knowable only in relation to humans. The deeds of his which history recounts take place within historical, not mythic, time. The covenant, the Exodus, the revelation of the Law, and even creation itself are events in the lives of humans, not of God. Creation marks the birth of the world and of humans, not of God; the covenant, the elevation of Israel, not of God; the Exodus, the liberation of Israel, not of God; the revelation of the Law, its revelation to Israel, not to God. These events alter history but not God himself. More important, they are irreversible. They may be commemorated annually, but they do not recur. The rituals which commemorate them may re-establish contact with God, but they do not duplicate his deeds.

The Pentateuch itself speaks little of eschatology. Israel awaits only entry into the Promised Land. As the fulfillment of the covenant going back to Abraham, that event signifies the fulfillment of history. The Prophets do espouse eschatologies, and those eschatologies usually involve not only the destruction of the Kingdom, Northern or Southern, but also its restoration. Nevertheless, the end, as the destruction of the Kingdom and not of the world, is wholly historical. Life is slated to revert not to primordial time but to the time prior to the establishment of the Kingdom. Moreover, humans, not God, are responsible for the end. Their disobedience breaks the covenant, and their obedience will one day repair it.

Admittedly, Eliade at times seems to acknowledge that Israelite history, independent of myth, is meaningful. For example, having noted the parallels drawn by various scholars between the Babylonian New Year Festival, at which history was abolished and the world recreated, and a reconstructed Jewish New Year Festival, at which the same phenomenon supposedly occurred, he cautions that "obviously, the symbolic reiteration of the cosmogony at the New Year in Mesopotamia and in Israel cannot be put on the same plane. Among the Jews the archaic scenario of the periodic renewal of the world was progressively historicized, while still preserving something of its original [mythic] meaning" (Eliade 1968a:49). By "progressive historicization" Eliade means not, however, that history ceased being periodically abolished and the world periodically renewed but the opposite: that the periodic renewal of the world was read into "such historical events as the exodus and the crossing of the Red Sea, the conquest of Canaan, the Babylonian captivity and the return from exile, etc." (Eliade 1968a:49). He concludes that "however great the differences between the Mesopotamian and Jewish cult systems, they still obviously share a common hope for the annual or periodic regeneration of the World" (Eliade 1968a:50) – and therefore for the abolition of history.

Even if Eliade were to say that the world finally ceased being renewed annually or periodically, his postulation of a "progressive historicization" would still be moot. For pitted against every Biblicist who believes that the meaning of the Jewish New Year Festival was originally the recreation of the world and was only progressively historicized is at least another who maintains the reverse: that the New Year Festival originally celebrated a historical event or series of events and was only later "mythicized."[7]

Eliade cites "recent studies" of Psalms which show that the Festival originally "commemorated the triumph of Yahweh, leader of the forces of light, over the forces of darkness (the chaos of the sea, the primordial monster Rahab). This triumph was followed by the enthronement of Yahweh as king and the repetition of the cosmogonic act. The slaying of the monster Rahab and the victory over the waters ... were equivalent to the creation of the cosmos ..." (Eliade 1959:60). The studies he cites, however, are exclusively those of myth ritualists, who hardly constitute the consensus of Biblicists. For at least as many other scholars, the forces over which God triumphs are from the outset physical rather than divine ones, are creations rather than rivals of God, or are only metaphors for the human enemies of Israel.

Without distinguishing between worldly and otherworldly brands of eschatology, Eliade speaks collectively of "Judaeo-Christian eschatological visions." He does note that "Judaeo-Christianity makes an innovation of the first importance" over previous eschatologies: "the End of the World will occur only once, just as the cosmogony occurred only once." He even speaks of the end as "the triumph of a Sacred History." But then he says that "the Cosmos that will reappear after the catastrophe will be the same Cosmos that God created at the beginning of Time ..." (Eliade 1968a:64-65). Once again, he will concede no significance to history itself.

In nonapocalyptic Jewish eschatology history certainly triumphs: it witnesses the progressive improvement of humanity, which the eschatology merely completes. Yet even in apocalypticism, where the world progressively degenerates and divine intervention is necessary not to complete but to overturn the course of history, history triumphs, and its triumph is still the realization of the eschatology. For the degeneration of the world becomes part of God's plan for the world: degeneration proves as prerequisite to the realization of the apocalyptic eschatology as improvement is to the realization of the nonapocalyptic one. The apocalyptic obsession with reading the present back into the past evinces the need to know how *history* is heading. The world may be under the temporary control of Satan, but his reign, too, is part of God's plan.

---

[7]For a summary of these different interpretations and an attempted reconciliation of them see Cross.

Nor is the end a return to primordial time. It is the fulfillment of the covenant made with the apocalyptic group, a fulfillment that now takes place on a cosmic rather than merely human scale. Whether the meaning accorded history is in fact a rationalization for its inherent meaninglessness is not here the issue, which is rather whether history even *seemingly* has meaning, rationalized or not.

At one point Eliade goes so far as to title the Prophetic view of history "history regarded as theophany" (Eliade 1959:102) – an impressive concession for one who otherwise dismisses history as profane. The Prophets, he says, were the first, the first "in history," to "affirm" "the idea that historical events have a value in themselves, insofar as they are determined by the will of God. This God of the Jewish people is no longer an Oriental divinity, creator of archetypal gestures, but a personality who ceaselessly intervenes in history, who reveals his will through events (invasions, sieges, battles, and so on). Historical facts thus become 'situations' of man in respect to God, and as such they acquire a religious value that nothing had previously been able to confer on them" (Eliade 1959:104). The Prophets not only were the first to place value on history itself but also "for the first time ... succeeded in transcending the traditional vision of the cycle (the conception that ensures all things will be repeated forever), and discovered a one-way time" (Eliade 1959:104).

Yet even "in the Israel of the Messianic prophets, historical events could be tolerated" only "because, on the one hand, they were willed by Yahweh, and, on the other hand, because they were necessary to the final salvation of the chosen people" (Eliade 1959:106-7). That salvation might come only once and not annually, but "when the Messiah comes, the world will be saved once and for all and history will cease to exist" (Eliade 1959:107). Eliade states outright that "Messianic beliefs in a final regeneration of the world themselves also indicate an antihistoric attitude. Since he can no longer ignore or periodically abolish history, the Hebrew tolerates it in the hope that it will finally end, at some more or less distant future moment. The irreversibility of historical events and of time is compensated by the limitation of history to time" (Eliade 1959:111). Having begun by singling out the Israelite view of history as unique, Eliade ends by lumping it with the longing of everyone else to overcome history.

How does Eliade know that the meaning which "the Hebrew" finds in history is only a device for tolerating it? How can Eliade foreclose the possibility that history gets tolerated because it is meaningful in the first place? Eliade cannot argue that the meaning of history for Israel transcends history, for he himself notes that the meaning of history for Israel lies within history. He must argue that history culminates in the abolition and thereby the rejection of itself. And so, as seen, he does.

Not only, however, has it seemed far from clear that the end of history for Israel necessarily means its abolition, but it is hardly clear that even the abolition of history would mean its rejection rather than fulfillment. If it is not clear that the abolition of history necessarily represents its rejection, then it is not clear that humans, Israelite or other, necessarily want to reject history, in which case it is not clear that in the meantime they seek simply to tolerate history, in which case it is not clear that the meaning history has for them is other than its genuine meaning.

J. H. Plumb's View of History

Recently, the English historian J. H. Plumb has lamented what he calls "the death of the past" and its replacement by sheer "history," or the past as dead. From the earliest recorded time, he explains, the past has been "a living past, something which has been used day after day, life after life, never-endingly," for a variety of purposes: "... to explain the origins and purpose of human life, to sanctify institutions of government, to give validity to class structure, to provide moral example, to vivify cultural and educational processes, to interpret the future, to invest both the individual human life or [sic] a nation's with a sense of destiny" (Plumb, 11). By contrast, "history" denotes a detached, professional stance toward the past, which no longer exerts any authority over the present. The past becomes a time distinct from our own, a subject of analysis rather than of either veneration or emulation. As Plumb puts it, history cannot do what the past did: dictate what one should believe and do.

Clearly, the relationship for Plumb between history and the past is like that for Eliade between history and myth. But where Eliade rejects history altogether, Plumb scurries to defend it. Even if history lacks the authority of the past, it can, he argues, reveal truths which increase humans' awareness of themselves. Its power lies in the fact that it *is* critical and objective, beholden to no tradition and free to seek the truth. Here history is more than, as mythic humans purportedly conceive it, a succession of "meaningless conjunctures or infractions of [archetypal] norms" (Eliade 1959:154). It is what has shaped the present, even if it no longer dictates the present. It lives on in the consequences it has for the present and is important just because it cannot be effaced. When blacks and others demand to know their own history, they only underscore the significance of history for all humans.

The Limits of Eliade's Theory of Millenarianism

Even if Eliade were able to show that every eschatology evinces a desire to abolish history and revert to primordial time, he would still have to explain the two characteristics which distinguish millenarianism from ordinary eschatology: the imminence of the eschatology, and the frequent adoption of a new eschatology rather than the realization of the existing one.

If, according to Eliade, humans are by nature potentially millenarian, why do they become millenarian when they do? Even if till now they have been merely tolerating history rather than truly finding meaning in it, why do they suddenly cease tolerating it? If they have always sought to overcome history, why do they succeed only now? Millenarianism may for Eliade be only the long-sought realization of an inherent longing, but it nevertheless *is* the realization of that longing. Why does it come when it does?

Most, perhaps all other, theorists of millenarianism have scant difficulty answering this question, for they deem millenarian yearnings the product of new rather than old conditions – social, political, economic, or other. Millenarian yearnings do not exist potentially in humans, merely awaiting realization. They do not previously exist at all. They *arise* as yearnings about to be realized. Eliade alone, perhaps, deems these yearnings innate and therefore latent. To explain their realization must he not, then, resort to something beyond a permanent human desire to do so, and does not his refusal to explain that realization make his theory of millenarianism inadequate?

In the case of the cargo cults it does not, and for that reason the example is misleading. Eliade need not explain why *this* particular millennium is realized when it is because it just *is* realized. He need not explain what new conditions trigger the millennium because the only conditions that could be said to trigger it – the arrival of the whites in cargo-laden ships – are for the natives not the cause of the millennium but the millennium itself, which for them is therefore a *fait accompli*. True, the natives must *interpret* these events as millenarian, but so they do: the appearance of the whites in ships with cargo is for them neither the cause of the millennium nor even a sign of it but the millennium itself.

The question is whether Eliade can cite any other millenarian movement in which the millennium simply arrives, the arrival of which he need therefore not explain. If there are few other instances of the unannounced realization of the millennium, he must explain why, in the light of an innate eschatological drive, humans act on that drive when they do.

It is unclear whether Eliade is even aware of this problem and therefore whether he intends either of the two possible solutions to it implicit in his writings. The first solution is the subsumption of the secular conditions connected with millenarianism under the millenarian instinct itself. The second solution is the opposite: the severance of these conditions from millenarianism itself and the relegation of them to the status of mere triggers of the instinct.

Either solution is inferable from Eliade's words: "Of course, all these millenarist movements in Oceania arose as a sequel to precise historical situations, and express a desire for economic and political independence. Numerous works have explained the socio-political context of the 'cargo-cults'. But the historico-religious interpretation of these millenarist minor religions has hardly begun. Now, all these prophetic phenomena become completely intelligible only in the perspective of the history of religions. It is impossible to discover the significance and assess the extraordinary success of the 'cargo-cults' without taking into account one mythico-ritual theme which plays a fundamental part in Melanesian religions: the annual return of the dead and the cosmic renewal that it implies" (Eliade 1969a:132). According to the first solution, the native desire for independence is really a desire for the recreation of the world, for starting life afresh. According to the second solution, this same desire for independence is itself secular and merely sparks the desire for the recreation of the world.

Both solutions are problematic. The first solution, exactly by subsuming the desire for independence under the desire for the millennium, fails to explain what it is supposed to explain: why the millenarian desire as a whole surfaces when it does. To say that the millenarian desire surfaces the moment the desire for independence does – the only conceivable explanation – is to abandon the first solution for the second.

But once Eliade acknowledges that the activator of millenarianism is secular, he can no longer blithely maintain that the activator is merely the activator and that millenarianism itself, like all other religious phenomena, is essentially, if not wholly, religious. That Eliade wants to do so is transparent from his continual dismissal of secular explanations of religion generally. Hence he implores his fellow religionists not "to submit to the audacious and irrelevant interpretations of religious realities made by psychologists, sociologists, or devotees of various reductionist ideologies" (Eliade 1969b:70). Yet insofar as something secular precipitates millenarianism, why is millenarianism, as a response to that precipitant, nevertheless at heart a religious rather than secular enterprise? Surely the reverse seems more reasonable: that millenarianism is at heart a secular activity and that religion is merely the means by which that secular activity expresses itself – for example, the means by which nationalism vents itself. Eliade thus faces a dilemma: either to refuse to explain the imminence of the millennium, in which case his theory is inadequate, or to explain it nonreligiously, in which case his theory is no longer primarily, let alone solely, religious.

The dilemma Eliade faces holds for his explanation of not only millenarianism but also religion generally. True, Eliade continually emphasizes that no religious phenomenon exists outside of historical time and space: "There is no such thing outside of history as a 'pure' religious datum" (Eliade 1968b:250). Eliade stresses that no religious phenomenon is even *understandable* outside of its historical context: "In sum, a religious phenomenon cannot be understood outside of its 'history,' that is, outside of its cultural and socioeconomic contexts" (Eliade 1968b:250). But Eliade's analysis of the origin and function, not to mention the meaning, of any religious phenomenon is nevertheless essentially, if not exclusively, religious, as his denunciation of "the audacious and irrelevant interpretations [or: explanations] of religious realities" made by social scientists evinces. Yet for all Eliade's zeal to ignore the secular world, he cannot do so. He must choose between explaining religion at least partly nonreligiously and explaining it inadequately.

Eliade can no more explain religiously the frequent supplanting of the traditional eschatology by a new one than he can the imminence of the eschatology. Eliade's explanation of the imminence of the eschatology may be unclear, but his explanation of the change in eschatology is unambiguous: he denies any change. Hence he assumes that the natives identify the cargo brought by the whites with the goods traditionally to be brought by the ancestors, and he assumes that the natives continue to identify the whites' goods with the ancestors' even after they have ceased to identify the whites themselves with the ancestors.

Among others, the anthropologist Kenelm Burridge agrees that the natives, if only *ex post facto,* see the cargo as part of the abundance traditionally expected from the ancestors. But Burridge also stresses the novelty of the cargo – the way it devalues existing notions of abundance. The cargo may fulfill the traditional hope for abundance per se, but in unprecedented form.[8]

Furthermore, not only is the hope for the cargo new; so is the hope for its return. The fact that the natives justify their demand for the cargo on the grounds that it represents the traditional abundance promised them does not obviate the newness of their state of dispossession and their longing to end it. Just, then, as Eliade blurs the distinction between the hope for traditional goods and the hope for the cargo, so he blurs the distinction between the hope for abundance, in whatever form, and the hope for *return* of the cargo. In the millennium, he says, "the natives will once more be masters of their islands" – the new hope – "and will no longer work, for the dead will bring them fantastic quantities of provisions" – the traditional hope (Eliade 1969a:129). In fact, the hope for regained mastery is no more tied to the hope for abundance than the hope for cargo is tied to the hope for traditional goods. In both respects, the eschatology now sought goes beyond the eschatology formerly sought, and Eliade's theory fails to explain the change.

The Distinctiveness of Eliade's Theory of Millenarianism

Eliade's inability to explain either the imminence or the novelty of the end does reveal the distinctiveness of his theory of millenarianism: its focus on the continuity rather than the discontinuity of millenarianism with everyday life.

To ask why the millennium comes now rather than before and why a new eschatology often replaces the old one is to ask why the present is different from the past. It is to search for not merely new but exceptional conditions like acute deprivation, whatever the kind, which alone can explain both why a previously nonmillenarian society suddenly becomes millenarian and why a new eschatology suddenly replaces an old one. It is, as a consequence, to emphasize the unnaturalness of millenarianism: its strangeness, its bizarreness, its fabulousness – in brief, those characteristics which distinguish it from ordinary life.

---

[8]See Burridge (passim).

Eliade, by contrast, is almost blasè. He sees millenarianism not as the supplanting of traditional values and habits but as their final fulfillment. He sees millenarianism as the product not of new conditions but of old ones, at last realized: an innate human desire to abolish history and return to primordial time. He emphasizes the naturalness of millenarianism, its conformity with conventional hopes and practices. For Eliade, millenarianism is no desperate response to unsettling circumstances but the long-awaited opportunity to effect the keenest human urges.

REFERENCES

ALLEN, DOUGLAS
1984   "Ist Eliade antihistorisch?" In *Die Mitte der Welt,* ed. Hans Peter Duerr, pp. 106-27. Frankfurt am Main: Suhrkamp.

BURRIDGE, KENELM
1969   *New Heaven, New Earth.* New York: Schocken.

CROSS, FRANK MOORE, JR.
1966   "The Divine Warrior in Israel's Early Cult." In *Biblical Motifs,* ed. Alexander Altmann, pp. 11-30. Cambridge, Mass.: Harvard University Press.

ELIADE, MIRCEA
1959   *Cosmos and History.* Tr. Willard R. Trask. Bollingen Series XLVI. New York: Harper Torchbooks. Original publ. of tr.: *The Myth of the Eternal Return:* New York: Pantheon, 1954.

1968a   *Myth and Reality.* Tr. Willard R. Trask. New York: Harper Torchbooks. Original publ. of tr.: New York: Harper, 1963.

1968b   "Comparative Religion: Its Past and Future." In *Knowledge and the Future of Man,* ed. Walter J. Ong, pp. 245-54. New York: Holt, Rinehart.

1969a   "Cosmic and Eschatological Renewal." In Eliade, *The Two and the One,* pp. 125-59. Tr. J. M. Cohen. New York: Harper Torchbooks. Original publ. of tr.: *Mephistopheles and the Androgyne:* New York: Sheed & Ward, 1965.

1969b   *The Quest.* Chicago: University of Chicago Press.

PLUMB, J. H.
1969   *The Death of the Past.* London: Macmillan.

SEGAL, ROBERT A.
1983   "In Defense of Reductionism." *Journal of the American Academy of Religion* 51 (March):97-124. Reprinted in revised form in the present book as ch. 1.

Chapter Four

Have the Social Sciences Been Converted?

Once considered hostile to religion, the social sciences are now considered friendly. Historians of religions consider contemporary social scientists kindred souls. The reason is not that social scientists once considered religion false and now consider it true. The truth or falsity of religion is ordinarily a philosophical rather than social scientific issue. Even if many earlier social scientists personally judged religion false, contemporary ones by no means necessarily judge it true. Rather, they typically shun the issue altogether and confine themselves to what for them is properly social scientific: the origin and function, not the object, of religion.

At the same time the reason for their embrace by historians of religions is not that they consider the function of religion positive rather than negative. Some earlier social scientists – notably, Marx and Freud – did consider religion harmful, but most – for example, Tylor, Durkheim, Malinowski, and Jung – considered it most helpful. For them, religion was one of the best, if not the best, means of serving its function. Contemporary social scientists grant religion no greater due.

The real reason for the embrace of "contemporaries" is the assumption that they explain religion the way historians of religions do: from the standpoint of believers themselves. Believers, assume historians, explain religion irreducibly religiously: as originating and functioning to link them to the sacred, which they seek not as the means to an end but as the end itself. Certainly all of the earlier social scientists mentioned explained religion otherwise. Religion for all of them arose to serve an economic, psychological, social, or explanatory end, not a uniquely religious one. The issue is whether the contemporary social scientists embraced most effusively by historians of religions – Peter Berger, Clifford Geertz, Robert Bellah, Mary Douglas, Victor Turner, and Erik Erikson – are any different. I claim that they, too, explain religion nonreligiously. In the language of the trade they remain "reductionistic," or "reductive."

To reduce religion to one of the social sciences is to translate its manifest, religious nature into something nonreligious. It is to account for its religious nature nonreligiously. To be sure, only the origin and function, not the object, of religion get reduced, for the social sciences can usually explain no more. They can usually explain only why, not what, believers believe. They can explain *belief* in the object of religion but usually not the object itself.[1]

There are at least two ways of being nonreductive. One way is merely to *capture* the believer's point of view. The other is to *accept* the believer's point of view. The first approach is that of the humanities. The second is that of one strand of the social sciences: interpretive social science. The phenomenology of religion espouses the first approach but actually practices the second. The first approach seeks to figure out why believers *think* they are religious – itself no easy task. The second approach seeks to understand why they really *are* religious – the answer simply coinciding with theirs. The first approach is "nonjudgmental": it tries only to render accurately the believer's own explanation of religion. The second approach is evaluative: it claims – better, assumes – that the believer's own explanation of religion is correct.

I am not questioning here, as I have elsewhere,[2] whether a social scientific explanation of religion either should or even can be nonreductive. I am questioning only whether recent social scientific explanations touted as nonreductive really are.

Insofar as interpretive social scientists, like humanists, seek the actor's point of view, their explanations[3] might seem automatically nonreductive. Yet from the standpoint of historians of religions they are not. Where historians attribute religion to a yearning for the sacred itself, interpretive social scientists attribute it to a yearning for, most often, a meaningful life. The reason for the difference may be that interpretive social scientists do not limit the believer's point of view to the believer's conscious point of view. Yet historians do not do so either. They even detect the yearning for the sacred in overt atheists, for whom any yearning is by definition unconscious. Whatever accounts for the difference in explanations, historians must, I assert, pronounce those of interpretive social scientists reductive.

In works like *The Sacred Canopy, A Rumor of Angels,* and *The Heretical Imperative* Peter Berger argues that religion, for better or for worse, serves to make human life meaningful. A meaningful life is one not merely explained but also outright justified. Suffering, above all death, mocks the justifications

---

[1]See Segal (1980).
[2]See Segal (1983:109-15).
[3]I am here using "explanation" in the most straightforward sense of the term: as an account of why believers are religious. In a second, more restricted sense of the term an explanation is a specific kind of account: one in terms of physical rather than mental causes. In a third, more sophisticated sense of the term an explanation is likewise a particular kind of account: one in terms of mental *or* physical causes rather than, defined strictly, "meanings." In a rejoinder (Segal 1986) I try to rebut the argument of Anthony Blasi, who most likely is using the term in the second sense, that interpretive social scientists are "interpreting" *rather than* "explaining" religion.

offered by secular society. Ascribing all events to the will of god, religion offers far sturdier justifications. Ritual implants and confirms those justifications. Both because every human being needs, not simply wants, meaning, or meaning*fulness,* and because no secular society can fully provide it, religion is indispensable for all.

Yet even if indispensable, religion is only a means to a secular end. For Berger, humans crave meaning in general, not religious meaning in particular. They seek not the sacred itself but only the justifications it bestows. Religion serves not the irreducibly religious purpose of giving humans religious meaning but the secular purpose of giving them meaning per se. From the standpoint of historians of religions, Berger's explanation of religion is therefore reductive. In the earlier *Sacred Canopy* Berger maintains that he is neutral, but his neutrality applies to the object, not the origin and function, of religion. In the later *Rumor of Angels* and *Heretical Imperative* Berger abandons his neutrality in favor of belief: religion now originates in response to "signals" of transcendence. But its function nevertheless remains secular and so reductive: to provide meaning per se.

Like Berger, Clifford Geertz, in works like *Islam Observed, The Interpretation of Cultures,* and *Local Knowledge,* says that humans need a meaningful life and that religion provides it. By a meaningful life Geertz means one not necessarily justified, as for Berger, but simply explained or endured. Threats to meaning can come not only, as for Berger, from suffering, or what Geertz calls "unendurable events," but also from merely inexplicable events, where Geertz locates death, and from outright unjustifiable ones like the Holocaust. Where unjustifiable events need to be outright justified, inexplicable ones need only to be explained and unendurable ones only to be endured.

For Geertz, as for Berger, religion arises only once the efforts of secular society have failed. For Geertz, those secular efforts take the form of common sense, which vainly tries to explain, alleviate, or justify troubling experiences. Religion arises to provide a far more cogent and powerful explanation, alleviation, or justification of those experiences. For Berger, secular culture limits itself to justifying ordinary, social activities like marriage and never even attempts to cope with the traumatic experiences of suffering and death. Religion for Berger therefore arises less to replace the failed justifications of secular society, as for Geertz, than to offer justifications for the first time. Geertz calls those justifications a "world view." In justifying – or, alternatively, explaining or alleviating – wrenching experiences, the world view for Geertz simultaneously serves not only to reinforce *existing* social life, as for Berger, but also to offer a model for creating a *new* life, or "ethos": a new set of values, customs, and institutions. Ritual fuses the world view with the ethos.

Geertz argues strenuously that, in sanctioning society, religion serves not only the social function of keeping humans in their social place, as it does secondarily for Berger as well, but primarily the existential one of giving them a meaningful place. Geertz maintains that his recognition of an existential need served by religion makes him nonreductive, but that need is, as for Berger, for meaning in general, not for religious meaning in particular. Because of its divine clout religion for Geertz, as for Berger, best provides that meaning – better than any of the other "cultural systems" that Geertz, unlike Berger, enumerates. Religion may even, as for Berger, be indispensable. But it remains only a means to a secular end.

In *Beyond Belief* Robert Bellah calls his new approach to religion "symbolic realism" and distinguishes it from three others. "Historical realism" deems religion cognitive, literal, and true: religion is a true explanation of the physical world. The most conspicuous historical realists are, presumably, fundamentalists. "Consequential reductionism" deems religion cognitive, literal, but false: religion is superstition. But consequential reductionism focuses more on the effect of religion on society when the superstition is believed true. Max Weber, Talcott Parsons, and the earlier Bellah himself fall here. "Symbolic reductionism" deems religion false when taken cognitively and literally but true when taken noncognitively and symbolically: as the disguised expression of something real in the individual, society, or the physical world. Symbolic reductionists are most of the earlier social scientists cited: Marx, Freud, Tylor, Durkheim, and Malinowski.

In contrast to all of these approaches stands "symbolic realism," with which Bellah associates Paul Tillich, Martin Buber, Norman O. Brown, Michael Polanyi, Herbert Fingarette, and Paul Ricoeur. Though not mentioned by Bellah, Jung, too, would likely fall here. The true pioneering symbolic realists are, however, Freud and Durkheim, both of whom, according to the view Bellah takes from Parsons, began as symbolic reductionists but ended as symbolic realists. Like historical realism, symbolic realism purports to capture the believer's point of view. Unlike historical realism, it deems that point of view symbolic rather than literal. Taken symbolically, religion describes not the world itself but the meaning humans find in it. Taken symbolically, religion expresses, not explains, that meaning. Insofar as religion accurately captures this meaning, it is true. But because religion makes no truth claims about the world itself, it is "beyond belief."

Even though Bellah distinguishes his concern with the *meaning* of religion for believers from the concern of consequential reductionists with the social *function* of religion, the "meaning" seems indistinguishable from the individual, meaning-giving function for Berger and Geertz. For him, as for them, religion serves not merely to express but even more to implant humans' attitudes toward the world. It functions to give meaning to life as well as to express the meaning given. In his new approach, in contrast to his old one, Bellah never says what threatens meaning, how religion provides it, or whether anything else provides it. Whether he, like Berger and perhaps Geertz, thinks religion indispensable to the provision of meaning is therefore uncertain.

Because symbolic realism seeks the meaning of religion for believers, it is for Bellah identical with nonreductionism. Whether Bellah in fact captures the believer's point of view is not, however, the issue. Whether that point of view is, as for historians of religions, irreducibly religious is. Clearly, it is not, and for the same reason that it is not for Berger and Geertz: religion is only a means, however invaluable, to a secular end. As symbolic realist, Bellah vigorously opposes the reduction of religion to something secular, but he is committed to the irreducible religiosity of whatever believers experience rather than, like historians of religions, to the reality of a need to experience it.

Admittedly, in his various essays and books on civil religion Bellah does argue that religion fulfills an irreducibly religious function: that of serving god by serving one's country. But this function stems from no *need* to serve god or otherwise link up with the sacred, as it does for historians of religions. What its origin is, Bellah never says.

In *Purity and Danger, Natural Symbols, Implicit Meanings,* and other works Mary Douglas maintains that religion arises and functions to fulfill the human need less for existential than for intellectual meaning, or order. Humans need not merely to explain, endure, or justify their experiences, as for Berger and Geertz, but more fundamentally simply to organize them. Religion, like other domains of culture, organizes experience by categorizing it. Without categories life would not be merely baffling, painful, or unjust. It would be incoherent. For Douglas, as for Berger and especially Geertz, rituals are the means by which order gets imposed. Rituals are exactly those actions that categorize, or demarcate, boundaries – of time, space, group, and status. Rituals do not primarily explain, justify, or express experience but constitute it.

Where Geertz denies that religion serves only a social, Durkheimian function and Bellah denies that it serves only a psychological, Freudian one, Douglas denies that it serves only a magical, Frazerian one. Religion, which means religious ritual, serves less to control than to organize experience. To take Douglas' most famous example, Jewish dietary laws serve to prohibit the eating of animals that violate the categories into which living things are divided.

Religion for Douglas is not the sole means of organizing experience. On the contrary, she is eager to prove that various secular activities like spring cleaning are in actuality ritualistic. Yet even if religion were, as for Berger, the sole means of serving its function, that function would still be nonreligious. Religion would be indispensable to ordering experience in general, not to ordering religious experience in particular.

What is true of Berger, Geertz, Bellah, and Douglas is, I think, true of Turner and Erikson as well. If so, then interpretive social scientists and historians of religions stand far apart. I am not here asserting here that they must do so but only that they do. The heralded reconciliation of the social sciences with religion has yet to occur.

REFERENCES

BELLAH, ROBERT N.

1970   *Beyond Belief.* New York: Harper.

1975   *The Broken Covenant.* New York: Seabury.

1976   "The Revolution and the Civil Religion." In *Religion and the American Revolution,* ed. Jerald C. Brauer, pp. 55-73. Philadelphia: Fortress Press.

BELLAH, ROBERT N., AND PHILLIP E. HAMMOND

1980   *Varieties of Civil Religion.* San Francisco: Harper.

BERGER, PETER L.

1969   *The Sacred Canopy.* Garden City, N.Y.: Doubleday Anchor Books. Original publ.: Garden City, N.Y.: Doubleday, 1967.

1970   *A Rumor of Angels.* Garden City, N.Y.: Doubleday Anchor Books. Original publ.: Garden City, N.Y.: Doubleday, 1969.

1980   *The Heretical Imperative.* Garden City, N.Y.: Doubleday Anchor Books. Original publ.: Garden City, N.Y.: Doubleday, 1979.

DOUGLAS, MARY

1970   *Purity and Danger.* Baltimore: Penguin Books. Original publ.: London: Routledge & Kegan Paul, 1966.

1973   *Natural Symbols.* Second ed. New York: Vintage Books. Original publ. of first ed.: New York: Pantheon, 1970.

1975   *Implicit Meanings.* London and Boston: Routledge & Kegan Paul.

GEERTZ, CLIFFORD

1968   *Islam Observed.* New Haven, Conn.: Yale University Press.

1973   *The Interpretation of Cultures.* New York: Basic Books.

1983   *Local Knowledge.* New York: Basic Books.

SEGAL, ROBERT A.

1980   "The Social Sciences and the Truth of Religious Belief." *Journal of the American Academy of Religion* 48 (September):403-13. Reprinted in revised form in the present book as ch. 7.

1983   "In Defense of Reductionism." *Journal of the American Academy of Religion* 51 (March):97-124. Reprinted in revised form in the present book as ch. 1.

1986   "Response to Blasi and Nelson." *Journal for the Scientific Study of Religion* 24 (September):369-72. Reprinted in revised form in the present book as ch. 6.

Chapter Five

Erik Erikson: Psychologist or Historian of Religions?

There have been many books and essays by "religionists" and others praising Erik Erikson for his approach to religion. The excellent anthology at hand, *Encounter with Erikson,* offers further tribute. Five of the fifteen essays – by Lindbeck, Bellah, Spitz, Geertz, and Donald Capps – assess Erikson's studies of Martin Luther and Mahatma Gandhi. Two – by Hay and Newhall – extend Erikson's study of Gandhi. Four – by Strout, Bushman, Capps (again), and Michaelsen – apply his approach to the lives of various American figures deemed religious – among them Jonathan Edwards, the Beecher and James families, and Abraham Lincoln. The last four essays – by Dittes, Reynolds, Kaplan, and Walter Capps – are theoretical: they either defend or extend Erikson's brand of psychology.

Of the fifteen essayists, only Lindbeck and Spitz are critical of Erikson, and even they offer as much praise as criticism. The essayists admire most, first, Erikson's concept of "identity" and, second, his positive view of religion, which they invariably contrast to Freud's.

The significance of Freud for the psychology of religion exceeds his significance for psychology generally. With him begins the animosity between psychology and religion. Freud objects to religion as both fallacious and harmful, though not fallacious because harmful. Religion is fallacious because it explains the world in supernatural, pre-scientific terms and, more important, because it purports to be about the world at all. It is really about human beings, who project themselves onto the world in the form of god.

In *Totem and Taboo, Moses and Monotheism,* and *Civilization and Its Discontents* Freud deems religion harmful because it demands the excessive repression of sexual and aggressive instincts. The survival of society requires the denial of the Oedipal desire to commit incest and murder, but religion, by which Freud means above all the Christianity of his day, unnecessarily and vainly prohibits not only incest but all sex outside of marriage, and not only murder but even plain ill will: one must "love" one's neighbor. Religion thereby exacerbates the inevitable tension between the individual and society.

In *The Future of an Illusion* and again in *Civilization and Its Discontents* Freud deems religion harmful because it exacerbates the inevitable tension

In *The Future of an Illusion* and again in *Civilization and Its Discontents* Freud deems religion harmful because it exacerbates the inevitable tension between the individual and the world. Here the tension involves not one's reluctant acceptance of repression but one's reluctance to accept the cruelty and indifference of the physical world. By attributing the vicissitudes of life to a just and merciful god, religion creates the fantasy of a fair, kind world and thereby discourages humans from accepting the world as it really is.

Where Freud invariably finds religion harmful, Erikson ordinarily finds it most helpful. Where Freud assumes the falsity of religion, Erikson declares its veracity a metaphysical matter beyond his ken. In both respects Erikson is like Carl Jung, but unlike Jung he strives to supplement, not reject, Freud, who remains his mentor.

Erikson retains Freud's final division of the psyche into ego, id, and superego, but he views the ego much more positively than does Freud. It is naturally strong, not weak, and is substantially independent of the id. It represents an existential, "meaning-seeking" side of human nature, a side separate from the instinctual one. In above all *The Future of an Illusion* Freud clearly recognizes the craving for meaning, or meaningfulness, but scorns it as infantile and surmountable. By contrast, Erikson considers the craving both mature and insurmountable – and as important as the craving for sex. Moreover, these two sides of human nature can and must develop together, and develop both internally and externally.

Internally, according to Erikson, humans seek more than a Freudian compromise among their parts: ego, id, and superego. They seek the full, positive integration of those parts. Externally, they similarly seek full, positive acceptance into society rather than merely a Freudian truce between themselves and society.

Internally and externally alike, humans, according to Erikson, seek an "identity" above all. That identity represents not, as for Freud, a child's wholly unconscious identification with the parent of the same sex but an adolescent's considerably conscious self-definition as a distinct, unified person – the master not only of one's instincts, as for Freud, but also of one's place in society. One's identity expresses itself concretely in yuppie form: in a career.

Religion abets the attainment of identity by providing an ideology, which explains and justifies one's place in both society and the world. Religion thereby facilitates, not hinders, adjustment to both. It neither furthers repression nor furnishes escape but enables one to "cope."

Erikson was surely not the first to suggest either that every person seeks an identity or that religion provides one. His contribution lies far more in his link of identity to a whole meaning-seeking side of human nature and, even more, in his link of that side to the instinctual, Freudian side. Yet most of the essayists isolate the concept of identity from the instinctual side of human nature. One would thereby assume that Erikson had broken altogether with Freud, despite his belabored efforts at reconciling himself with Freud.

More important here than Erikson's vaunted reconciliation of himself with Freud is his purported reconciliation of psychology with religion. If most of the essayists ignore his reconciliation with Freud, they take for granted his reconciliation with believers. Only Lindbeck questions his success. He is certainly right to do so, for Erikson in fact skirts the issue.

In *Young Man Luther,* for example, Erikson ascribes to the adolescent Martin a nonreligious conflict with his father which Martin's subsequent theology at once reflects, parallels, and partly resolves. Erikson conspicuously fails to say, however, whether reflects means "is caused by," whether parallels means "stands for," and whether resolves means "arises to resolve." Erikson maintains that Luther's conflict with his father is not merely a sexual, Oedipal struggle but also a struggle over Luther's career and therefore over his identity. He never says, however, whether the religious identity Luther forges serves an irreducibly religious need or a psychological one, be that psychological one existential or instinctual.

The essayists praise Erikson for what are in fact contradictory achievements: accounting for religion psychologically on the one hand yet not reducing it to psychology on the other. If Erikson merits praise for accounting for religion as the solution to a quest for identity, he has necessarily reduced religion to psychology – to the extent, that is, that he *has* accounted for it. If, alternatively, Erikson deserves praise for not reducing religion to psychology, he has necessarily not accounted for religion psychologically and therefore not explained it at all. A complete reduction of religion to psychology would not, to be sure, preclude the truth of religion: to say otherwise would be to commit the genetic fallacy. But a complete reduction would either preclude or obviate an irreducibly religious origin and function of religion – a consequence ignored by the essayists.

Finally, the essayists presuppose rather than justify the *impropriety* of reducing religion to psychology. The only legitimate objection can be that, in origin, function, or meaning, religion is really more than psychological, but the only legitimate proof of its irreducibility is the failure of attempts to reduce it to psychology. The proper objection to Freud's reduction should not, then, be that he tries to reduce religion to psychology but that he fails. In sum, not only may Erikson, despite his disavowal, prove to be reductive, but if he does not, he warrants praise only if reductionism itself has been proved impossible.

REFERENCES

CAPPS, DONALD, WALTER H. CAPPS, AND M. GERALD BRADFORD, EDS.
1978   *Encounter with Erikson: Historical Interpretation and ReligiousBiography.* The American Academy of Religion and The

Institute of Religious Studies Joint Series on Formative Contemporary Thinkers, No. 2. Missoula, Mont.: Scholars Press.

ERIKSON, ERIK H.

1958   *Young Man Luther*. New York: Norton.

1969   *Gandhi's Truth*. New York: Norton.

Chapter Six

Interpreting and Explaining Religion:
A Response to Blasi and Nelson

In a rejoinder to the essay in chapter four sociologist Anthony Blasi distinguishes sharply between "interpreting" and "explaining" cultural phenomena and denies that interpretive social scientists do what explanatory social scientists do: "seek origins and functions" (Blasi, 365). Says Blasi: "The crux of Segal's misunderstanding of interpretive social science is his assumption that interpretive social scientists seek to *explain* social phenomena (i.e., causally account for them) .... Historians of religion may or may not explain religion; I would be surprised if they did. But interpretive social scientists do not explain when they are being interpretive; they interpret" (Blasi, 365).

According to Blasi, interpretive social scientists are distinctive, first, in "placing cultural phenomena in their social structural contexts" (Blasi, 365). But who does otherwise? Noninterpretive social scientists may *subsequently* go beyond the context to either comparison or criticism, but they, too, at least *start* with the context. Moreover, many renowned interpretive social scientists have been comparativists. Conversely, social scientists who proceed to criticism may be exceeding their status as social scientists.

According to Blasi, interpretive social scientists are distinctive, second and far more important, in employing the "criterion of meaning-adequacy" rather than causality (Blasi, 365). Few social scientists or philosophers contest the equation of interpretation with "meaning" and of explanation with "cause." At issue is the *definition* of meaning and cause. There are at least three possibilities. The most straightforward and most common definition equates the meaning with the *message,* or *theme,* of religion and equates the cause, or origin, with whatever *brings about,* or *accounts for,* religion. Distinguished this way, interpretation and explanation run askew.

If Blasi is distinguishing meaning from cause in this first way, it is hard to see whom he has in mind. The figures I named as interpretive social scientists – Peter Berger, Robert Bellah, Clifford Geertz, Mary Douglas, Victor Turner, and Erik Erikson – he dismisses as "not all people whom one would plausibly label 'interpretive social scientists'" (Blasi, 364). But he himself names only one figure: Max Weber, who will be considered shortly. Since at least Berger, Geertz, and Bellah conventionally get characterized as leading interpretive social scientists, surely at least they qualify. Yet none of them refrains from accounting for religion.

When Berger says that there is "a human craving for meaning that appears to have the force of instinct" (Berger, 22) and that in bolstering the threatened meaning of secular society "religion thus serves to maintain the reality of that socially constructed world" (Berger, 42), he is surely trying to *account for* religion. He is surely claiming that a universal need for meaning, or meaning*fulness,* is what gives rise to religion. The processes of externalization, objectivation, and internalization are his account of *how,* not just *why,* there is religion. Berger is claiming not simply that believers happen to find meaning through religion but also that they *need* to find meaning because of their unfinished state at birth.

When Clifford Geertz says that "whatever else religion may be, it is in part an attempt ... to conserve the fund of general meanings in terms of which each individual interprets his experience and organizes his conduct" (Geertz, 127), he, too, is surely asserting that a need for meaning gives rise to religion – whatever, if anything, gives rise to that need itself. For him, ritual accounts for *how,* not just *why,* there is religion. Yet Geertz calls his own effort an "interpretation." If Blasi is equating an account with an explanation, he can scarcely declare categorically that "interpretive social scientists do not explain when they are being interpretive; they interpret" (Blasi, 365).

When Robert Bellah says of religious symbols that "they are born out of the tragedy and the suffering, the joy and the victory of men struggling to make sense out of their world" (Bellah, 195), he is likewise surely contending that religion, for which he is therefore accounting, arises to provide meaning. Though less often labeled interpretive social scientists, Mary Douglas, Victor Turner, and Erik Erikson say the same. If Blasi chose to distinguish them from Berger, Geertz, and Bellah, by what criterion could he do so?

The second possible distinction between meanings and causes is that between meanings and physical causes. Here meanings *as well as* causes seek to account for religion, but meanings do so in terms of *mental* rather than physical states. Mental states are voluntary and intentional; physical states, involuntary and mechanical.

Insofar as Weber for Blasi epitomizes interpretive social science, Blasi must be distinguishing meanings from causes in this second way: as the difference between meanings and physical causes. This second distinction between meanings and causes will become clearer after the third possible one gets drawn: that between meanings and causes per se, mental or physical. This distinction is the one drawn by philosophical proponents of interpretation like R. G. Collingwood (1946), William Dray (1957), and Peter Winch (1958).

According to them, the principal difference between meanings and causes is not, as in the second distinction, that meanings are mental and causes physical but that meanings are linked to behavior differently from the way causes are. Where a cause is separate from what it effects, a meaning is inseparable, so that what it effects is really the *expression* rather than the *effect* of it. To use Collingwood's example, to say that the *cause* of Brutus' stabbing Caesar was a hunger for power would be to say that power-hungering was a trait in Brutus distinct from the stabbing, which was the effect of that trait. To say that the *meaning* of Brutus' stabbing Caesar was a hunger for power would be to say that power-hungering was a trait expressed outwardly in the stabbing. The deed becomes part of the meaning, or *definition*, of power-hungering.

As a cause, power-hungering says merely what brought about the deed. As a meaning, power-hungering also characterizes, or classifies, the deed *as* power-hungering. Indeed, to say *what* Brutus did – sought power – is to say *why* he did it.[1]

Suppose one says causally that any power-hungry person will in certain circumstances stab others. If in such circumstances Brutus had not stabbed Caesar, he would not have been power-hungry. But suppose one *defines* a power-hungry person as one who in those circumstances will stab others. If in such circumstances Brutus had not stabbed Caesar, not only would he have been other than power-hungry, but his behavior would have contradicted the meaning of the term.

For some "interpretivists," the same mental state – power-hungering – can be either a meaning or a cause. But even for those interpretivists for whom all mental states are meanings, a meaning is not just mental rather than physical but also connected differently to a behavior than a cause is.

Both the second and the third ways of distinguishing meanings from causes have been severely criticized. Against the second way it has been argued that mental as well as physical states can be causes, in which case meanings are simply mental causes. Against the third way it has, in addition, been argued that mental states *must* be causes in order to be meanings.[2] The issue at hand, however, is not whether the distinction that Blasi's interpretive social scientists are making between meanings and causes is tenable but simply what that distinction is.

Of the six figures I labeled interpretive social scientists, all, as argued, are concerned with accounting for religion. None, then, uses the first possible distinction: a meaning as the message or theme of religion; a cause as whatever brings about religion. Conversely, none of the six save Geertz seems even aware of the third possible distinction: a meaning as whatever defines as well as brings

---

[1]See Collingwood (214).
[2]See Segal (forthcoming₁).

about religion; a cause as simply whatever brings about religion. With the exception of Geertz all the figures I cited straightforwardly treat meanings as causes: they say that a need for meaning is *fulfilled* by religion rather than *expressed* by it.[3]

I argue elsewhere that in practice even Geertz violates this third way of distinguishing meanings from causes.[4] But I want to focus here on Weber. For Blasi labels him not only a true interpretive social scientist but "the most influential interpretive social scientist" (Blasi, 365). I want to show that even Weber employs the second, tame distinction between meanings and causes rather than either the first or the third, both of which are much more radical and so much more significant.

Undeniably, Weber claims to be seeking to "understand" religious "behavior ... from the viewpoint of the subjective experiences, ideas, and purposes of the individuals concerned" (Weber 1963:1). But in saying next that "the ends of the [earliest] religious and magical actions are predominantly economic" (Weber 1963:1), he is using the believer's own view of the world to *account for* religion: earliest believers apply the idea that the world is controlled by spirits to secure basic necessities. Later believers apply the idea that the world ought to be just to secure a different end: purpose, or meaning*fulness*. The fact that Weber accounts for religion in terms of ideas hardly means that he is not accounting for it. Because ideas, or meanings, *account for* religion, Weber cannot be employing the first possible distinction between meanings and causes.

Moreover, Weber cites material factors, social and economic, which account for the ideas which account for religion, though for Weber an account provides only necessary, never sufficient, conditions. For example, religion after the earliest, magical stage arises only once there is a priesthood, which itself arises only once there is a permanent congregation.[5] Conversely, the occupation of peasants bars the development of religion beyond the magical stage: "The lot of peasants is so strongly tied to nature ... and economically so little oriented to rational systematization that in general the peasantry will become a carrier of [post-magical] religion only when it is threatened by enslavement or proletarization ..." (Weber 1963:80). Having argued that one consequence of ascetic Protestantism was the spirit of capitalism, Weber adds that "Protestant Asceticism was in turn influenced in its development and its character by the totality of social conditions, especially economic" (Weber 1958:183).

If nothing else, Weber's sheer juxtaposition of ideas with physical causes to account for both religious and secular behavior suggests that he treats ideas, or meanings, as causes. Because ideas and material conditions together bring about both religious and nonreligious behavior, it is hard to see how they can be

---

[3]See Segal (forthcoming$_1$).
[4]See Segal (forthcoming$_1$; forthcoming$_2$).
[5]See Weber (1963:28-31).

connected to that behavior in the logically distinct ways demanded by the third possible distinction. Moreover, Weber himself seems oblivious to the distinction and indeed has been criticized for effacing it.[6] In short, even Weber, Blasi's paradigmatic interpretive social scientist, not only invokes physical causes alongside mental states in accounting for religion but also treats mental states *as* causes. Even if Weber attributed religion to only mental states, it would be arbitrary to label those states meanings rather than causes. For to Weber the sole difference between them and physical causes is that they are mental, not that they are noncausal in any other respect. Blasi is free to employ this second, innocuous distinction between meanings and causes, but what is the point of doing so?

In any case Weber is no bedfellow of Mircea Eliade's. For Eliade, religion arises to satisfy a need for religious meaningfulness itself. For Weber, even later religion arises to satisfy a need for meaningfulness per se, not for religious meaningfulness in particular, and that need presupposes a certain social organization. Contact with the sacred is not, as for Eliade, the believer's end but only the believer's means.

In a second rejoinder to my essay sociologist Lynn Nelson assumes that I am arguing *against* contemporary social scientific explanations *because* they are reductive and that I consider them reductive because "they are ignoring a nonempirical 'reality' which is the core of religion" (Nelson, 367): hence "Segal argues that social science can appropriately explain religion only if the social scientists are themselves believers" (Nelson, 367). Nelson objects to the introduction of the believer's or social scientist's metaphysical beliefs or disbeliefs into a properly empirical inquiry: "What Segal misunderstands is that being a believer or a nonbeliever is beside the point in that process of inquiry. That is because any religious experience which is so personal that only a believer can comprehend or describe it is too idiosyncratic to be evidence of religion's usefulness in the social order" (Nelson, 367).

Nelson seems to be responding less to my "Perspectives" essay[7] than to my reductionism one,[8] and he *reverses* its point. In my "Perspectives" essay I argue neither for nor against social scientific accounts of religion. I argue only that the contemporary social scientific accounts praised by historians of religions as irreducibly religious are in fact reductive. I say explicitly that only the origin and function, not the object, of religion are being reduced, so that I am scarcely claiming that the figures I consider "are ignoring a nonempirical reality."

In my reductionism article I argue not, as Nelson assumes, that social scientists can never account for the irreducibly religious origin and function of any aspect of religion but, on the contrary, that the true origin and function of

---

[6]See Winch (116-17), Schutz (28-29, 87).
[7]See Segal (1985).
[8]See Segal (1983).

any aspect of religion may not be irreducibly religious. I fault Eliade and others for dogmatically assuming that the believer's own, purportedly religious account of religion is the true one. By embracing that account, Eliade excludes exactly the accounts of reductive social scientists, whom I am *defending* rather than, as Nelson assumes, *dismissing*.

In my reductionism essay I argue not, as Nelson assumes, that "social science can appropriately account for religion only if the social scientists are themselves believers" (Nelson, 367) but the opposite: that the history of religions *rather than* social science can explain religion only if its practitioners are themselves believers. Social science, by contrast, ordinarily requires neither belief nor disbelief. Historians of religions must, I argue, be believers because the views they seek to duplicate presuppose belief. In another article[9] I argue that historians must be believers for another reason: because they say that religion not just seeks to make contact with the sacred but succeeds, in which case the sacred must for them exist.

REFERENCES

BELLAH, ROBERT N.
1970   *Beyond Belief.* New York: Harper.

BERGER, PETER L.
1969   *The Sacred Canopy.* Garden City, N.Y.: Doubleday Anchor Books. Original publ.: Garden City, N.Y.: Doubleday, 1967.

BLASI, ANTHONY J.
1986   "Comment on Segal's 'Have the Social Sciences Been Converted?'" *Journal for the Scientific Study of Religion* 25(September):364-66.

COLLINGWOOD, R. G.
1946   *The Idea of History.* Ed. T. M. Knox. New York: Oxford University Press.

DRAY, WILLIAM H.
1957   *Laws and Explanation in History.* Oxford: Clarendon Press.

GEERTZ, CLIFFORD
1973   *The Interpretation of Cultures.* New York: Basic Books.

NELSON, LYNN D.
1986   "Comment on Segal's 'Have the Social Sciences Been Converted?'" *Journal for the Scientific Study of Religion* 25 (September):367-68.

[9]See Segal (1987).

SCHUTZ, ALFRED

1967   *The Phenomenology of the Social World*. Trs. George Walsh and Frederick Lehnert. Evanston, Ill.: Northwestern University Press.

SEGAL, ROBERT A.

1983   "In Defense of Reductionism." *Journal of the American Academy of Religion* 51 (March):97-124. Reprinted in revised form in the present book as ch. 1.

1985   "Have the Social Sciences Been Converted?" *Journal for the Scientific Study of Religion* 24 (September):321-24. Reprinted in revised form in the present book as ch. 4.

1987   "Are Historians of Religions Necessarily Believers?" *Religious Traditions* 10 (July):71-76. Reprinted in revised form in the present book as ch. 2.

forth-coming₁   "Comment on Steven Kepnes' 'Bridging the Gap Between Understanding and Explanation Approaches to the Study of Religion'." *Journal for the Scientific Study of Religion*.

forth-coming₂   "Interpreting and Explaining Religion: Geertz and Durkheim." *Soundings*.

WEBER, MAX

1958   *The Protestant Ethic and the Spirit of Capitalism*. Tr. Talcott Parsons. New York: Scribner.

1963   *The Sociology of Religion*. Tr. Ephraim Fischoff. Boston: Beacon Press.

WINCH, PETER

1958   *The Idea of a Social Science and Its Relation to Philosophy*. London: Routledge & Kegan Paul.

Chapter Seven

The Social Sciences and the Truth
of Religious Belief

There are two kinds of assessments of religious belief, or belief in the existence of god: those which assess religious belief itself and those which assess the holders of religious belief. The assessment of religious belief itself is the task of philosophy. The assessment of the holders of religious belief is the task of the social sciences. Philosophy assesses the truth and, less germane here, the logical meaningfulness of religious belief. The social sciences assess the origin and, less germane here, the function of religious belief.

More precisely, the social sciences assess the truth of religious *explanations* of religious belief. Philosophy determines whether the reasons believers provide for believing are sound reasons for believing. The social sciences determine whether the reasons believers provide for their *coming* to believe are truly the reasons for which they have come to believe.

The issue is whether an evaluation of the reasons believers give for coming to believe has any bearing on an evaluation of the reasons they give for believing. Put more simply, the issue is whether a social scientific explanation of the origin of religious belief has any bearing on the truth of the belief.

Seemingly, a social scientific explanation has no bearing at all. Seemingly, it cannot establish that religious belief is either true or false but, at best, that a believer's account of the origin and function of the believer's belief is.

Take, for example, Sigmund Freud's explanation of religious belief in *The Future of an Illusion*.[1] Freud argues that the helplessness which all humans experience in the face of an impersonal, arbitrary, and amoral world makes them long less for maternal love than for paternal security – the protection their fathers provided during childhood.[2] That longing impels most of them to project their fathers onto the world in the form of supreme deities. Religious belief thus originates in the inability to accept the unfriendliness and indifference of the

---

[1] In *Totem and Taboo* and *Moses and Monotheism* Freud presents an entirely different, truly "Freudian" explanation of religious belief.

[2] In *The Future of an Illusion* the frustration which humans experience in the face of a repressive society is an additional, but secondary, cause of religious belief.

world. It originates in the human yearning to transform that harsh, adult world
into the comforting one of childhood. For Freud, religious belief is illusory not
in the sense of false, though false it is, but in the sense of originating and
functioning to fulfill a wish: the wish to make the world nicer than it is.[3]

The first question to be asked is whether Freud's explanation of religious
belief is true. One can certainly challenge Freud's explanation on many grounds
– for example, by arguing that religion sometimes makes the world less rather
than more palatable. Moreover, Freud's explanation in even *The Future of an
Illusion* depends partly on his general psychoanalytic theory,[4] which may well
be either false[5] or unprovable.[6] What matters here is whether Freud's
explanation would refute the truth of religious belief if both his overall theory
and his theory of religion were at once provable and true. Assume, then, that
both[7] are.

The second question to be asked is whether, if accepted, Freud's explanation
of religious belief refutes a believer's own explanation. Believers likely attribute
their belief to either a supernatural origin – for example, the experience of god –
or a naturalistic cause different from Freud's – for example, the inheritance of
familial belief. Freud's explanation might well be compatible with a believer's
own naturalistic explanation. The inheritance of familial belief would explain
similarities in the depiction of the divine father. Freud's explanation might prove
compatible with even a believer's supernatural explanation. The experience of a
hostile world as the origin of all religious belief would be incompatible with the
experience of god as the *direct* origin but would not be incompatible with an
indirect supernatural source – god's orchestration of the experience as a means of
inculcating belief. The acceptance of Freud's explanation would not, then,
automatically refute a believer's own.

---

[3]In contrast to *Totem and Taboo* and *Moses and Monotheism,* the prime wish in
The Future of an Illusion is neither sexual nor repressed.

[4]For a careful breakdown of the explanation in *The Future of an Illusion* into
psychoanalytic and nonpsychoanalytic components see Grünbaum (1987:156-69).
I confine myself to the nonpsychoanalytic component, which in *The Future of an
Illusion* is the dominant one.

[5]For assessments of the truth of Freud's general psychoanalytic theory see, con,
Sears, Eysenck (ch. 3), Eysenck and Wilson, Grünbaum (1985); pro, Kline, Fisher
and Greenberg, Wallace (1986); con and pro, Grünbaum and Caplan.

[6]For assessments of the provability of Freud's general psychoanalytic theory see,
con, Popper (34-38); pro, Glymour (1974; 1980:176-78, 263-77), Grünbaum
(1985:chs. 1, 11), Edelson, Wallace (1986); con and pro, Hook (pts. I, IV),
Grünbaum and Caplan.

[7]For assessments of the truth and provability of Freud's explanation of religious
belief in *Totem and Taboo* see, con, Kroeber (1920; 1939), Alston (65-82, 93-
96), Banks (410-12); pro, Wallace (1983); con and pro, Küng (66-75, 93-109).
For assessments of the truth and provability of Freud's explanation of religious
belief in *The Future of an Illusion* see, con, Alston (75-76), Grünbaum (1987:153-
69); con and pro, Küng (75-80, 93-109).

The third and most important question to be asked is whether Freud's explanation refutes the *truth* of religious belief.[8] Suppose that Freud *could* refute a believer's own explanation of religious belief. The fact that a believer would have misunderstood how the believer had acquired the belief would hardly seem to falsify the belief itself. To say otherwise would seemingly be to fail to distinguish between the *origin* of one's holding a belief and the *justification* for holding it. It would be to commit the genetic fallacy.

Not only believers but also philosophers of religion invoke the genetic fallacy to dismiss the would-be encroachment of the social sciences on the truth of religious belief. Most famous is William James' sneering objection to what he calls "medical materialism": "Medical materialism seems indeed a good appellation for the too simple-minded system of thought which we are considering. Medical materialism finishes up Saint Paul by calling his vision on the road to Damascus a discharging lesion of the occipital cortex, he being an epileptic. It snuffs out Saint Teresa as an hysteric, Saint Francis of Assisi as an hereditary degenerate" (James, 14). Less famously, James Ross invokes the genetic fallacy against Freud himself: "It may very well be that the forces of nature and of the human mind determine that certain individuals have religious beliefs. Does that mean that such beliefs cannot be true or cannot be knowledge?... To infer from the ignoble or irrational origin of belief to its falsity or improbability is to commit the psychogenetic fallacy, the fallacy of assuming that just because we can account ... for someone's having a certain belief, his belief is less likely to be true" (Ross, 61-62).

Surely true as well as false beliefs of any kind can have a secular or irrational origin, so that the secular or irrational origin of a belief in no way entails its falsity. Otherwise many beliefs true on all other grounds would thereby be false.[9] The fact that an "ignoble or irrational origin" would likely contradict a believer's own view of the origin of the believer's belief is beside the point, which is, again, that the belief can be true even when the believer's account of its origin is not.

Not only philosophers but even social scientists themselves spurn the relevance of the social sciences to the truth of religious belief. For example, Carl Jung on the one hand maintains that religious belief originates in the projection of archetypes of the collective unconscious onto the world yet on the other hand denies that this explanation has any consequence for the truth of the belief: "I approach psychological matters from a scientific and not from a philosophical standpoint. In as much as religion has a very important psychological aspect, I am dealing with it from a purely empirical point of view, that is, I restrict

---

[8]On the ramifications of Freud's explanation of religious belief for the truth of religious belief see Alston (82-96) and Banks (415-20). The fact that both Alston and Banks focus on the explanation in *Totem and Taboo* rather than the one in *The Future of an Illusion* does not alter their general conclusions.

[9]See Alston (83).

myself to the observation of phenomena and I refrain from any application of metaphysical or philosophical considerations" (Jung 1938:2).[10] Similarly, Peter Berger asserts that "religion constitutes an immense projection of [wished for] human meanings into the empty vastness of the universe," yet adds that "it is impossible within the frame of reference of scientific theorizing to make any affirmation, positive *or* negative, about the ultimate ontological status of this alleged reality. Within this frame of reference, the religious projections can be dealt with only as such, as products of human activity and human consciousness, and rigorous brackets have to be placed around the question as to whether these projections may [or may] not *also* be something else than that (or, more accurately, *refer* to something else than the human world in which they empirically originate)" (Berger, 100).[11] How extraordinary it is that these social scientists are so eager, not just obliged, to restrict the ramifications of their own discoveries.

In any case these statements sum up the conventional view of the relationship between the social sciences and religious belief. As self-evident as they seem, they do not in fact rule out the relevance of the social sciences to the truth of religious belief. The social sciences, I argue, can challenge the truth of religious belief without committing the genetic fallacy.[12]

The relevance of the social sciences to not the truth but the origin of religious belief is the first issue. Admittedly, not all believers explain the origin of their beliefs supernaturally. But any naturalistic explanations that they accept *are* social scientific ones. At the same time many believers doubtless explain the origin of their religions, even if not of their own religiosity, supernaturally. Again, a social scientific explanation, even if accepted, could not refute an indirect supernatural one – the use by god of the experience of the world as a device for instilling belief. But a social scientific explanation would make that indirect supernatural explanation superfluous.

As for a direct supernatural explanation, a naturalistic, social scientific explanation is superior to it for at least two reasons. First, a naturalistic explanation of religious belief, like a naturalistic explanation of the physical world, is simpler than a supernatural one. In attributing religious belief, like the world itself, to god, a supernatural explanation postulates an entity, however conceived, in *addition* to all the ones already postulated, not in *place* of any of them. No matter how direct a cause of religious belief god is, even god must utilize naturalistic mechanisms to reach humans – mechanisms ranging from

---

[10]See also Jung's response (1976) to Martin Buber, who charges him with atheism.
[11]See also Berger (1969:88-89, 179-85; 1970:46-47). To be sure, in subsequent works Berger more often argues from the *supernatural* origin of religion to the *existence* of god: see Berger (1970:52-97; 1980:58-60, ch. 5).
[12]Whether the social sciences can *support* the truth of religious belief without committing the genetic fallacy is a possibility I am not considering here.

ears to feelings to projection. Indeed, the line between god as the direct cause and god as an indirect one thereby becomes blurry. At the same time the addition of god to the world is the addition of an entity far different from all other ones. The postulation of god does not simply add one more entity to the universe but incalculably complicates it. By contrast, social scientific explanations either use already postulated entities – whatever mechanism in humans is deemed responsible for projection – or at most propose new ones comparable with the ones already postulated – a new mechanism in humans responsible for projection. The issue is not, of course, whether the universe itself is complex but whether, among competing accounts of its complexity, the simpler account is preferable.

Second, a social scientific explanation of religious belief has a higher prior probability than a supernatural one. For it is linked to natural science, which has provided the most persuasive explanation so far of the physical world. Social science, here *including* interpretive social science, extends to the study of humans the nonsupernatural framework of natural science.[13] A social scientific explanation therefore carries a higher prior probability than a supernatural one and so, in a choice between the two, "deserves the nod."

A social scientific explanation, once accepted, renders the truth of religious belief improbable. Take the explanations of Freud, Berger, and Jung. To say, as all three do, that religious belief originates in projection is to say that it originates in error. For to *project* god onto the world is by definition to ascribe to the world that which is in humans rather than the world. To project something onto the world is to confuse what is in oneself – whether a wish, as for Freud and Berger, or an image, as for Jung – with what is in the world. To project is to project falsely.

In denying that their explanations of religious belief refute the truth of religious belief, Berger and Jung are denying that the objects of projections are necessarily nonexistent. Incontestably, they are correct. But even if the object of a projection can yet exist on its own, the projection itself still constitutes an error. Whoever projects god onto the world does not discover god in the world but imposes god on it. Should god turn out to exist after all, the projection would represent no insight on the believer's part. It would represent mere coincidence. The extraordinariness that such a coincidence would represent is what, I suggest, challenges the truth of religious belief. Projection challenges the truth of religious belief not because projection itself fails to establish the truth of the belief but because a belief originating in projection is statistically unlikely to be true.

---

[13]Even those who sharply distinguish social from natural science scarcely consider social scientific explanations, or interpretations, supernatural rather than naturalistic.

Freud most of all perceives this challenge. On the one hand he, like Jung and Berger, recognizes the logical distinction between the origin of religious belief and the truth of religious belief. He thus acknowledges that "to assess the truth-value of religious doctrines does not lie within the scope of the present [social scientific] enquiry" (Freud 1964:52), which is concerned with only the origin of those doctrines.[14] He distinguishes between the illusory status of religious belief, which refers to its origin, and its delusory status, which refers to its truth-value. Religious belief is for him delusory as well as illusory, but it is delusory on nonpsychological grounds.[15]

On the other hand, and in contrast to Jung and Berger, Freud recognizes a connection between the origin and the truth of religious belief. The mechanism on which he happens to focus is not, however, projection but wish fulfillment, and of its consequence for the truth of religious belief he says: "We know approximately at what periods and by what kind[s] of men religious doctrines were created. If in addition we discover the motives which led to this, our attitude to the problem of religion will undergo a marked displacement. We shall tell ourselves that it would be very nice if there were a God who created the world and was a benevolent Providence, and if there were a moral order in the universe and an after-life; but it is a very striking fact that all this is exactly as we are bound to wish it to be" (Freud 1964:52-53).

Assuming wish fulfillment as the origin of religious belief, Freud is noting its ramifications for truth. He is saying that it would be an extraordinary coincidence if our wishes about the world, constituting as they do "the oldest, strongest and most urgent wishes of mankind" (Freud 1964:47), matched the world itself, just as it would be an extraordinary coincidence if our projections onto the world, originating as they do in error, proved to be true projections about the world. The challenge to religious belief stems not from the origin of

---

[14]At times Freud says that psychoanalysis *can* refute the truth of religious belief: "Nothing that I have said here against the truth-value of religions needed the support of psycho-analysis; it had been said by others long before analysis came into existence. If the application of the psycho-analytic method makes it possible to find a new argument against the truths of religion, *tant pis* for religion ..." (1964:60). If Freud is referring to his argument from coincidence, he is arguing from origin to falsity without committing the genetic fallacy.

[15]Freud usually *presupposes* the decisive refutation of religious belief by philosophy and the natural sciences and then invokes psychoanalysis to explain why humans succumb and remain "succumbed" to so conspicuous a delusion: "... religious ideas, in spite of their incontrovertible lack of authentication, have exercised the strongest possible influence on mankind. This is a fresh psychological problem. We must ask where the inner force of those doctrines lies and to what it is that they owe their efficacy, independent as it is of recognition by reason. I think we have prepared the way sufficiently for an answer to both these questions. It will be found if we turn our attention to the psychical origin of religious ideas" (1964:45-47). Rather than delusory because illusory, religious belief here is illusory because delusory.

belief in human wishes – to say otherwise would be to commit the genetic fallacy – but from the rarity with which humanity's mildest, let alone fondest, wishes get fulfilled.[16] A wish to believe that god exists does not *preclude* the existence of god, but it does make the existence of god improbable.[17]

Not every social scientific explanation of religious belief, to be sure, involves either wish fulfillment or projection. But every one does involve a naturalistic rather than supernatural origin. Where a supernatural origin automatically justifies as well as explains belief in the existence of god, a naturalistic origin, once accepted, automatically challenges the justification as well as the explanation of that belief. A naturalistic cause reduces, or tends to reduce, the would-be supernatural effect to error. The error lies not in the postulation of a being who does not exist but in the postulation of a being on a basis, be it a wish or projection, which does not warrant the postulation. Should that being exist in fact, the postulation would, again, represent a remarkable coincidence. The unlikelihood of the coincidence constitutes the challenge.[18]

So far, it has been argued that, once accepted, a naturalistic, or social scientific, account of religious belief provides one argument against the truth of religious belief: the improbability that a belief originating in error is true. But in addition, a social scientific account, once accepted, provides an argument against one commonly offered *justification* for the truth of religious belief: the supernatural origin of that belief. The social sciences not only argue directly against the truth of religious belief, whatever the justification offered for the belief, but also argue against one conventional justification offered for that belief: its supernatural origin.

Doubtless countless believers cite other justifications for their beliefs – for example, logical proofs for the existence of god. But surely many believers cite as justification the supernatural origin of their belief: the experience of god. To

---

[16]Singling out Freud's stress on the antiquity rather than, like me, the strength of the wishes, Grünbaum (1987:169-73, 152-53, 160-61), like me, shows how Freud uses the "wishful" origin of religious belief to refute the truth of it without committing the genetic fallacy.

[17]Strictly, Freud himself says only *that*, not *why*, it would be too coincidental for our wishes to match the world itself: even though he does note that "examples of illusions which have proved true are not easy to find" (1964:49), he does not explicitly appeal to the infrequency of true illusions as justification for the likely falsity of illusions. But perhaps he is simply taking the point for granted. So I am assuming. Grünbaum (1987:170-72), by contrast, assumes that for Freud the *antiquity* of our wishes, which Freud indeed calls "the oldest ... wishes of mankind" (1964:47), is what makes them likely false: the religious beliefs which express our wishes go back to antiquity and therefore likely rest on evidence long since made tenuous by science. But why newer, more cogent evidence could not be adduced for hoary wishes Freud would, then, have to say.

[18]Of course, one could argue from coincidence to the *probability* of the existence of god on the grounds that any widespread belief is more likely than not to be true. I thank Richard Gale for this point.

accept a social scientific explanation of religious belief would automatically be to reject a supernatural one – as either superfluous or outright incompatible.

A believer might respond that origin and truth have gotten confused: even if, say, projection *causes* the experience, the experience can still *be* of god. But the experience cannot be of god unless god is at least a partial cause of it: god need not cause one to *seek* god, but god must be at least one cause of the experience's *being* an experience of god. As William Alston puts it: "... the presence of x somewhere (not too far back) in the chain of causes giving rise to a certain experience is one necessary condition of that experience being involved in a perception of x.... If a thick brick wall was so placed as to prevent light waves from a house from reaching my eyes, then I could not have seen that house at that time" (Alston, 89).[19] The social scientist would be claiming to offer only a sufficient, not a necessary, cause of religious experience. He would be challenging the believer's claim that god is a necessary cause of every religious experience.

Admittedly, not all social scientific explanations of religious belief are, formally, explanations of religious experience, just as not all social scientific explanations utilize either wish fulfillment or projection. Indeed, only Jung, not Freud or Berger, is primarily concerned with religious experience. But the explanations which Freud and Berger offer of religious belief certainly apply to religious experience: to explain religious belief as a wish to believe that god exists is readily to explain religious experience as the fulfillment of that wish. The same is true of other social scientific explanations of religious belief. All of them apply to religious experience, and in explaining it naturalistically rather than supernaturally they undermine one standard justification for the truth of religious belief.

The extent to which the social sciences undermine the genetic justification for the truth of religious belief is the extent to which believers appeal to the supernatural origin of their belief to justify that belief. Insofar as believers appeal to the experience of god to justify their belief, denying the truth of the belief on the grounds that the source of the experience was not necessarily god involves no genetic fallacy. Insofar as believers appeal to more or other than the experience of god to justify their belief, denying the truth of the belief on the grounds that the source of the experience was not necessarily god commits the genetic fallacy. The social sciences can at most refute one justification for the truth of religious belief. They cannot refute all justifications.[20]

---

[19] Against Alston see Wainwright (69-73).
[20] As Alston says of Freud's explanation: "... even if there are certain ways of justifying theistic beliefs which could be discredited by psychological explanations ... there would always remain the possibility that there were other modes of justification which would turn out to be valid" (90).

The desire of more recent social scientists like Jung and Berger to circumvent the issue of truth distinguishes them from their predecessors, who were not the least reluctant to pronounce religious belief false. To be sure, those predecessors – for example, Edward Tylor, James Frazer, Karl Marx, and Émile Durkheim – did not, like Freud, argue for the falsity of religious belief on the grounds of its origin or function. Rather, they did the reverse: they argued for a secular origin and function and, even more, for the harmfulness or futility of the function on the grounds of its falsity,[21] which they established independently. Not only Jung and Berger but also Clifford Geertz and Victor Turner, among many other contemporaries, do not argue relativistically that religious belief is true. Rather, they confine themselves to the issues of function and, even more, meaning.[22]

REFERENCES

ALSTON, WILLIAM P.
1964   "Psychoanalytic Theory and Theistic Belief." In *Faith and the Philosophers,* ed. John Hick, pp. 63-102. New York: St. Martin's Press.

BANKS, ROBERT
1973   "Religion as Projection: A Re-appraisal of Freud's Theory." *Religious Studies* 9 (December):401-26.

BELLAH, ROBERT N.
1970   *Beyond Belief.* New York: Harper.

BERGER, PETER L.
1969   *The Sacred Canopy.* Garden City, N.Y.: Doubleday Anchor Books. Original publ.: Garden City, N.Y.: Doubleday, 1967.

1970   *A Rumor of Angels.* Garden City, N.Y.: Doubleday Anchor Books. Original publ.: Garden City, N.Y.: Doubleday, 1969.

1980   *The Heretical Imperative.* Garden City, N.Y.: Doubleday Anchor Books. Original publ.: Garden City, N.Y.: Doubleday, 1979.

DOUGLAS, MARY
1975   *Implicit Meanings.* London and Boston: Routledge & Kegan Paul.

---

[21]See Segal (1985).

[22]To be sure, the later Robert Bellah (1970:252-53) outright proclaims religion true, but its truth is its accurate depiction of humans' experience of the world, not its explanation of the world itself: see Segal (1983; 1986). In her relativistic writings Mary Douglas (1975: ix-xxi; 1979) comes far closer to proclaiming true the religious and other beliefs of alien cultures. As noted, the later Berger argues for the truth of religion.

1979   "World View and the Core." In *Philosophical Disputes in the Social Sciences*, ed. S. C. Brown, pp. 177-87. Sussex, Eng.: Harvester Press; Atlantic Highlands, N.J.: Humanities Press.

EDELSON, MARSHALL
1984   *Hypothesis and Evidence in Psychoanalysis*. Chicago: University of Chicago Press.

EYSENCK, H. J.
1965   *Fact and Fiction in Psychology*. Harmondsworth, Middlesex, Eng.: Penguin Books.

EYSENCK, HANS J., AND GLENN D. WILSON, EDS.
1973   *The Experimental Study of Freudian Theories*. London: Methuen.

FISHER, SEYMOUR, AND ROGER P. GREENBERG
1977   *The Scientific Credibility of Freud's Theories and Therapy*. New York: Basic Books.

FREUD, SIGMUND
1950   *Totem and Taboo*. Tr. James Strachey. New York: Norton.

1964   *The Future of an Illusion*. Tr. W. D. Robson-Scott, rev. James Strachey. Garden City, N.Y.: Doubleday Anchor Books.

1965   *Moses and Monotheism*. Tr. Katherine Jones. New York: Vintage Books.

GLYMOUR, CLARK
1974   "Freud, Kepler, and the Clinical Evidence." In *Freud*, ed. Richard Wollheim, pp. 285-304. Modern Studies in Philosophy. Garden City, N.Y.: Doubleday Anchor Books.

1980   *Theory and Evidence*. Princeton, N.J.: Princeton University Press.

GRÜNBAUM, ADOLF
1985   *The Foundations of Psychoanalysis*. Berkeley: University of California Press.

1987   "Psychoanalysis and Theism." *Monist* 70 (April):152-92.

GRÜNBAUM, ADOLF, AND ARTHUR CAPLAN ET AL.
1986   "Precis of *The Foundations of Psychoanalysis*." With Commentary by Arthur Caplan et al. *Behavioral and Brain Sciences* 9 (June):217-84.

HOOK, SIDNEY, ED.
1959   *Psychoanalysis, Scientific Method, and Philosophy*. Second Annual New York University Institute of Philosophy. New York: New York University Press.

JAMES, WILLIAM
1936   *The Varieties of Religious Experience*. New York: Modern Library.

JUNG, CARL G.

1938   *Psychology and Religion.* New Haven, Conn.: Yale University Press.

1976   "Religion and Psychology: A Reply to Martin Buber." In *The Collected Works,* eds. Sir Herbert Read and others, trs. R. F. C. Hull and others. Bollingen Series XX. Vol. XVIII, *The Symbolic Life.* Princeton, N.J.: Princeton University Press. Pp. 663-70.

KLINE, PAUL

1981   *Fact and Fantasy in Freudian Theory.* Second ed. London: Methuen.

KROEBER, ALFRED L.

1920   "Totem and Taboo: An Ethnologic Psychoanalysis." *American Anthropologist,* N.S., 22 (January-March):48-55.

1939   "Totem and Taboo in Retrospect." *American Journal of Sociology* 45 (November):446-51.

KÜNG, HANS

1979   *Freud and the Problem of God.* Tr. Edward Quinn. New Haven, Conn.: Yale University Press.

POPPER, KARL R.

1962   *Conjectures and Refutations.* New York: Basic Books.

ROSS, JAMES F.

1969   *Introduction to the Philosophy of Religion.* New York: Macmillan.

SEARS, ROBERT R.

1943   *Survey of Objective Studies of Psychoanalytic Concepts.* New York: Social Science Research Council.

SEGAL, ROBERT A.

1983   "Have the Social Sciences Been Converted?" *Journal for the Scientific Study of Religion* 24 (September):321-24. Reprinted in revised form in the present book as ch. 4.

1985   "A Jungian View of Evil: A Review Essay of John Sanford's *Evil.*" *Zygon* 20 (March):83-89. Reprinted in revised form in the present book as ch. 8.

1986   "The 'De-Sociologizing' of the Sociology of Religion." *Scottish Journal of Religious Studies* 7 (Spring):5-28. Reprinted in revised form in the present book as ch. 10.

WAINWRIGHT, WILLIAM J.

1981   *Mysticism.* Madison: University of Wisconsin Press.

WALLACE, EDWIN R., IV

1983   *Freud and Anthropology.* Psychological Issues, Monograph 55. New York: International Universities Press.

1986   "The Scientific Status of Psychoanalysis: A Review of Grünbaum's *The Foundations of Psychoanalysis.*" *Journal of Nervous and Mental Disease* 174 (July):379-86.

Chapter Eight

A Jungian View of Evil: A Review Essay of John Sanford's *Evil*

Carl Jung maintains relentlessly that he is only a psychologist and not a philosopher: "... I approach psychological matters from a scientific and not from a philosophical standpoint. Inasmuch as religion has a very important psychological aspect, I deal with it from a purely empirical point of view, that is, I restrict myself to the observation of phenomena and I eschew any metaphysical or philosophical considerations. I do not deny the validity of these other considerations, but I cannot claim to be competent to apply them correctly" (Jung [1958] 1969a:6).[1] In deeming himself only a psychologist, Jung is saying that he can explain only the origin and function, not the truth, of religion. He can determine only why believers believe, not whether what they believe is true. Indeed, he is saying that he cannot determine even the ultimate origin and function of religion. He can therefore neither prove nor disprove any ultimate role by god in causing believers to believe. He can at most determine only the direct role of psychological processes in causing believers to believe.

These two restrictions are not unrelated. The heart of religion for Jung is not belief but experience, albeit experience guided by belief. To believe in god is to encounter god – less often directly, as in Moses at the burning bush, than indirectly, through rituals and myths. Religion is true when religious experience is really of god, but religious experience is of god only when god is at least partly the cause of one's experience. God need not be the cause of one's *seeking* god but must be at least part of the cause of one's *experiencing* god.[2]

Despite Jung's denial that psychology has any bearing on metaphysics, he himself waxes metaphysical. The question is whether he does so on psychological grounds. In, notably, the case of synchronicity, or the coincidence of an individual's psychological state with an external event in the individual's life, he does not: synchronicity refers to the coincidence itself, not to its cause, and the coincidence is an entirely empirical matter. Furthermore, Jung necessarily argues for the coincidence on nonpsychological as well as

---

[1]See also Jung ([1956] 1967:231; [1961] 1962:349-50; 1976:663-70).
[2]See Alston (88-90). But against Alston see Wainwright (69-73).

psychological grounds: he must cite not just an individual's psychological state but also the external event itself.[3]

By contrast, Jung's professions of religious belief are unabashedly metaphysical. For example, he thanks God daily for permitting him "to experience the reality of the *imago Dei* in me" (Jung 1979:209). "From the beginning," he says, he had "the conviction that it was enjoined upon me to do what God wanted and not what I wanted.... Often I had the feeling that in all decisive matters I was no longer among men, but was alone with God" (Jung [1961] 1962:48). Best known is Jung's answer to the question whether he believed in God: "I *know*. I don't need to believe. I know" (Jung 1977:428).

In none of these passages, however, does Jung appeal to psychology to support his belief. Whether he or his followers do so in the case of not god but evil is the question prompted by Jungian John Sanford's recent book, *Evil*.[4] On the one hand Sanford criticizes Jung's understanding of the Christian view of evil. On the other hand he follows Jung in using psychology to evaluate that view. Whether either he or Jung uses psychology to evaluate the *truth* of that view is the issue.

The Social Scientific Evaluation of Religion

As a social scientist, Sanford can legitimately evaluate religion in several ways. First, he can account for the origin and function of religion. Second, he can evaluate the believer's own explanation of religion: he can determine whether religion arises and operates for the reasons the believer gives. Third, he can evaluate the utility of religion: he can determine whether religion really serves a function, whether it serves the function for which it was intended, whether the function it serves is helpful, whether the function it serves is important, and how important religion is to the serving of that function.

As a social scientist, Sanford cannot, however, ordinarily evaluate the truth of religion. Function and truth are usually distinct. Religion can be true yet dysfunctional or functional yet false. To be functional, religion must be *believed* true by believers, through whom it must operate, but it need not be true in fact. A belief believed true is no less efficacious when actually false than when true.

Whether *origin* and truth are distinct is a more complicated question than whether function and truth are. The case of religious experience most forcefully prompts the question. Admittedly, a naturalistic, or social scientific, account of the origin of a would-be experience of god would, if accepted, prove only that god did not cause the experience. It would hardly prove that apart from the experience god does not exist. Yet insofar as some believers muster their experience as justification for their belief in god, a sufficient naturalistic account

---

[3]On synchronicity see Jung ([1960] 1969b:417-519, 520-31).
[4]All unidentified citations in the chapter are to this book.

of that experience, while still not *precluding* god as the ultimate object and therefore ultimate cause of that experience, would render god superfluous: one would not need to invoke god to account for the experience, which need not therefore be of god. A sufficient naturalistic explanation, whether from psychology or another social science, would, then, constitute one case against the existence of god.[5]

Many classical social scientists assess the truth of religion, but they do not do so on grounds of the origin and function of religion. For Marx, religion is dysfunctional – not, however, because it fails to accomplish its intended function but because the escapist and justificatory functions it accomplishes are more harmful than helpful. Religion would not, however, be escapist if Marx believed in the place of escape: heaven. Marx does, then, deem religion dysfunctional because false, but he does not deem religion false because dysfunctional. Someone else might invoke economic harm as an argument against the existence of either a just or a powerful god, in which case the dysfunctional effect of religion would argue for the falsity of religion. But Marx himself disbelieves in god of any kind and does so on other grounds.

For the Freud of *The Future of an Illusion,* religion is, as for Marx, dysfunctional despite the fact that it accomplishes its intended function. But where for Marx religion is dysfunctional because the accomplishment of its function is harmful, for Freud religion is dysfunctional simply because the accomplishment of its function presupposes a false belief in a kind and just god. Like Marx, Freud disbelieves in god on independent grounds, not on the grounds of its effect. By vaunting a benevolent god, religion does not so much exacerbate human suffering as deny it. Still, Freud, like Marx, is saying that religion is dysfunctional because false: the comfort religion provides would be unobjectionable if Freud believed in god. But like Marx as well, Freud is not saying that religion is false because dysfunctional.[6]

For the Freud of *Totem and Taboo* and to a lesser extent *Moses and Monotheism,* religion is dysfunctional because, more straightforwardly, it fails to accomplish its intended function: alleviating guilt over parricidal deeds or urges. At the same time religion here is not even dysfunctional because false. Even though Freud here, too, scarcely believes in god, he objects to what believers do in the name of god: vainly attempt to repress irrepressible desires – an attempt that would be no less vain and no less harmful if god did exist.

Among classical social scientists, James Frazer above all considers religion dysfunctional because false. Certainly religion for him is not dysfunctional

---

[5]See Segal (1980). See also Alston (87-90).

[6]To be sure, in *The Future of an Illusion* Freud does deem religion false because of its *origin:* the origin of religion in a wish renders the truth of it improbable (52-53). Conversely, the blatant falsity of religion for Freud supports the claim that it originates in a wish, for only the eagerness to believe something so dubious can account for the belief (45-47). See Segal (1980).

because of its intended function: providing food. Rather, religion is dysfunctional because it fails utterly to accomplish that function, and it fails because god, whom believers ask for food, does not, for Frazer, exist. Frazer assumes not that believers thereby starve but that religion is not what gets them food. Yet precisely because he judges religion dysfunctional because false, he least of all judges religion false because dysfunctional.

For Edward Tylor, no less than for Frazer, religion is false science, but for Tylor its falsity does not preclude its utility – for Tylor, as an explanation of the world. For Frazer, the function of religion is inseparable from the falsity of it: religion can scarcely provide food when the would-be source of it does not exist. For Tylor, the function of religion is largely separable from the falsity of it: religion provides a rational and comprehensive, even while false, explanation of the world. Doubtless a true explanation would be even more effective, but a false one is not, as for Frazer, worthless because false.

By contrast to classical social scientists, most contemporary ones shun the issue of truth altogether, and do so on the same grounds as Jung: that the issue is beyond their social scientific ken. Just like Jung, Peter Berger says that the social sciences can determine neither the ultimate origin nor, as a consequence, the truth of religion.[7] More frequently, contemporary social scientists avoid the issue of origin altogether and focus entirely on function, which, they assume, has even less bearing on truth. One conspicuous exception is Mary Douglas, who on occasion uninhibitedly assesses the truth of the religious beliefs of at least alien cultures.[8]

For Jung, religion provides a most effective, if unconscious, vehicle for the expression of archetypes. Religion is functional in all the respects noted: it serves a function, it serves the function for which it was at least unconsciously intended, the function it serves is not just helpful but indispensable, and religion is an exceedingly useful means of serving that function. Jung does not go so far as to say that religion is the lone or even the best means of serving its function: art and dreams are equally effective unconscious means, and they, together with the "active imagination," also operate as even more effective conscious means.

So insistent is Jung on the distinction between utility and truth that he refrains from broaching the question of truth with any patient for whom religion works. The efficacy of religion depends on the patient's believing religion true, not on its being true: "If, therefore, a patient is convinced of the exclusively sexual origin of his neurosis, I would not disturb him in his opinion because I know that such a conviction ... is an excellent defence against an onslaught of immediate experience with its terrible ambiguity. So long as such a defence

---

[7]See Berger (1969:88-89, 100, 179-85). To be sure, in subsequent, less neutral works Berger argues that the social sciences can *establish* a supernatural origin, hence referent, of religion: see Berger (1970:52-97; 1980:58-60, ch. 5).
[8]See Douglas (1975:ix-xxi; 1979:177-87).

works I shall not break it down, since I know that there must be cogent reasons why the patient has to think in such a narrow circle.... In the same way and for the same reason I support the hypothesis of the practising Catholic while it works for him. In either case, I reinforce a means of defence against a grave risk, without asking the academic question whether the defence is an ultimate truth. I am glad when it works and so long as it works" (Jung [1958] 1969a:44-45).

For Jung, *religion* must be believed literally in order to work psychologically, but *myth* need not. A myth translated from literal, metaphysical terms into symbolic, psychological ones can still work psychologically. One need believe in only its *psychological* truth. One need believe that the Oedipus myth, for example, describes a psychological state of humans, not that there ever was a person named Oedipus. Many theorists of myth contend that the true meaning of myth is nonliteral. Jung, together with Rudolph Bultmann, is distinctive in contending that myth works even when no longer taken literally.

Jung's Criticism of Christianity

Jung faults Christianity on two counts. He argues, first, that Protestantism in particular, by eliminating most sacraments and other rituals, has eliminated fixed, safe channels for the expression of archetypal energy: "Protestantism, having pulled down so many walls carefully erected by the Church, immediately began to experience the disintegrating and schismatic effect of individual revelation. As soon as the dogmatic fence was broken down and the ritual lost its authority, man had to face his inner experience without the protection and guidance of dogma and ritual, which are the very quintessence of Christian as well as of pagan religious experience. Protestantism has, in the main, lost all the finer shades of traditional Christianity: the mass, confession, the greater part of the liturgy, and the vicarious function of priesthood" (Jung [1958] 1969a:21).

Jung argues, second, that Christianity in general, by excluding from the Trinity both Mary and Satan, has denied channels for the realization of what he calls the anima archetype in males and the shadow archetype in all: "Medieval iconology ... evolved a quaternity symbol in its representations of the coronation of the Virgin and surreptitiously put it in place of the Trinity. The Assumption of the Blessed Virgin Mary ... is admitted as ecclesiastical doctrine but has not yet become dogma" (Jung [1958] 1969a:170).[9] "But the Christian definition of God as the *summum bonum* excludes the Evil One right from the start, despite the fact that in the Old Testament he was still one of the 'sons of God.' Hence the devil remained outside the Trinity as the 'ape of God' and in opposition to

---

[9]On the exclusion of the feminine in Christianity see Jung ([1958] 1969a:62-63, 170-71; [1953] 1968a:150-51). See also Philp (70-72, 79-80, 216, 219), White (113-14), Moreno (89-90, 117), Dry (204-5), Heisig (64-68), Sanford (120-21, 139-40).

it.... The devil is, undoubtedly, an awkward figure: he is the 'odd man out' in the Christian cosmos. That is why people would like to minimize his importance by euphemistic ridicule or by ignoring his existence altogether; or, better still, to lay the blame for him at man's door" (Jung [1958] 1969a:172).[10] For Jung, even Catholicism fails to give Mary and therefore the anima sufficient due, for it grants neither her nor any other female a place in the pantheon. Similarly, Christianity generally fails to accord Satan and therefore the shadow any place in heaven.[11] By humans' evil side Jung and Sanford alike mean the shadow – more precisely, the collective rather than the personal one.[12]

To be sure, Jung distinguishes sharply between Christian *mythology* and *institutionalized* Christianity. The mythology of Christianity, found above all in the Bible, fully recognizes both Mary and Satan and therefore both the anima and the shadow. It is institutionalized Christianity which denies its own mythology: "Our myth has become mute, and gives no answers. The fault lies not in it as it is set down in the Scriptures, but solely in us, who have not developed it further, who, rather, have suppressed any such attempts" (Jung [1961] 1962:332).

Sanford's Assessment of Jung's Criticism

Sanford considers neither Jung's criticism of Christianity in general for ignoring the anima nor his criticism of Protestantism in particular for ignoring the unconscious as a whole. Jung's criticism of Christianity for ignoring the shadow he deems onesided. Christianity, he argues, has various, disparate views of evil rather than a single, doctrinal one.

Sanford distinguishes, first, between the view of the Synoptic Gospels and that of both Paul and Revelation (35-48, 67-84). For Sanford, the Synoptic Jesus' acceptance of sinners, acceptance of the body, and refusal to blame sin on a Satan distinct from God all symbolize acceptance of evil amidst good and thereby acceptance of the shadow. By contrast, Paul's intolerance of sin in himself and others, his Gnostic-like rejection of the body, and his ascription of evil to Satan rather than to God all constitute a denial of evil and therefore a denial of the shadow. For Sanford, the same is true of Revelation.

On the one hand Sanford criticizes Jung for overlooking the Synoptic view, which acknowledges evil. On the other hand he grants that Paul and Revelation

---

[10]On the exclusion of evil in Christianity see Jung ([1958] 1969a:107-200, 355-470; [1959] 1968c:36-71; [1961] 1962:327-34, 337-38). See also Philp (passim), White (95-114, 141-65), Bertine (54-67, 243-63), Jaffé (95-127), Moreno (85-101, 145-60), Hostie (188-209), Dry (203-6), Heisig (54-59, 76-78), Cox (271-84).

[11]Correctly or not, Jung not only castigates at least mainstream Christianity but also praises Gnosticism on this ground: see Segal (1986:esp. 138-42).

[12]On the shadow see Jung ([1959] 1968b:255-72; [1959] 1968c:8-10).

deny evil and that, moreover, their view has proved the dominant one in Christianity.

Sanford distinguishes, second, among three distinct Patristic views of evil (129-55). The first blames evil wholly on humans and thereby preserves God's sheer goodness. The second, that of both Irenaeus and Origen, ascribes evil to God but considers it a necessary means to a good end. The third, that of Origen as well and above all that of Augustine, relegates evil to *privatio boni,* or the denial of good.

On the one hand Sanford criticizes Jung for taking the Augustinian view of evil as the sole Patristic one. On the other hand he criticizes Jung for taking even the Augustinian view as a dismissal of evil. On the contrary, he argues, Augustine presupposes the reality of evil and uses the denial of good to explain it. Evil vis-à-vis good is like illness vis-à-vis health: real, just parasitical on its opposite.[13] Consistently or not, Sanford argues that all three Patristic views acknowledge evil yet also that the view of Paul and Revelation is the main Christian one, in which case Sanford as well as Jung faults Christianity for denying evil.

Sanford: Social Scientist or Metaphysician?

The issue at hand is not whether Sanford correctly characterizes the Christian view of evil. To cite a single instance, Paul does not, like the Gnostics, reject the body as evil: Paul's antithesis of spirit and flesh does not correspond to the Gnostic antitheis of soul and body – or, alternatively, of spirit and soul plus body. Nor is the question even whether Sanford correctly characterizes Jung's view of the Christian view. To cite another example, Jung's frequent invocation of the Synoptics suggests strongly that he is not overlooking them. Moreover, Sanford never distinguishes between Jung's view of institutionalized Christianity and his view of Christian mythology.

The real issue, however, is whether Sanford, as a social scientist, can determine the reality of evil. "Jung," he says, "justly criticizes the Church for neglecting the task of dealing with evil" (145). Is Sanford thereby criticizing Christianity on only psychological grounds or outright metaphysical ones? Does he consider the denial of evil merely dysfunctional or outright false? Does he want evil acknowledged in order to serve only human needs or also cosmic truth?

On the one hand Sanford, like Jung, says repeatedly that he is restricting himself to the psychology of religion: "... the theme that runs throughout the book is the nature of evil as seen from the vantage point of religion and psychology ..." (2). Thus he says that "from the vantage point of psychology ... the legend [of Lucifer] describes a fateful split in the human psyche ..." (114-15).

---

[13]On the view of evil as *privatio boni* see Jung ([1958] 1969a:168-80, 304-5; [1959] 1968c:41-71). For a similar criticism of Jung's interpretation of *privatio boni* see many of the references in note 10. For a defense of Jung see Lambert.

Sanford not only separates the metaphysical viewpoint from the psychological one but even argues that the Biblical story of Balaam, for example, expresses both: "So the story illustrates both the dark, daemonic side of Yahweh in the Old Testament, and also the dark side of the Self" (31).

On the other hand Sanford, whether or not Jung as well, in fact discusses metaphysics as if psychology bore on it. Sometimes he claims that psychology can elucidate the nature of God: "... if we can gain a deeper insight into the nature of and reasons for [human] evil, we may also learn more about the nature of God. It is with this hope that this book has been written" (3). One might assume that Sanford, like many other Jungians, is arguing that the human psyche is, or contains, an image of God, so that evil in humans *mirrors* evil in God. That claim would itself clearly transcend the bounds of psychology. But instead Sanford is arguing, even more boldly, that human evil, by which he means evil done *to* humans rather than *by* them, is *caused* by an evil God: "When we first encounter the dark side of the Self we may feel that we are confronting evil. Certainly the problem that is tormenting us – our illness, anxiety, depression, or phobia – is experienced as an evil condition .... Most conventional Christian training today encourages us to dissociate this evil state of affairs with [sic] God. God's intentions, we are assured, are too benign to send such darkness upon us .... The biblical story of Balaam, though, is only one of many parts of the Bible which tells [sic] us that God has this dark side too, and that if we persevere in the wrong course in life we can run into the Wrath of God which will destroy us" (32). Clearly, here, too, Sanford is venturing beyond the immediate, psychological origin of human affliction to its ultimate, metaphysical one.

Other times Sanford argues, no less metaphysically, the opposite: not that psychology reveals the nature of god but that psychology reveals god to be only a human projection. In the fashion of Ludwig Feuerbach, Sanford asserts that the evil ascribed to god matches too closely that in humans to be merely coincidental: "Yahweh has His dark side .... This image of God as light and dark corresponds so closely to the archetype of the Self ... that we cannot simply dismiss it as primitive. Rather, we must look to the ancient Hebrew image of God as a totality of light and dark, as an [projected] expression of one aspect of the truth about the relationship between [human] good and [human] evil" (32-33).

Satan likewise proves to be only a human projection: "... the devil is a personification of the power drive of the ego. There is within us something that wants to set the ego up against the Self, the human against the Divine Will. Legend personified this as Lucifer, whose power drive led to his expulsion from heaven" (127). Dualism in the cosmos gets reduced to a projection of human good and evil: "The extreme Dualism of the Book of Revelation suggests a violent and unsolved split in the psychological attitude of the early Church. It is as though the psyche of the early Church was split, and this split projected itself into the metaphysical apocalyptic imagery of the teaching of the Antichrist" (43-44).

At most, it would seem, psychology can explain only evil done by humans, not evil done to them. Though Sanford notes evil done to them – for example, natural catastrophes, physical diseases, and even mental ones (133, 32) – he not coincidentally concentrates on evil done by them – the kind of evil attributed to the shadow. Jung himself, however, invokes synchronicity to explain evil done to humans as well: whatever happens to one in the external world parallels, though admittedly not necessarily causes, something within one. Even if, then, synchronicity does not say why humans suffer evil, it does say that some connection exists between their suffering and their psychological state. Even if synchronicity never says that suffering is punishment for something awry in one, it does say that suffering is not random: the state of one's psyche may not cause one's death in a plane crash, but it does make one's death other than accidental. Still, Jung is not thereby going beyond psychology to metaphysics, let alone using psychology to do so. For, again, synchronicity is only the correlation of inner with outer events, not the ultimate or even direct explanation of the correlation.

Unlike Sanford, Jung, as a Kantian, insists on separating social scientific inquiries from metaphysical ones. If he errs, he errs not, like Sanford, in taking psychology too far but in not taking it far enough. Like other contemporary social scientists, he errs in not seeing the possible metaphysical ramifications of empirical inquiries.

REFERENCES

ALSTON, WILLIAM P.
1964   "Psychoanalytic Theory and Theistic Belief." In *Faith and the Philosophers,* ed. John Hick, pp. 63-102. New York: St. Martin's Press.

BERGER, PETER L.
1969   *The Sacred Canopy.* Garden City, N.Y.: Doubleday Anchor Books. Original publ.: Garden City, N.Y.: Doubleday, 1967.

1970   *A Rumor of Angels.* Garden City, N.Y.: Doubleday Anchor Books. Original publ.: Garden City, N.Y.: Doubleday, 1969.

1980   *The Heretical Imperative.* Garden City, N.Y.: Doubleday Anchor Books. Original publ.: Garden City, N.Y.: Doubleday, 1979.

BERTINE, ELEANOR
1967   *Jung's Contribution to Our Time.* Ed. Elizabeth C. Rohrbach. New York: Putnam.

COX, DAVID
1959   *Jung and St. Paul.* London: Longmans, Green.

DOUGLAS, MARY

1975   *Implicit Meanings.* London and Boston: Routledge & Kegan Paul.

1979   "World View and the Core." In *Philosophical Disputes in the Social Sciences,* ed. S. C. Brown, pp. 177-87. Sussex, Eng.: Harvester Press; Atlantic Highlands, N.J.: Humanities Press.

DRY, AVIS M.

1961   *The Psychology of Jung.* New York: Wiley.

FREUD, SIGMUND

1964   *The Future of an Illusion.* Tr. W. D. Robson-Scott, rev. James Strachey. Garden City, N.Y.: Doubleday Anchor Books.

HEISIG, JAMES W.

1979.   *Imago Dei.* Cranbury, N.J.: Bucknell University Press.

HOSTIE, RAYMOND

1957   *Religion and the Psychology of Jung.* Tr. G. R. Lamb. New York: Sheed & Ward.

JAFFÉ, ANIELA

1975   *The Myth of Meaning.* Tr. R. F. C. Hull. Baltimore: Penguin Books.

JUNG, CARL G.

[1953]   *The Collected Works.* Eds. Sir Herbert Read and others. Trs. R. F. C.
1968a   Hull and others. Bollingen Series XX. Vol. XII, *Psychology and Alchemy.* Second ed. Princeton, N.J.: Princeton University Press.

[1956]   *The Collected Works.* Vol. V, *Symbols of Transformation.* Second ed.
1967   Princeton, N.J.: Princeton University Press.

[1958]   *The Collected Works.* Vol. XI, *Psychology and Religion: West and East.*
1969a   Second ed. Princeton, N.J.: Princeton University Press.

[1959]   *The Collected Works.* Vol. IX, part I, *The Archetypes and the Collective*
1968b   *Unconscious.* Second ed. Princeton, N.J.: Princeton University Press.

[1959]   *The Collected Works.* Vol. IX, part 2, *Aion.* Second ed. Princeton, N.J.:
1968c   Princeton University Press.

[1960]   *The Collected Works.* Vol. VIII, *The Structure and Dynamics of the*
1969b   *Psyche.* Second ed. Princeton, N.J.: Princeton University Press.

[1961]   *Memories, Dreams, Reflections.* Ed. Aniela Jaffé. Trs. Richard and Clara
1962   Winston. New York: Vintage Books.

1976   *The Collected Works.* Vol. XVIII, *The Symbolic Life.* Princeton, N.J.: Princeton University Press.

1977   *C. G. Jung Speaking.* Eds. William McGuire and R. F. C. Hull. Bollingen Series XCVII. Princeton, N.J.: Princeton University Press.

1979   *Word and Image.* Ed. Aniela Jaffé. Bollingen Series XCVII:2. Princeton, N. J.: Princeton University Press.

LAMBERT, KENNETH
1960   Review of Philp, *Jung and the Problem of Evil. Journal of Analytical Psychology* 5 (July):170-76.

MORENO, ANTONIO
1970   *Jung, Gods, and Modern Man.* Notre Dame, Ind.: University of Notre Dame Press.

PHILP, H. L.
1958   *Jung and the Problem of Evil.* London: Rockliff.

SANFORD, JOHN A.
1982   *Evil: The Shadow Side of Reality.* New York: Crossroad.

SEGAL, ROBERT A.
1980   "The Social Sciences and the Truth of Religious Belief." *Journal of the American Academy of Religion* 48 (September):403-13. Reprinted in revised form in the present book as ch. 7.

1986   *The Poimandres as Myth.* Religion and Reason Series, No. 33. Berlin: Mouton de Gruyter.

WAINWRIGHT, WILLIAM J.
1981   *Mysticism.* Madison: University of Wisconsin Press.

WHITE, VICTOR
1960   *Soul and Psyche.* New York: Harper.

Chapter Nine

Fustel de Coulanges:
The First Modern Sociologist of Religion

It has been said that the first sociologist of religion was Plato in Book X of the *Laws*. Whatever Plato's status, the first *modern* sociologist of religion was surely Numa Denis Fustel de Coulanges.[1] While William Robertson Smith and Émile Durkheim get vaunted as rivals to Fustel, one elementary fact militates against the claims made on their behalf: chronology. *The Ancient City*,[2] Fustel's main and in fact only work on the sociology of religion, was first published in 1864.[3] Smith's principal work on the subject, *Lectures on the Religion of the Semites,* was first published only in 1889. His sole other work bearing on the sociology of religion was first published only four years earlier. Durkheim's writings on religion date from 1899, but his central tome, *The Elementary Forms of the Religious Life,* did not appear until 1912.

Moreover, Fustel was Durkheim's teacher and deeply influenced him.[4] By contrast, it is unclear whether Smith was even aware of Fustel.[5] Fustel did write before the emergence of sociology as a discipline and did see himself as a historian instead. Still, he was concerned with the same sociological issues as Durkheim and therefore deserves the title of first modern sociologist of religion.[6]

---

[1]On Fustel de Coulanges see, in addition to the works listed in the references, the bibliographies in Herrick (130-37), Thompson (363n8), Momigliano (1977:341n4; 1980:xv).

[2]All unidentified citations in the chapter are to the edition of this book cited in the references.

[3]In later works Fustel downplays the importance of religion.

[4]On Fustel's influence on Durkheim see, for example, Alpert (22-23), Evans-Pritchard (50-51), Lukes (58-63), Momigliano (1977:339-40), Nisbet (1965:75, 76-77, 80; 1966:238-43; 1974:27-28, 78, 163, 172-73), Pickering (47, 56-58, 116, 524).

[5]Lukes states that "Smith's theory" (and therefore Smith) "was influenced by Fustel de Coulanges' *La Cité antique,* via Smith's friend J. F. McLennan" (238; see also 450n1). But Lukes cites no evidence, and Beidelman declares that he himself has yet to find any evidence to support Lukes' claim (68n142).

[6]Nevertheless, sociologists of the stature of Malinowski (168) and Radcliffe-Brown (181), for example, regard Smith, not Fustel, as the first modern sociologist of religion. And Beidelman, having confidently said the same, adds:

The argument over who was first prompts the question of what constitutes the sociology of religion. Answering that the field deals with the relationship between society and religion may be tautological, but it does prompt the further question of what that relationship is. That the relationship is close all sociologists of religion by definition assume. They disagree over which phenomenon is the cause and which the effect. Some believe that society acts on religion. Others – Smith, Bronislaw Malinowski, A. R. Radcliffe-Brown, and Peter Berger among them – believe that religion acts on society. Still others, including Durkheim and especially Max Weber, believe that religion and society act on each other. Fustel believes uncompromisingly in a one-way relationship: religion acts on society, not vice versa.

Among sociologists of religion who believe that religion either wholly or partly acts on society, there are two camps. One camp views religion as a "passive" cause; the other, as an "active" one. For Smith, Malinowski, Radcliffe-Brown, Berger, and in part Durkheim, religion acts "passively" on society: it bolsters, not creates, society. It causes not society itself but the support members accord society. For Weber and again in part Durkheim, religion acts "actively" on society: it outright establishes, not merely sustains, society. Fustel is a grand exemplar of the "active" camp.[7]

In *The Ancient City* Fustel seeks to prove that religion creates not, as for the "activist" Durkheim, the cognitive categories of society but, more tangibly, the customs, laws, and institutions of society. Although he restricts himself to ancient Greece and Rome, Fustel clearly means to generalize to all ancient, albeit not modern, societies: he rigidly distinguishes ancient piety from modern atheism. Indeed, he even charges contemporary historians, who in his day dismissed ancient religion as mere poetry or politics (205, 166, 213), with projecting their secular outlook onto the ancient world. Exactly because *ancients* took religion seriously, it had, he claims, the influence that it did.

The first social institution that Fustel considers is marriage. He does not, to be sure, assert that religion created marriage, but he does assert that religion made marriage a grave event. In leaving her family, a bride was above all leaving her religion. For her religion was the worship of her family's ancestors. She had therefore to be accepted into the religion of her husband. Marriage was above all initiation into that religion.

If religion did not cause marriage itself, it did, according to Fustel, cause numerous other familial practices and regulations: the near-prohibition of

---

"The only contender to his claim would be Numa Denis Fustel de Coulanges and clearly even in France Fustel's work seems to have had less impact than that of Smith" (68n142) – a debatable rationale for dethroning Fustel.

[7]I am not using "active" and "passive" cause the way Mary Douglas (ch. 1) does: with whether theories of religion deem individuals free or determined. I am concerned with whether theories credit religion with outright creating or merely perpetuating society.

divorce, the prohibition of male celibacy, the mechanism of adoption, the right to private property, the right of primogeniture, the authority of the father, morality, the gens, and class divisions. Several of these practices and regulations arose as ways of protecting familial religion from extinction. For example, male celibacy was forbidden in order to insure the continuation and therefore the worship of the family, traced as it was through the male. Likewise the mechanism of adoption was instituted to insure a male heir when marriage failed to yield one.

Other activities and rules were sheer consequences of religion, not means of safeguarding it. The right to private property, for instance, developed out of the family's obligation to retain the land on which its hearth was located and beneath which its ancestors resided. The right of primogeniture was the extension of the eldest son's succession to the family priesthood. The authority of the father rested on his religious authority.

Gradually, society grew from family to gens to phratry to tribe to city. The gods grew with it from domestic to, eventually, municipal deities. At the same time nature gods, who had been overshadowed by their ancestral counterparts, came at last to the fore. Though at times Fustel implies otherwise (for example, 13), religion apparently did not so much cause the expansion of society as expand with it. Still, the expansion of society required the expansion of religion: operating now as a "passive" rather than "active" cause, common worship was needed to unify society at each stage, and was needed *before* society could expand rather than just to support new expansion.

Within the city, religion was responsible for innumerable phenomena: all festivals, the calendar, the census, the power of the king and later of the magistrate, the nature of all laws, the determination of citizenship, class divisions, the degree of patriotism, the fear of exile, the authority of the city over its citizens, and the inability of cities to merge. Other phenomena religion did not so much cause as either govern – war – or pervade – meetings of the assembly and of the courts. Still other phenomena – various ceremonies and laws – were religious in themselves. Above all, there loomed the continuous need to appease the gods.

Having charted the rise of the ancient city, Fustel next plots its fall, which he attributes to four causes.[8] First, traditional religion, which had unified society, slowly declined (353-60). Second, class conflict developed and led to four successive revolutions, each further weakening traditional authority (225-351). Third, Rome's conquest of the cities subordinated municipal loyalties to imperial ones (360-88). Last, the triumph of Christianity marked the universalizing of local religion and, if only temporarily, the splitting of the union of church and state (389-96).

---

[8]Fustel speaks twice of two causes (224, 352-53) but actually names four.

Fustel pursues his thesis of the significance of ancient religion with a boldness and a relentlessness that make few works more worthy of the phrase *tour de force*. Yet as dazzling as his effort is, it prompts questions of both fact and logic. The questions of fact concern ancient Greece and Rome exclusively and are less important here than the questions of logic, which concern Fustel's approach to religion generally. Still, classical scholarship since Fustel's day has rendered untenable much of his characterization of ancient life. In particular, his reconstruction of the earliest stage of classical religion and classical society has proved entirely speculative, and most scholars have long since abandoned the search for the origin of either.[9]

As for questions of logic, Fustel does not always argue consistently for his thesis that ancient religion determined ancient society. He ascribes an almost uniformly causal role to religion within the family, but its role within the city proves more mixed. Religion thus regulated rather than caused war and permeated rather than caused meetings of the assembly and the courts. As noted, Fustel appears to be saying that religion accommodated rather than caused the expansion of society from the family to, ultimately, the city – as if religion were the effect instead of the cause (for example, 118, 131-32). Even to say, as Fustel does (for example, 118, 131-32), that society could not have expanded without the expansion of religion is still to make religion only an indispensable effect, or merely a "passive" cause: the expansion of religion merely sustained, not produced, the expansion of society.

Finally, only the first and fourth causes of the fall of the city, the decline of ancient religion and the triumph of Christianity, are religious. The third cause, Rome's conquest of the cities, has nothing to do with religion. The second cause, class conflict, might have had a religious cause in turn but is itself a political or economic cause.[10] Indeed, Fustel attributes the first cause, the decline of traditional belief, to something entirely secular: the natural intellectual maturation of humanity.

Although these departures from Fustel's uncompromising thesis are serious, far more serious is the one logical fallacy he commits unremittingly: the confusion of mere correlation with cause, the *cum hoc, propter hoc* fallacy.[11] Distinguishing cause from correlation is not easy, but to prove that religion alone shaped ancient society Fustel must clearly prove first that other correlates did not. Fustel recognizes this obligation and tries to meet it by refuting three rival correlates conventionally offered as causes: birth, natural affection, and the

---

[9]See, for example, Guthrie's remarks (21) on ancestor worship as the origin of Greek religion.

[10]It is, then, hard to fathom Fustel's seeming declaration at the end of the book that religion was the sole cause of the fall of the ancient city: "We have written the history of a belief. It was established, and human society was constituted. It was modified, and society underwent a series of revolutions" (396).

[11]Thompson as well (II:366) notes this fallacy.

inherent authority of the father (41-42). But his refutation is tenuous. The fact that none of these three correlates can explain all of ancient society hardly means that each cannot explain some of it. Fustel simply takes for granted that a single cause underlay all of ancient society.

Further, Fustel never even proves that religion actually antedated the phenomena it allegedly caused. *Merely* to show that it antedated its would-be effects would not prove causality, and to say that it did would be to commit the *post hoc, propter hoc* fallacy. But not to show that religion even antedated its would-be effects would not preclude its having been their mere correlate, the *cum hoc, propter hoc* fallacy, or even their effect, the *pro hoc, propter hoc* fallacy.

Take the first two phenomena Fustel considers: marriage and divorce. He maintains that religion was the cause of the momentousness of marriage. His only evidence, however, is the simple correlation of the bride's change of family as a change of worship with her change of family as a momentous event. That correlation scarcely proves causality. Perhaps the change of family itself was momentous and the change of worship only a concomitant or a consequence of it.

Similarly, Fustel contends that religion made divorce nearly impossible. His sole evidence, however, is the correlation of religious opposition to divorce, which broke the sacred bonds of marriage, with the secular prohibition of it. That correlation does not prove that divorce was almost impossible because it was religiously unconscionable. Perhaps divorce was proscribed for economic reasons, and religious opposition was a mere concomitant. Perhaps religious opposition was imposed *ex post facto* to rationalize economic opposition. Supporting rather than creating the proscription, religion would here be a "passive" rather than active cause. The issue is not whether ancients themselves deemed marriage grave and divorce difficult for religious reasons but what directly or indirectly caused them to do so. Fustel's explanation of the role of religion in ancient society might well be more persuasive than alternatives, but his obliviousness to the need to entertain rival explanations makes his own dogmatic.

There are, finally, logical questions about Fustel's most general brand of sociology of religion: his view that religion acts on society, actively or passively, rather than vice versa. For even if religion were in fact the cause of every phenomenon he assigns to it, society would still remain at least partly the cause of religion. Surely not only the prior existence but also the prior importance of the family can account for worship by and of the family.[12] What accounts for the eldest son's succession to the priesthood if not his prior secular status? Is it really religion itself that elevates sons over daughters and eldest sons

---

[12]Fustel does concede that "Religion ... did not create the family" (42), but this concession is insufficient: why assume that religion even "gave the family its rules" (42)?

over younger ones? What accounts for the father's religious authority if not his prior secular authority? Is it really religion that makes the father the head of the family? Few aspects of religion seem immune to "sociologizing" of this kind.

Fustel is able to argue that religion shaped society and not the reverse only by arbitrarily taking religion as the given. But if one begins with society, religion readily seems shaped by it. Whether religion is really the cause of society or society really the cause of religion should be settled by research, not dogmatism. Maybe religion and society will prove to be partly the cause and partly the effect of each other, as they are for Weber above all.

As severe as all of these criticisms are, they do not challenge Fustel's standing as the first modern sociologist of religion. His attempt to prove ancient religion wholly responsible for ancient society may be futile and even misconceived, but his attempt to link ancient religion at all with ancient society, not the specific link he draws, makes him a sociologist.

Whatever the exact influence of Fustel on Smith and Durkheim, the three of them together constitute the first generation of modern sociologists of religion. What unites them, and unites them with their successors, are their concerns with the place of religion within society; the function rather than origin, or mere origin, of religion; the integrative function of religion; the communal rather than individual nature of at least ancient religion; and the practical rather than theoretical, or purely theoretical, side of religion.[13] What allies them with not

---

[13]There are many other similarities as well as considerable differences between Fustel and each of them. Like Fustel, Smith (1) is concerned with only the function, not the origin, of religion; (2) is concerned with only the impact of religion on society, not the reverse; (3) sees religion as functioning to unify society; (4) deems at least ancient religion collective rather than individualistic; (5) assumes the fundamental religious unit to be based on kinship; (6) considers rituals far more important than either myths or creeds; and (7) stresses the differences between ancient and modern society, hence between ancient and modern religion. Unlike Fustel, Smith (1) is concerned with religion for its own sake as well as for its social consequences; (2) nevertheless sees religion as only one part, not the whole, of ancient society and therefore does not equate the religious with the social; (3) sees religion as only "passively" unifying society, not also "actively" creating it; (4) deems totemism, not ancestor worship, the earliest form of religion; (5) deems the clan, not the family, the fundamental social unit; (6) regards ancient religion as amoral and materialistic, not moral and spiritual; (7) sees religion as still alive in the modern age, simply transformed from a collective to an individual phenomenon, rather than dead because no longer collective; and (8) generalizes from Semitic rather than classical society.

Like Fustel, Durkheim (1) is interested in religion not for its own sake but for its social consequences; (2) regards religion as the decisive factor in society – ancient society alone for Fustel; (3) sees religion as partly functioning "passively" to unify society; (4) regards religion as the key to the survival of society; (5) sees religion as "actively" creating, not just "passively" maintaining, society; (6) outright equates the religious with the social; (7) considers rituals more important than either myths or creeds; (8) defines the prime object of religion as the

only their fellow sociologists of religion but also historians of religions is that they take religion seriously.

REFERENCES

ALPERT, HARRY
1961   *Émile Durkheim and His Sociology*. New York: Russell & Russell. Pp. 22-23.

BEIDELMAN, T. O.
1974   *W. Robertson Smith and the Sociological Study of Religion*. Chicago: University of Chicago Press. P. 68.

BLOCH, MARC
1931   "Fustel de Coulanges, Numa-Denis." In *Encyclopaedia of the Social Sciences* 6:543.

DOUGLAS, MARY
1982   *In the Active Voice*. London and Boston: Routledge & Kegan Paul.

DURKHEIM, ÉMILE
1915   *The Elementary Forms of the Religious Life*. Tr. Joseph Ward Swain. London: Allen & Unwin.

EVANS-PRITCHARD, E. E.
1965   *Theories of Primitive Religion*. Oxford: Clarendon Press. Pp. 50-51, 53.

FINLEY, M. I.
1977   "The Ancient City: From Fustel de Coulanges to Max Weber and Beyond." *Comparative Studies in Society and History* 19 (July):305-27.

FUSTEL DE COULANGES, NUMA DENIS
1956   *The Ancient City*. Tr. Willard Small. Garden City, N.Y.: Doubleday Anchor Books. Original publ. of tr.: Boston: Lothrop, Lee, 1873.

impersonal sacred – embodied for Fustel in the hearth; and (9) stresses the reality of religion for believers. Unlike Fustel, Durkheim (1) is concerned with the origin as well as the function of religion; (2) regards religion as the product of society as well as vice versa, though religion is the product of society less in *The Elementary Forms of the Religious Life* than in *The Division of Labor in Society;* (3) is thereby concerned with the impact of society on religion as well as vice versa; (4) takes religion to be the reflection of society, not the reverse; (5) sees religion as creating sentiments and cognitive categories more than customs, laws, and institutions; (6) deems totemism, not ancestor worship, the earliest form of religion; (7) deems the clan, not the family, the fundamental social unit; (8) is interested in religious symbolism; (9) sees religion, in traditional or modern guise, as naturally present in every society, though at times says that in modern society it must be created; and (10) generalizes from aboriginal rather than classical society.

Reprint: Baltimore: Johns Hopkins University Press, 1980 – with foreword by Arnaldo Momigliano and S. C. Humphreys.

GLOTZ, G.
1929   *The Greek City and its Institutions.* Tr. N. Mallinsen. London: Kegan Paul. Pp. 2-5.

GUIRAUD, PAUL
1896   *Fustel de Coulanges.* Paris: Hatchette.

GUTHRIE, W. K. C.
1950   *The Greeks and Their Gods.* Boston: Beacon Press.

HERRICK, JANE
1954   *The Historical Thought of Fustel de Coulanges.* Washington, D.C.: Catholic University of America Press.

HUMPHREYS, S. C.
1978   *Anthropology and the Greeks.* London and Boston: Routledge & Kegan Paul. Ch. 8.

1980   "Foreword" to *The Ancient City.* Baltimore: Johns Hopkins University Press. Pp. xv-xxiii.

1987   "Fustel de Coulanges, N. D." In *Encyclopedia of Religion* 3:459-60.

LATOUCHE, ROBERT
1968   "Fustel de Coulanges, Numa Denis." In *International Encyclopedia of the Social Sciences* 6:43-44.

LUKES, STEVEN
1975   *Émile Durkheim.* Harmondsworth, Middlesex, Eng.: Penguin Books. Pp. 58-63.

MALINOWSKI, BRONISLAW
1944   *A Scientific Theory of Culture and Other Essays.* Chapel Hill: University of North Carolina Press.

MOMIGLIANO, ARNALDO
1977   *Essays in Ancient and Modern Historiography.* Middletown, Conn.: Wesleyan University Press. Ch. 19.

1980   "Foreword" to *The Ancient City.* Baltimore: Johns Hopkins University Press. Pp. ix-xv.

NISBET, ROBERT A.
1965   *Émile Durkheim: With Selected Essays.* Ed. Nisbet. Englewood Cliffs, N.J.: Prentice-Hall. Pp. 73, 75, 76-77, 80.

1966   *The Sociological Tradition.* New York: Basic Books. Pp. 55, 73, 238-43.

1974   *The Sociology of Émile Durkheim.* New York: Oxford University Press. Pp. 27-28, 78, 115, 130-31, 161-63, 172-73.

PICKERING, W. S. F.

1984   *Durkheim's Sociology of Religion.* London and Boston: Routledge & Kegan Paul. Pp. 47, 56-58, 116, 192, 524.

RADCLIFFE-BROWN, A. R.

1958   *Method in Social Anthropology.* Ed. M. N. Srinivas. Chicago: University of Chicago Press.

SMITH, WILLIAM ROBERTSON

1889   *Lectures on the Religion of the Semites.* Edinburgh: A. and C. Black.

THOMPSON, JAMES WESTFALL

1942   *A History of Historical Writing.* 2 vols. New York: Macmillan. II:362-73.

TOURNEUR-AUMONT, JEAN M.

1931   *Fustel de Coulanges.* Paris: Boivin.

TURNER, BRYAN S.

1971   "Sociological Founders and Precursors: The Theories of Émile Durkheim, Fustel de Coulanges, and Ibn Khaldun." *Religion* 1 (Spring):34-48.

Chapter Ten

The "De-Sociologizing"
of the Sociology of Religion

The sociology of religion goes back to at least the turn of the century. The biggest change in the field from then to now has, I assert, been the "de-sociologizing" of it. Contemporary sociologists see religion as much less of a social phenomenon, and therefore much less of a subject for sociology, than early ones did. Certainly contemporary sociologists continue to see religion as a considerably social activity. Otherwise they would scarcely remain sociologists of religion. They simply see religion as much less social in nature than their predecessors did.

There are two main sociological – more generally, social scientific – questions: one of origin and one of function. The question of origin is twofold: not only "why" but also "how" religion arises. The question of function is likewise twofold: not only "why" but also "how" religion operates.

A third question posed by some social scientists is that of content, or subject matter: to what object religion, properly understood, refers. Because this question blurs with the philosophical one of the existence of that object, it is less distinctively social scientific.

I am not contending that the sociology of religion has become less sociological by turning from the issues of origin and function to other issues like "meaning." I am taking for granted that sociologists of religion still focus on origin and function. Indeed, I argue elsewhere that the easy distinction between origin and meaning sometimes rests on facile definitions of both terms.[1] At the same time I am certainly not presuming to say that the issue of meaning, when properly delineated, is less sociological in nature than the issues of origin and function.

I am asserting only that the sociology of religion has become less sociological in its answers to the questions of origin and function. The field, I assert, has come to give a less sociological answer to not the "how" but the "why" side of both questions. Where early sociologists gave a largely, often

---

[1]1. See Segal (1986; forthcoming).

exclusively, sociological answer to the "why" of these questions, contemporary ones give a largely, though rarely exclusively, nonsociological one.

By sociologists of religion I mean not only sociologists proper but also social anthropologists for whom either the origin or the function of religion is at least partly social. By early sociologists of religion I mean classical ones: above all Émile Durkheim, A. R. Radcliffe-Brown, and Max Weber. By "contemporaries" I mean above all Clifford Geertz, Peter Berger, Victor Turner, Robert Bellah, and Mary Douglas.

The contrast between the two groups is stark but not rigid. For the classical anthropologist Bronislaw Malinowski (1925), for example, the origin and function of religion are as much individual as collective: religion arises as much to enable individuals to endure privation as to impel them to serve society. For Karl Marx and Friedrich Engels (1957), religion may conspicuously manage to preserve society, but only as a consequence of offering individuals either justification for economic misery or future escape from it. The sociologist Gaston Richard (1975), Durkheim's once well-known contemporary, berates him for ignoring the individual origin and function of religion. Fustel de Coulanges (1873), sometimes considered the *first* sociologist of religion,[2] goes far beyond even contemporary sociologists in deeming the origin, whether or not the function, of religion entirely nonsocial: for him, society does not shape religion at all; religion overwhelmingly shapes society. Conversely, various contemporary sociologists – notably, Guy Swanson (1960; 1967) – follow early sociologists in deeming the origin, not to say the function, of religion overwhelmingly social: for them, society shapes religion, and religion, once created, shapes society in turn. The difference between the two camps is, then, only a tendency, not a rule. To present it I will take an eminent representative of each camp: Durkheim and Geertz.

Émile Durkheim

For Durkheim (especially 1965), the origin, function, and content of religion are entirely social. Using primitive religion as the simplest and therefore clearest instance of religion generally,[3] Durkheim argues that religion originates socially because, to begin with, it originates in a group. Ordinarily, members of society – more precisely, of the totemic clan – live apart. Whenever they gather, their sheer contact with one another creates an extraordinary feeling of energy and power. They feel infused, uplifted, omnipotent: "The very fact of the concentration acts as an exceptionally powerful stimulant. When they are at once come together, a sort of electricity is formed by their collecting which quickly transports them to an extraordinary degree of exaltation" (Durkheim 1965:246-47). "In the midst of an assembly animated by a common passion, we become

---

[2]See Segal (1976).
[3]See Durkheim (1965:15-21).

susceptible of acts and sentiments of which we are incapable when reduced to our own forces ..." (Durkheim 1965:240).[4]

Knowing that individually they lack this power, primitives ascribe it not to themselves collectively but to possession by something external: "One can readily conceive how, when arrived at this state of exaltation, a man does not recognize himself any longer. Feeling himself dominated and carried away by some sort of an external power which makes him think and act differently than in normal times, he naturally has the impression of being himself no longer" (Durkheim 1965:249). Looking about, primitives spot the totemic emblem, which they know is only a symbol of their totem[5] yet which they nevertheless take as the object of worship. They even value it above the totem itself: "All that he [the primitive] knows is that he is raised above himself and that he sees a different life from the one he ordinarily leads. However, he must connect these sensations to some external object as their cause. Now what does he see about him? On every side those things which appeal to his senses and strike his imagination are the numerous images [emblems] of the totem.... How could this image, repeated everywhere and in all sorts of forms, fail to stand out with exceptional relief in his mind?... The sentiments experienced fix themselves upon it, for it is the only concrete object upon which they can fix themselves" (Durkheim 1965:252).[6]

Because the supernatural power which primitives attribute to the totemic emblem is in fact their own collective power, the true origin of religion is their experience of themselves: "So it is in the midst of these effervescent social environments and out of this effervescence itself that the religious idea seems to be born" (Durkheim 1965:250).[7] Surely no origin could be more social!

The aspect of the origin described so far is, however, simply that of the means, not the ends: the "how," not the "why." But in fact there is no "why." Religion arises accidentally: as the false ascription of power to the emblem, which thereby becomes god. Durkheim *is* explaining the origin of religion. Even though often considered the pioneering functionalist, he is not, like many of his successors, concerned with the function *rather than* the origin of religion. He is concerned with both. The origin of religion, while still the origin, is simply unintentional. Religion does not arise *in order* to serve society. Society for Durkheim may be an autonomous entity, but it is not a thinking entity. Rather than intentionally created by society, religion serves society, and serves society indispensably, only *once* it arises.

The function of religion mirrors the origin. The "how" of the function is social because religion operates exclusively collectively: above all in ritual, not

---

[4]See also Durkheim (1965:236-51, 463-65).
[5]See Durkheim (1965:149, 251).
[6]See also Durkheim (1965:252-54, 239).
[7]See also Durkheim (1965:465).

myth or creed.[8] Taken as an intent, there is no more a "why" of function than a "why" of origin. Because religion arises accidentally, it secures loyalty only coincidentally. In a narrow sense of the term there is therefore no function, or *intended* effect, at all. Durkheim is still explaining the effect of religion, and the effect is still the satisfaction of a need. The effect is simply unintentional. But in the looser, professionally more common, sense of the term an unintended effect is still a function.

The effect of religion on society is the instillment or, better, intensification of a sense of dependence on society. Members of society are in fact beholden to it for everything: their morality, language, tools, values, thoughts, categories of thought, and concept of objectivity.[9] As much as individuals benefit from these phenomena, Durkheim himself is concerned with only the social origin of the phenomena, not with their effect on individuals. Knowing that none of these phenomena, any more than their own effervescent state, is their individual creation, members ascribe them, too, to something external, on which they are therefore dependent. Everyday life confirms their dependence, but religion confirms it most intensely. For only during religious activity are members not just confronted but possessed by something external. Here, too, Durkheim hardly denies the effect of religion on individuals. He even stresses the energy, confidence, and security that the feeling of possession implants. Nevertheless, he cares far more about the consequence of that feeling for society itself.

The external cause of possession is taken to be god, not society,[10] but god is taken to be the god of society. Moreover, god is credited with not only possession but all the other social phenomena noted: language, tools, values, and so on.[11] In depending on god for everything, members are in fact depending on society itself, which in its relationship to them *is* like god to worshipers: "In a general way, it is unquestionable that a society has all that is necessary to arouse the sensation of the divine in minds, merely by the power that it has over them; for to its members it is what a god is to his worshippers. In fact, a god is, first of all, a being whom men think of as superior to themselves, and upon whom they feel that they depend.... Now society also gives us the sensation of a perpetual dependence" (Durkheim 1965:236-37). From dependence on god, and so on society, comes loyalty and so unity – the ultimate effect of religion. The society that prays together stays together.

Durkheim never claims that religion alone unifies society. Indeed, society must be sufficiently united for its members to assemble and thereby create religion in the first place. Religion is, however, the best means of preserving

---

[8]See Durkheim (1965:bk. III).
[9]See Durkheim (1965:242-43, 22-32, 169-70, 488-90, 480-87; Durkheim and Mauss).
[10]See Durkheim (1965:236-40).
[11]To be sure, Durkheim says (1965:21-22, 476-80, 493-95) that religion is really the source of at least science and the categories of the mind.

and, more, intensifying that unity. So indispensable is it that Durkheim at times writes as if society, with a mind of its own, creates religion in order to foster unity: "There can be no society which does not feel the need of upholding and reaffirming at regular intervals the collective sentiments and the collective ideas which make its unity and its personality" (Durkheim 1965:474-75).[12]

Yet however much religion shapes society, it itself remains a social product. The origin of religion is not individual because there is no individual – more precisely, no innate one. In primitive society the link, or "solidarity," among members is "mechanical": occupationally alike, members have no distinctive identity and therefore no individuality. Their sole identity is as members of society. Only in modern society is there a division of labor and therefore the specialization which constitutes individuality. There remains solidarity – Durkheim never pits the individual against society – but it is now "organic": members are related not just to society itself but, as specialized workers, to one another. They are like organs in an organism.[13]

Durkheim does not, then, deny the existence of individuality. He denies the innateness of it. For him, individuality both originates and functions socially: its cause is the division of labor, and its operation requires formal recognition of the individual by society.

More important, Durkheim denies individuality any place in traditional religion, which deals entirely with the mechanical, pre-individualistic side of social life.[14] In modern society that side, and so traditional religion, will continue to diminish as organic solidarity grows. Traditional religion will also continue to decline as science grows.[15]

On the one hand Durkheim predicts the eventual emergence of a new, secular religion to replace Christianity. That religion will perhaps be akin to the one created during the French Revolution: "In a word, the old gods are growing old or are already dead, and others are not yet born.... But this state of incertitude and confused agitation cannot last for ever.... We have already seen how the French Revolution established a whole cycle of holidays to keep the principles with which it was inspired in a state of perpetual youth.... But though the work may have miscarried, it enables us to imagine what might have happened in other conditions; and everything leads us to believe that it will be taken up again sooner or later" (Durkheim 1965:475-76).

On the other hand Durkheim proposes the *creation* of a secular religion – a religion worshiping not god but humanity.[16] He envisions a cult of the

---

[12]See also Durkheim (1965:465-66).
[13]See Durkheim (1933).
[14]Durkheim thus equates (1933:78, 92-93, 159-64, 169-70) the communal laws of mechanical solidarity with religious laws.
[15]See Durkheim (1965:478).
[16]See Durkheim (1975).

individual, but by the individual he means the nonegoistic individual, who reveres rather than violates the rights of others and who thereby promotes rather than threatens the group. Coinciding with the harmonious individuality of organic solidarity, Durkheim's new religion would thus serve the same social function as the old one: "Now all that societies require in order to hold together is that their members fix their eyes on the same end and come together in a single faith; but it is not at all necessary that the object of this common faith be quite unconnected with individual persons. In short, individualism thus understood is the glorification not of the self, but of the individual in general. Its motive force is not egoism but sympathy for all that is human .... Is this not the way to achieve a community of good will?" (Durkheim 1975:64)[17]

Both because modern society creates the individual and because religion, modern or traditional, is a collective activity, religion for Durkheim scarcely alienates individuals from their true selves, as it does for Marx and Ludwig Feuerbach. Because religion is a consummately social activity, participants scarcely cede their private selves to it. Religion does involve projection, as for Marx and Feuerbach, but the projection onto god is of social, not private, experience.

Durkheim does grant the existence of individual worship: worship by less than all of society. But he labels it magic rather than religion and deems it parasitic on true, social religion.[18]

Durkheim gives a wholly sociological analysis of not only the origin and function but also the content of religion. God is imagined in exactly the fashion that society is experienced during group gatherings: as an extraordinary power on whom one is dependent.[19] Similarly, the number of gods reflects the number of sources of power in society: in primitive society there are many gods because clans are more powerful than the tribes of which they are parts. Not until a tribe becomes fully united does its god become singular.[20]

A. R. Radcliffe-Brown

No early sociologist of religion is so relentlessly sociological as Durkheim. Radcliffe-Brown (especially 1922) comes closest. But in contrast to Durkheim, he restricts himself to function and refuses to consider origin – on the grounds that no information exists and that speculation is idle.[21] He ignores the "why" as well as the "how" of origin. Consequently, there is no "why" of function and

---

[17]See also Durkheim (1933:172-73, 407-9).
[18]See Durkheim (1965:57-60, 472-74).
[19]Because the conception of god expresses the extraordinary rather than ordinary experience of society, god symbolizes ideal, not everyday, society: see Durkheim (1965:467-71).
[20]See Durkheim (1965:225-26).
[21]See Radcliffe-Brown (1922:229; 1958:19-20).

therefore, as for Durkheim, no intended effect. The unintended effect of religion is, as for Durkheim, the cultivation of loyalty to society. Like Durkheim, Radcliffe-Brown says that religion is outright indispensable to society: "... the ceremonial customs [of religion] are the means by which the society acts upon its individual members and keeps alive in their minds a certain system of sentiments. Without the ceremonial those sentiments would not exist, and without them the social organisation in its actual form could not exist" (Radcliffe-Brown 1922:324). Radcliffe-Brown goes so far as to say that religion, like any other social institution, exists only *because* it serves society. But he, like Durkheim, does not thereby say that religion arises *in order* to serve society. How religion arises he, unlike Durkheim, never says.

For Radcliffe-Brown, the "how" of the function is the same as for Durkheim. As the prior quotation says, religion works by instilling – better, intensifying – feelings, or "sentiments," of dependence: "... what is expressed in all religions is what I have called the sense of dependence" (Radcliffe-Brown 1952:177).[22] Where for Durkheim the object of those feelings is society itself, for Radcliffe-Brown it is food, rain, marriage, and other phenomena of importance to society – phenomena with a "social value," positive or negative. Toward those phenomena religion arouses feelings of not only dependence, as for Durkheim, but also love or hate: "... the function of the belief in the protective power of such things as fire and the materials from which weapons are made is to maintain in the mind of the individual the feeling of his dependence upon the society; but viewed from another aspect the beliefs in question may be regarded as expressing the social value of the things to which they relate.... Value may be either positive or negative, positive value being possessed by any thing that contributes to the well-being of the society, negative value by anything that can adversely affect that well-being" (Radcliffe-Brown 1922:264).[23] For Radcliffe-Brown, as for Durkheim, ritual, not myth or creed, stirs social feelings.[24]

For Durkheim, totemic emblems become gods because they are coincidentally present during group gatherings. For Radcliffe-Brown, the phenomena that become gods are exactly those with the highest social value – above all forces of nature like the sun.[25] Insofar as society for Durkheim is worshiping randomly chosen gods, the content of religion is less significantly social than it is for Radcliffe-Brown. But insofar as society is, through those gods, really worshiping itself, the content is far more deeply social than it is for Radcliffe-Brown.

Unlike Durkheim, Radcliffe-Brown never considers modern society and, with it, individuality. For him, all solidarity is mechanical, so that no new religion is

---

[22]See also Radcliffe-Brown (1922:257-58, 275, 277-78, 319-20).
[23]See also Radcliffe-Brown (1922:277-78, 297, 315-16).
[24]See Radcliffe-Brown (1952:155).
[25]See Radcliffe-Brown (1922:356, 380-81, 402-5).

required to accommodate a new form of society. Moreover, religion is an entirely social phenomenon. The feelings of dependence it elicits might seem instinctive responses by individuals, but even they are implanted by society: "In human society the sentiments in question are not innate but are developed in the individual by the action of the society upon him" (Radcliffe-Brown 1922:234).

Max Weber

Less sociological than either Durkheim's or Radcliffe-Brown's explanation of religion is Weber's (especially 1963). Where Durkheim and Radcliffe-Brown, as "methodological holists," consider society an autonomous causal force, Weber, as a "methodological individualist," reduces all social events to the actions of individuals. Where for Durkheim and Radcliffe-Brown society is the given, for Weber individuals are. Where for Durkheim and Radcliffe-Brown individuals are the product of society, for Weber society is the product of individuals. Still, society for Weber not only certainly exists – above all as both social organization and values – but also influences individuals, who may be the direct agents of events but who do not act in a void.

On the one hand, then, individuals for Weber create religion and do so to serve individual ends. On the other hand society still plays an enormous role: it shapes the ends they seek. Society determines the "why," not to mention the "how," of the origin and function of religion.

For Weber, the most primitive stage of religion is magic, which, as for James Frazer, is the coercion of the divine for immediate, physical ends: food, clothing, shelter, and health. The magician may well serve all of society and not just, as for Durkheim, a portion of it. But because he is self-employed and therefore hired anew each time, he develops no systematic doctrines, only concrete techniques.

Not until there emerges a stable clientele of worshipers – a congregation, or cult – does a priesthood emerge. Not until priests succeed magicians does metaphysics – a comprehensive explanation of the world – emerge in place of mere techniques. Likewise not until priests arise does ethics – ends achieved through obedience – emerge in place of coercion – ends achieved through techniques. The combination of metaphysics and ethics makes religion "rational" rather than *ad hoc* and constitutes the stage of religion after magic: "It is more correct for our purpose ... to set up as the crucial feature of the priesthood the specialization of a particular group of persons in the continuous operation of a cultic enterprise, permanently associated with particular norms, places and times, and related to specific social groups. There can be no priesthood without a cult .... The full development of both a metaphysical rationalization and a religious ethic requires an independent and professionally trained priesthood, permanently occupied with the cult and with the practical problems involved in the cure of souls" (Weber 1963:30).

Finally, not until a cult emerges does the concept of a fixed god – singular, powerful, named, personal, and involved – emerge in place of the magical concept of multiple, weak, nameless, impersonal, and uninvolved fleeting gods: "Gods were not originally represented in human form. To be sure they came to possess the form of enduring beings, which is absolutely essential for them, only after the suppression of the purely naturalistic view still evident in the Vedas (e.g., that actual fire is a god, or is at least the body of a concrete god of fire) in favor of the view that a god, forever identical with himself, possesses all individual fires, controls them, or somehow incorporates them all within himself. This abstract conception becomes really secure only through the continuing activity of a 'cult' dedicated to one and the same god – through the god's connection with a continuing association of men, a community for which he has special significance as the enduring god" (Weber 1963:10). While the character of god does not, as for Durkheim, *mirror* society, it does *presuppose* something in society: a cult.

Social organization thus determines both the means – the "how" – and at least indirectly the content – the "what" – of religion but so far still not the "why." So far, religion originates and functions to serve an innate rather than implanted need: the need for food, clothing, shelter, and health.

Yet even if the need initially fulfilled by religion is innate rather than implanted, the need subsequently fulfilled by it is implanted, in which case society does determine the "why" of at least the stage of religion beyond magic. For only with the development of "rationalized" religion – a comprehensive explanation of the world, a prescribed means of securing long-term rewards, and a universal god permanently involved in human affairs – does there develop not so much a discrepancy between expectation and experience – there is a discrepancy whenever magic fails – as a desire to resolve that discrepancy systematically: "It is certainly true that not every religious ethic has crystallized a god of transcendental quality who created the universe out of nothing and directed it himself.... But the more the development tends toward the conception of a transcendental unitary god who is universal, the more there arises the problem of how the extraordinary power of such a god may be reconciled with the imperfection of the world that he has created and rules over" (Weber 1963:138-39).

That problem, or desire, is the desire for "meaning," or "meaningfulness": the demand for a coherent explanation and, more, justification of experience. The experience that, according to Weber, most needs justifying is suffering. A sufficient explanation for the failure of magic is that the technique has been misapplied. But "rationalized" religion must explain the failure of the gods to respond to the behavior they themselves have dictated. Because their failure means their failure to prevent or withhold suffering, the explanation sought is a theodicy.[26] The theodicy ultimately involves the provision of salvation,[27] which can take physical as well as spiritual form and which can therefore be as worldly as magic. But in contrast to magic, even worldly salvation is a long-term, not immediate, end and satisfies a desire for justice, or meaning, itself, not merely for the worldly end.

Since all human beings for Weber recognize the discrepancy between their expectations and their experience, all harbor the *potential* desire for meaning. But its *emergence* depends on rationalized religion, the emergence of which itself depends on a particular kind of religious leader – a priest – whose emergence depends in turn on a particular kind of social organization – a cult.

Yet even if the need for meaning is the work of society, the primitive, magical need for food and other immediate ends still seems instinctive. Even it, however, proves to be the product of a particular kind of social organization: one's class. For example, the religion of peasants, like that of primitives, is magical – not, however, because a cult has yet to develop and therefore to alter their naturally worldly and *ad hoc* "why," as in the case of primitives, but because their occupation makes or at least keeps their outlook worldly and *ad hoc*. For the goal of farming is necessarily not only physical but also short-term and unpredictable, so dependent is it on the vagaries of the elements. The occupation of peasants precludes the development of "rationalized" religion and, with it, of the need for meaning: "The lot of peasants is so strongly tied to nature, so dependent on organic processes and natural events, and economically so little oriented to rational systematization that in general the peasantry will become a carrier of [rationalized] religion only when it is threatened by enslavement or proletarization, either by domestic forces (financial, agrarian, or seignorial) or by some external political power" (Weber 1963:80).

Similarly, the religion of warrior lords is magical because the militaristic ethos of their vocation spurns as dishonorable submission to either gods or humans: "The life pattern of a warrior has very little affinity with the notion of a beneficent providence, or with the systematic ethical demands of a transcendental god. Concepts like sin, salvation, and religious humility have not only seemed remote from all elite political classes, particularly the warrior nobles, but have indeed appeared reprehensible to its sense of honor" (Weber 1963:85).

As decisive a cause of the origin, function, and content of religion as society is for Weber, it is never the only cause, as it is for both Durkheim and Radcliffe-Brown. Society is a necessary cause but not a sufficient one. Weber thus says that the emergence of a priesthood requires a cult but not that every cult produces a priesthood.[28] Nor does every cult produce the notion of a fixed god. Ideas as well as social conditions are necessary, and ideas are not the mere reflection of

---

[26]See Weber (1963:ch. 9).
[27]See Weber (1963:chs. 9-12).
[28]See Weber (1963:30).

social conditions, as they are for Radcliffe-Brown and especially Durkheim. To this limited extent, it might be noted, Weber is a nonreductionist: religion is the product of reflection as well as social setting. Still, the *secular* quest for either necessities or meaning spurs its creation.

Undeniably, Weber, like Durkheim and Radcliffe-Brown, is concerned not only with the direct or indirect impact of society on religion but also with the impact of religion on society. Like them, he is concerned not only with the creation of religion by society but also with the effect of religion, once created, on society. For him, as for them, that effect is unintentional. To cite Weber's most celebrated case, the role of ascetic Protestantism in creating capitalism was wholly coincidental. Defined strictly as intended consequence, the *function* of ascetic Protestantism was salvation for the individual. Capitalism was a mere *byproduct,* however monumental.[29] By the looser definition applied to Durkheim and Radcliffe-Brown, *both* capitalism and salvation were functions.

Edward Tylor

Before contrasting the less sociological approach of contemporary sociologists of religion to that of classical ones, I want to contrast to both an instance of an entirely nonsociological approach: that of the anthropologist Edward Tylor (1958:vol. II). For Tylor, both the "why" and the "how" of religion are wholly nonsocial. First, religion originates and functions to fulfill not simply an individual rather than, as for Durkheim and Radcliffe-Brown, a social need but also an innate rather than, as for Weber, an implanted one. That need is to explain the world. Second, society plays a dispensable rather than, as for Durkheim, Radcliffe-Brown, and Weber, an indispensable role in the creation of religion to fulfill that need. A whole society invariably *does* share a religion, but it *need* not. A solitary could invent and practice a religion. The credibility of the explanation a religion provides is in no way enhanced by its popularity, as it is for Durkheim above all. What is true of Tylor is also true of Max Müller, among others: for both, religion is either an entirely individual affair or else only coincidentally a social one.

If one *excludes* theorists for whom society plays no necessary part in religion, the difference between classical and contemporary sociologists could not be sharper. For classical sociologists, the "why" of the origin and function either is social itself, as for Durkheim and Radcliffe-Brown, or else is implanted by society, as for Weber. For contemporary sociologists, the prime "why" is neither. Not only does religion arise and function to serve a primarily individual rather than social need, but that need is innate rather than implanted. Were society to play no necessary role at all in religion, "contemporaries" would be like Tylor and would not be sociologists at all. Society does play a central role, but only in the "how," not also, as for classical sociologists, in the "why" of

---

[29] See Weber (1958).

religion: society is indispensable not to the creation of the prime need religion fulfills but only to the creation of religion to fulfill it.

Clifford Geertz

For Geertz (especially 1973:87-125, 126-41), a celebrated "contemporary," religion arises primarily to fulfill the same need as for Weber: a need for meaning, or, again, meaningfulness. "Whatever else religion may be," says Geertz, "it is in part an attempt ... to conserve the fund of general meanings in terms of which each individual interprets his experience and organizes his conduct" (Geertz 1973:127).[30] For Geertz, as for Weber, the need for meaning is clearly individual rather than social: an individual, not society, feels it. But for Geertz, in contrast to Weber, the need is innate. It presupposes no cult or particular class. It is found in every social organization and is the need religion fulfills wherever *religion* is found. Challenges to meaning are thus "challenges with which any religion, however 'primitive,' which hopes to persist must attempt somehow to cope" (Geertz 1973:100).

For Weber, the challenge to meaning comes above all from suffering, which must be not only explained but also justified. For Geertz, the challenge to meaning comes from two other sources as well. Merely inexplicable experiences – for example, death and dreams – need only to be explained, not also justified. Unendurable experiences – suffering – need to be not only explained but also borne. Put tautologically, only outright unjustifiable experiences – for example, the Holocaust – need to be outright justified, not merely explained and borne: "Bafflement, suffering, and a sense of intractable ethical paradox are all, if they become intense enough or are sustained long enough, radical challenges to the proposition that life is comprehensible and that we can, by taking thought, orient ourselves effectively within it ..." (Geertz 1973:100).[31]

On the one hand religion, in attempting to cope with all three kinds of experiences, covers a far wider range of life for Geertz than for Weber. On the other hand Geertz no more than Weber considers religion the sole, even if the best, source of meaning. In fact, Geertz, unlike Weber, enumerates at least three other sources, or "cultural systems": common sense, ideology, and art.[32]

Any cultural system for Geertz provides meaning by telling one not only what to believe about threatening experiences but also how to act in the wake of the beliefs. A cultural system must not only explain, make bearable, and justify threatening experiences but also prescribe behavior in the light of its explanation, alleviation, or justification. It must provide not only a conception of reality but also an accompanying way of life. Religion in particular, says

[30]See also Geertz (1973:140-41, 109).
[31]See also Geertz (1973:100-8). On the difference between Geertz and Weber see Geertz (1973:104-6; 1968b:101).
[32]See Geertz (1973:ch. 8; 1983:chs. 4, 5).

Geertz, provides not only a "world view" but also an "ethos,"[33] not only a "model of" reality but also a "model for" behavior, not only a set of convictions but also a set of "moods and motivations": "The Christian sees the Nazi movement against the background of The Fall which ... places it in a moral, a cognitive, even an affective sense [i.e., world view]. An Azande sees the collapse of a granary upon a friend or relative against the background of a concrete and rather special notion of witchcraft and thus avoids the philosophical dilemmas as well as the psychological stress of indeterminism.... But more than gloss, such beliefs are also a template. They do not merely interpret social and psychological processes in cosmic terms – in which case they would be [merely] philosophical, not religious – but they shape them. In the doctrine of original sin is embedded also a recommended attitude toward life, a recurring mood, and a persisting set of motivations [i.e., ethos]. The Azande learns from witchcraft conceptions not just to understand apparent 'accidents' as not accidents at all, but to react to these spurious accidents with hatred for the agent who caused them and to proceed against him with appropriate resolution" (Geertz 1973:123-24).[34] The invocation of witchcraft not only explains and makes bearable the friend's or relative's death but also spurs revenge.

To work, a cultural system must not only offer both a conception of reality and a way of life but also mesh the two. In the Christian and Azande examples in the quotation the two are in sync, but Geertz himself stresses how often they are at odds.[35] When in sync, the two reinforce each other. In the case of religion the world view makes the ethos natural, and in turn the ethos provides a concrete, living manifestation of the world view: "In religious belief and practice a group's ethos is rendered intellectually reasonable by being shown to represent a way of life ideally adapted to the actual state of affairs the world view describes, while the world view is rendered emotionally convincing by being presented as an image of an actual state of affairs peculiarly well-arranged to accommodate such a way of life" (Geertz 1973:89-90).[36]

To work, religion, as a cultural system, must, in addition, be the religion of a whole society. No one could either create or sustain a private religion, as Geertz's continuing reference to a "group's" world view and ethos suggests. Indeed, a solipsistic religion would be a contradiction in terms. For it would likely fail to account for exactly both the world view and the ethos which its adherent would confront daily: those of everyone around him. Geertz is well aware of *rival* religions and of the difficulties they create, but each is a collective enterprise. For Geertz, the "how" of the origin and function of religion must,

---

[33]Because Geertz applies these terms to only religion, it is not clear whether he is saying that the conception of reality and way of life provided by any other cultural system constitute less than a full-fledged world view and ethos.
[34]See also Geertz (1973:126-41, 87-125; 1968b:16-17, 98).
[35]See esp. Geertz (1968b).
[36]See also Geertz (1973:126-31; 1968b:39, 97-98, 114-15).

then, be social. For him, as for Durkheim and Radcliffe-Brown, the "how" of the function is not myth or creed but ritual, which both instills and fuses the world view and the ethos.[37]

Geertz never denies that religion serves a social as well as an individual "why." Indeed, religion serves society by serving the individual. For in conferring naturalness on the ethos, which includes group values, customs, and institutions, the world view musters support for it: "The force of a religion in supporting social values rests, then, on the ability of its symbols to formulate a world in which those values ... are fundamental ingredients.... [R]eligion, by fusing ethos and world view, gives to a set of social values what they perhaps most need to be coercive: an appearance of objectivity. In sacred rituals and myths values are portrayed not as subjective human preferences but as the imposed conditions for life implicit in a world with a particular structure" (Geertz 1973:131).

Moreover, in most of his earlier writings[38] Geertz is primarily concerned with the impact of religion on society, not on the individual. Still, even here the social impact depends on the individual one. Religion spurs conflict rather than consensus either when there are rival religions and therefore rival meanings held by individuals[39] or else when there is a disparity between the preaching of unity and the actual experience of division.[40] Where in his earlier writings Geertz is concerned most with the effect of division on society, in his later ones[41] he is concerned most with its disconcerting effect on individuals. Still, the later Geertz denies only that religion serves a social function primarily, not that it serves one at all.[42]

Like Durkheim and Weber, Geertz maintains that the nature of society shapes the content of religion. By the nature of society Geertz means not only, like Durkheim and Weber, social organization but, more broadly, "style," which, alas, seems indistinguishable from the ethos that religion purportedly provides society.[43] By the content of religion Geertz means not only, like Durkheim, the conception of god but also, like Weber, the manner of worship: "... particular kinds of faith (as well as particular kinds of doubt) flourish in particular kinds of

---

[37]See Geertz (1973:112-13; 1968b:100).
[38]See Geertz (1960; 1973:142-69, which originally appeared in 1959).
[39]See Geertz (1960).
[40]See Geertz (1973:142-69).
[41]See, e.g., Geertz (1968b). To be sure, Geertz is primarily concerned with the individual in some of his earliest writings: see Geertz (1973:126-41), which originally appeared in 1957.
[42]See Geertz (1973:125).
[43]See Geertz (1968b:98, 114). If "style" is in fact identical with "ethos," then ethos shapes religion rather than gets shaped by it, as Geertz says everywhere else. When, furthermore, Geertz says that religion functions "to synthesize a people's ethos ... and their world view" (1973:89), he implies that religion functions to synthesize an existing pair.

societies .... The material reasons why Moroccan Islam became activist, rigorous, dogmatic and more than a little anthropolatrous and why Indonesian Islam became syncretistic, reflective, multifarious, and strikingly phenomenological lie, in part anyway, in the sort of collective life within which and along with which they evolved" (Geertz 1973:20).[44] The goal of worship, by contrast, remains innate rather than implanted.

What is true of Geertz is also true of Berger, Turner, Bellah, Douglas, and other contemporary sociologists of religion: religion primarily originates and functions to fulfill the individual's innate need for meaning. Society still plays an indispensable part, but only in the creation of religion to fulfill the need, not in the creation of the need itself. Society deals with only the "how," not the "why," of the need. Religion is therefore far less the product of society, and so far less the subject of sociology, than it is for classical sociologists. "Contemporaries" differ with one another over what threatens meaning and over how religion provides it.

Peter Berger

According to Berger (especially 1969), "the religious enterprise of human history profoundly reveals the pressing urgency and intensity of man's quest for meaning" (Berger 1969:100). For Berger, as for Geertz, the quest for meaning is innate: "Men are congenitally compelled to impose a meaningful order upon reality" (Berger 1969:22). Seemingly, for Berger, as for Geertz, a meaningful experience may need only to be explained, not also either borne or justified. In fact, for Berger, as for Weber, every meaningful experience must be outright justified, and the experiences which most require justification are, as for Weber, suffering.[45]

For Geertz, religion provides meaning by providing both a world view and an ethos. Where the world view makes the ethos natural rather than arbitrary, the ethos makes the world view germane rather than irrelevant. For Berger, religion provides the equivalent of simply a world view: a justification for threatening experiences.

For Geertz, the ethos as well as the world view arises in response to such experiences. The world view explains, alleviates, or justifies not, strictly, the ethos itself but these experiences, and the ethos organizes behavior in light of the world view. Initially, secular culture, in the form of common sense, tries to make sense of these experiences, but it inevitably fails. It can neither alleviate nor justify nor perhaps even explain them. Without the equivalent of a world view the common-sense equivalent of an ethos collapses. Either religion or some other cultural system arises to replace common sense.

---

[44]See also Geertz (1968b).
[45]See Berger (1969:53; 1970:25).

For Berger, seculardom initially tries to provide only an ethos, not also a world view. The ethos seemingly gets established to fend off only potential threatening experiences rather than, as for Geertz, to meet current ones. Once established, the ethos fails for the same reason as for Geertz: because secular culture cannot then provide the equivalent of a world view – now, as for Geertz, in reaction to actual threats. Mentioning no other "cultural systems," Berger says that religion arises not, as for Geertz, to provide both a new ethos and a new world view but rather to strengthen the existing ethos by providing a world view for the first time. Strictly, the world view serves to justify not the ethos itself but, as for Geertz, the threatening experiences themselves. For Berger, those threats are, again, suffering – above all death. Because secular society for Berger does not even try to meet threats to meaning this profound, religion serves not, as for Geertz, to give a sturdier justification to threats already faced by seculardom but rather to give the first justification to threats skirted by seculardom. Secular society thus proves less frail than frivolous.

Even if for Geertz, too, the world view does not justify the ethos itself, it does make the ethos natural and thereby supports it. Because the ethos for Geertz is, moreover, the application of the world view, the ethos necessarily covers the same experiences as the world view. Because the ethos for Berger arises independently of the world view, it need not and does not cover the same experiences as the world view. For Geertz, the ethos and the world view may at times be out of sync, but because they give different responses to the same experiences. For Berger, the two are always out of sync because they treat different experiences altogether: the ethos treats everyday ones; the world view, extraordinary ones. For Berger, the ethos is secular and only the world view religious. For Geertz, both are religious.

Because religion for Berger not merely explains or alleviates but outright justifies death and other kinds of suffering, the meaning it provides constitutes, as for Weber, a theodicy.[46] The justifications, or "legitimations," provided by religion are the staunchest possible ones because they carry the unassailable authority of divinity: "Religion legitimates so effectively because it relates the precarious reality constructions of empirical societies with ultimate reality. The tenuous realities of the social world are grounded in the sacred *realissimum*, which by definition is beyond the contingencies of human meanings and human activity" (Berger 1969:32). In Berger's pet terms, religion confers on experience a "sacred canopy," or "plausibility structure."

Like Geertz, Berger grants that religion serves not only the individual function of giving meaning but also the social function of securing obedience.[47] But like Geertz as well, Berger concentrates on the individual function and, more, deems the social one a consequence of it. Even though religion justifies less the

---

[46]See Berger (1969:ch. 3, 1970:25-26).
[47]See Berger (1969:32, 90-91).

secular, everyday ethos itself than suffering, unjustified suffering threatens to trivialize even the most firmly sanctioned ethos: "Religion, then, maintains the socially defined reality [i.e., ethos] by legitimating marginal [i.e., asocial] situations in terms of an all-encompassing sacred reality. This permits the individual who goes through these situations to continue to exist in the world of his society – not 'as if nothing had happened' ... but in the 'knowledge' that even these events or experiences have a place within a universe that makes sense. It is thus even possible to have 'a good death,' that is, to die while retaining to the end a meaningful relationship with the nomos of one's society ..." (Berger 1969:44).

For Berger, as for Geertz, society is indispensable to the "how" of the individual as well as the social function of religion. No one could alone either invent or, more, sustain the legitimations which religion provides. Social support is, as for Durkheim, mandatory for validating those legitimations.[48] For Berger, as for Geertz and certainly Durkheim and Radcliffe-Brown, ritual, not myth or creed, instills the legitimations.[49]

In his earlier writings[50] Berger disapproves of the individual function of religion. The justifications it provides constitute for him Sartrean bad faith, which he wants supplanted by existential faith. In his more recent writings,[51] however, Berger approves of the individual function. For now he grants that, in the wake of the competing justifications offered by the modern world, the choice of any one of them requires a leap of faith. For Berger, as for Kierkegaard, religion is not incompatible with existentialism.

Victor Turner

Like Geertz, Turner (especially 1967; 1968; 1974; 1975)[52] shifts from an initial focus on the social function of religion[53] to a subsequent focus on the individual one.[54] Though he, even more firmly than Geertz or Berger, remains concerned with the social function, he, too, comes to consider the individual function primary. That function is, as for them, to make life meaningful.

Turner does not, like Geertz and Berger, list the threats to meaning, but the cases he cites seem akin to Geertz's. Transitional states – for example, from childhood to adulthood – are threatening because they are inscrutable. Life crises – for example, famine and disease – are threatening because they are both painful and unwarranted.

---

[48]See Berger (1970:34; 1980:16), Durkheim (1965:486-87).
[49]See Berger (1969:40-41).
[50]See Berger (1961a; 1961b; 1969:92-96).
[51]See Berger (1970:42-45; 1980:58-60, chs. 1, 5).
[52]On Turner see Segal (1983b).
[53]See Turner (1957).
[54]See Turner (1967; 1968; 1969; 1974; 1975; 1985; Turner and Turner).

For Geertz and especially Berger, the prime threats to meaning come from the cosmos – in the form, for example, of disease and mortality. Though life crises for Turner certainly constitute cosmic threats, for him the prime threats come from society – in its demand for new statuses and, even more, in its ill-treatment of some members. For Geertz and especially Berger, one's place in society is the application of one's place in the cosmos. For Turner, one's place in the cosmos is the extension of one's place in society.

For Turner, as for Berger and especially Geertz, ritual, not myth or creed, implants one's social and cosmic places alike. A ritual administered to a bewitched Ndembu thus functions not only socially to purge perennial tribal tensions, for which the afflicted was a scapegoat, but also individually to overcome the subject's own feeling of ostracism: "Ndembu ritual ... may be regarded as a magnificent instrument for expressing, maintaining, and periodically cleansing a secular order of society without strong political centralization and all too full of social conflict.... In the idiom of the rituals of affliction it is as though the Ndembu said: 'It is only when a person is reduced to misery by misfortune, and repents of the acts that caused him to be afflicted, that ritual expressing an underlying unity in diverse things may fittingly be enacted for him'" (Turner 1968:21-22).

For Turner, as for Geertz and Berger, society is indispensable to religion. Alone, no one could either create or maintain a religion.

Robert Bellah

Unlike Geertz, Berger, and Turner, Bellah (especially 1970a:pt. III) announces his change of views. In his earlier writings he, like them in theirs,[55] is concerned with the effect of religion on society, not on the individual. Like them, he is concerned with how religion provides meaning as a way of securing obedience rather than as an end in itself. For him, as for Geertz and Turner, religion provides meaning by providing the equivalent of both a world view and an ethos.[56]

Dealing, like Geertz and Turner, with changing societies, Bellah investigates, specifically, how religion either spurs or retards modernization. Tokugawa religion, he argues, constitutes the Japanese counterpart to Weber's Protestant Ethic: "As we have had repeated occasion to see, Japanese religion never tires of stressing the importance of diligence and frugality and of attributing religious significance to them, both in terms of carrying out one's obligations to the sacred and in terms of purifying the self of evil impulses and desires. That such an ethic is profoundly favorable to economic rationalization was the major point of Weber's study of Protestantism and we must say that it seems similarly favorable in Japan" (Bellah 1957:196). At the same time Bellah,

---

[55]See Bellah (1957; 1965; 1970a:pts. I, II).
[56]See, e.g., Bellah (1970a:12).

like Weber, is also concerned with the impact of society on religion, not just vice versa.[57]

Bellah calls his later approach to religion "symbolic realism" and distinguishes it from three other approaches: "historical realism," "consequential reductionism," and "symbolic realism."[58] Historical realism deems religion cognitive, literal, and true: religion is a true explanation of the physical world. Historical realists are, presumably, fundamentalists. Consequential reductionism considers religion cognitive, literal, but false: religion is superstition. But consequential reductionists are concerned less with the falsity of religion than with the effect of religion on society when it is believed true. Consequential reductionists are social functionalists like Malinowski and Radcliffe-Brown.

Symbolic reductionism also considers religion false when taken cognitively and literally but considers it true when taken noncognitively and symbolically: as the disguised expression of something real within individuals, society, or the physical world. Symbolic reductionists are nineteenth- and early twentieth-century social scientists – among them Tylor, Frazer, Marx, Durkheim, and Freud. One exception is Weber, who is rather a consequential reductionist: he is interested less in the reduction of religion to something underlying it than in the effect of religion on society. Bellah would presumably classify his own earlier self as a consequentialist, as he would at least partly his then-mentor, Talcott Parsons. Yet surely many symbolic reductionists are as interested in the effect of religion on either society or the individual as in the hidden reality either causing or incurring that effect.

In any case Bellah argues that at least Durkheim and Freud, together with Parsons, are themselves the pioneering symbolic realists. Bellah adopts Parsons' view that the attempts of Durkheim and Freud to reduce religion to something else fail. More accurately, Durkheim and Freud fail to reduce to something nonsymbolic the entity to which religion does get reduced: society for Durkheim and the unconscious for Freud. Both entities remain sets of symbols. Hence the term "symbolic realism," with which Bellah also associates Paul Tillich, Martin Buber, Norman O. Brown, Michael Polanyi, Herbert Fingarette, and Paul Ricoeur.

For Bellah, as for Carl Jung, symbols, at least religious symbols, are doubly symbolic. On the one hand they refer to an irreducibly nonempirical reality. On the other hand that reality is knowable and expressible only symbolically: "The canons of empirical science apply primarily to symbols that attempt to express the nature of objects, but there are nonobjective symbols that express the feelings, values, and hopes of subjects, or that organize and regulate the flow of interaction between subjects and objects, or that attempt to sum up the whole subject-object complex or even point to the context or ground of that

---

[57]See, e.g., Bellah (1970a:chs. 2, 4, 8).
[58]See Bellah (1970a:pt. III; 1970b; 1970c; 1970d).

whole. These symbols, too, express reality and are not reducible to empirical propositions. This is the position of symbolic realism" (Bellah 1970a:252).

What this symbolic reality is Bellah scarcely makes clear. It seems, alternatively, to be the meaning of life, metaphysical reality, mystical reality, the reality experienced by humans, the reality constructed by humans, and irrationality within humans. Why this reality is knowable and expressible only symbolically Bellah never makes clear either.

One difference between symbolic realism and the consequentialism of at least Parsons and the earlier Bellah is the focus of symbolic realism on the effect of religion on the individual rather than on society. But if only because other consequential as well as symbolic reductionists likewise focus on the individual function of religion, a sharper difference between symbolic realism and reductionism of either variety may be the focus of realism on the *meaning* rather than the *function* of religion, be the function individual or social.

In contrast to historical realism, which also seeks the meaning of religion for believers, symbolic realism deems that meaning symbolic rather than literal. Bellah is here like Rudolf Bultmann, who interprets the New Testament symbolically in the name of believers themselves. In contrast to historical realism as well, symbolic realism deems the meaning experiential rather than explanatory. Religion for believers themselves is not a scientific-like account of the world but an encounter with it: "For religion is not really a kind of pseudogeology or pseudohistory but an imaginative statement about the truth of the totality of human experience" (Bellah 1970a:244). "These [religious] symbols are not 'made up' by the human ego or deduced by rational reflection. They are born out of the tragedy and the suffering, the joy and the victory of men struggling to make sense out of their world. They tell us nothing at all about the universe except insofar as the universe is involved in human experience" (Bellah 1970a:195).

Yet the difference between meanings and at least the existential function of religion for Geertz, Berger, and Turner is blurry. What is the difference between Bellah's concern with the struggle of humans "to make sense out of their world" (Bellah 1970a:244) and the meaning-giving function of religion for Geertz, Berger, and Turner? Indeed, when Bellah in even his earlier writings seeks to "grasp even imperfectly the place a religion has in the thoughts, feelings, and aspirations of individuals" (Bellah 1957:1), the only difference between meaning and function seems to be that between the meaning-giving function as an end in itself and that same function as a means to a social end.

Because religion for Bellah *expresses* humans' *experience* of the world rather than *explains* the *world* itself, it is true: "If we define religion as that symbol system that serves to evoke ... the totality that includes subject and object and provides the context in which life and action finally have meaning, then I am prepared to claim that as Durkheim said of society, religion is a reality *sui generis*. To put it bluntly, religion is true" (Bellah 1970a:252-53). Because religion makes no truth claims about the world itself, it is "beyond belief."

Here the difference between symbolic realism and reductionism of either kind is neither the difference between meaning and function nor the difference between individual and social function. It is the difference between religion as true and religion either as functional when believed true – consequential reductionism – or as latently true – symbolic reductionism. But how can religion be true when "beyond belief"? Conversely, how is religion in symbolic reductionism, which also deems religion true when taken noncognitively and symbolically, any less true? In any case Bellah's concern with not only the origin and function but also the outright truth of religion sets him apart from his fellow "contemporaries," who at times venture beyond origin and function to content but who never, save at times for Berger and Douglas, venture beyond content to truth.

Though Bellah stresses the expressive function – for him "meaning" – of religion, religion for him, as for Geertz, Berger, and Turner, doubtless functions primarily to instill, not merely to express, humans' attitudes toward the world. Religion functions primarily to give humans a secure, clear place in the world and only thereafter to articulate the place they have. Whether, as for his fellow "contemporaries," religion also gives humans a place in society, later Bellah does not say. Nor does later he, like them, say what threatens meaning, how religion provides it, or whether anything else provides it.

In arguing for "civil religion" in America and elsewhere, Bellah[59] is certainly arguing that religion serves more than an individual function. Yet that function is not really social. Religion does not, as for Durkheim and Radcliffe-Brown, serve to weld people into a nation, at least as an end in itself. Rather, it welds them as a means of fulfilling the nation's ideals – for example, of peace and equality. The fulfillment of these ideals constitutes less a function than a duty – a duty not only to the nation but, at least in the case of America, to God, whose chosen nation America believes itself to be. This duty is therefore less social than irreducibly religious: serving one's country in order to serve God, who is the mentor rather than, as for Durkheim, the projection of society.

Mary Douglas

For Douglas (especially 1970; 1973), religion arises and functions to fulfill a need less for existential than for intellectual order. Insofar as the need for meaning, or meaningfulness, is necessarily existential rather than purely intellectual, Douglas is not, strictly, concerned with meaning. For her, humans need less to explain, endure, or justify their experience, as for her fellow contemporaries, than, more fundamentally, to organize it. Religion, like every

---

[59]See Bellah (1975; 1976; Bellah and Hammond).

other domain of culture, organizes experience by classifying it. Without classifications life would be not baffling, painful, or unjust but plain incoherent.

For Douglas, as for Geertz and Turner above all, ritual is the means by which order gets imposed. Ritual classifies, or demarcates, a boundary – of time, space, group, or status: "... a ritual provides a frame. The marked off time or place alerts a special kind of expectancy, just as the oft-repeated 'Once upon a time' creates a mood receptive to fantastic tales.... Framing and boxing limit experience, shut in desired themes or shut out intruding ones" (Douglas 1970: 78).

Ritual does not primarily explain, alleviate, justify, or express experience, as it does for Geertz and Turner, but in Kantian fashion constitutes it: "So it is not enough to say that ritual helps us to experience more vividly what we would have experienced anyway.... If it were just a kind of dramatic map or diagram of what is known it would always follow experience. But in fact ritual does not play this secondary role. It can come first in formulating experience. It can permit knowledge of what would otherwise not be known at all" (Douglas 1970:79-80).

Just as Geertz, Turner, and Bellah deny that religion serves only a social, Durkheimian function or only a psychological, Freudian one, so Douglas denies that it serves only a magical, Frazerian one, though at times she inconsistently insists that it does.[60] Religion, which means religious ritual, ordinarily serves less to control the world than to organize it: "Of course the Dinka hope that their rites will cause rain, healing rituals avert death, harvest rituals produce crops. But instrumental efficacy is not the only kind of efficacy to be derived from their symbolic action. The other kind is achieved in the action itself, in the assertions it makes and the experience which bears its imprinting" (Douglas 1970:84). A rain dance serves to divide time into rainy and dry seasons. To take Douglas' most famous example, Jewish dietary laws serve to prohibit the eating of animals which violate the classifications into which living things are divided: "Those species are unclean which are imperfect members of their class, or whose class itself confounds the general scheme of the world" (Douglas 1970:70).

No more than other "contemporaries" does Douglas deny that religion also serves a social function, but no less than they does she deem the individual one primary. At the same time she, too, deems society indispensable to the serving of it. No one alone could either create or sustain the religious and other classifications which it provides. Indeed, Douglas, following Durkheim and Mauss (1963), argues that all classifications are projections of the organization of society itself, in which case individuals clearly depend on society for their classifications.[61] In fact, where Durkheim and Mauss argue that the

---

[60]See Douglas (1970:86-89; 1973:69-73).
[61]See Douglas (1970; 1973; 1975; 1982; 1986).

classifications of modern society eventually develop independently of their social origin, Douglas argues that even they remain reflections of society.

Insofar as religious classifications for Douglas are projections of social ones, religion functions to reinforce society. For her, as for Geertz, Berger, and Turner, religion thus serves its social function while serving its individual one – not, as for them, by explaining and justifying social organization but simply by expressing that organization. Although Douglas never says, perhaps the pervasiveness of that organization throughout culture makes it seem natural and in that respect justified.

Mircea Eliade

In deeming the "why" of religion independent of society, contemporary sociologists of religion seem to be emulating historians of religions like Mircea Eliade (for example, 1959), who likewise stresses the autonomy not of the object, or referent, of religion but of its origin and function: why, not what, believers believe. According to Eliade, believers seek the sacred not as the means to an end but as the end itself. They seek the sacred because they seek the sacred. Their need for it is therefore irreducibly religious.

Contemporary sociologists in fact view religion differently. For them, religion arises and functions to satisfy a secular, not religious, need: the need for order, intellectual or existential. Humans do seek the sacred, but, consciously or unconsciously, as only a means to order. For most "contemporaries," religion is one of the best means of securing order, but even if it were the exclusive means, the end would still be order, not the sacred. Undeniably, the need for order is for "contemporaries" independent of society: it serves the individual rather than society and is innate rather than implanted. But it is not therefore independent of anything secular. It itself is secular, and religion arises and functions to fulfill it. Contemporary sociologists and historians of religions like Eliade thus remain far apart.[62]

Why the "De-Sociologizing" of the Sociology of Religion?

There are at least two possible explanations for the "de-sociologizing" of the sociology of religion. First, the change may be part of a general shift in the social scientific study of not only religion but culture as a whole from explanations which ignore or even contradict the participant's own view to explanations which accept it. Nineteenth-century theorists were not at all reluctant to explain human beliefs and actions in terms different from those of the participant. Twentieth-century theorists typically are. Striving to overcome their own professed biases, they accept as authoritative the participant's point of

---

[62]See Segal (1985).

view.[63] Even if contemporary sociologists of religion still stop short of what at least historians of religions like Eliade deem the believer's point of view, their accounts of religion are undeniably closer to the believer's presumed own than those of their predecessors. The fulfillment of an innate need for order is surely closer to the believer's own likely explanation of religiosity than the fulfillment of a need for a stable society.

A second possible explanation of the "de-sociologizing" may be the acknowledgment that past explanations of religion – the classical ones – have proved inadequate. Religion, it has perhaps therefore been concluded, is too complicated a phenomenon to be explained entirely or even considerably sociologically. For the "de-sociologizing" of the field involves exactly the assumption that sociology cannot explain all or even much of religion. I myself think neither of these possible explanations justification for the abandonment of a wholly sociological quest, but they may nevertheless account for the change.

REFERENCES

BELLAH, ROBERT N.

1957   *Tokugawa Religion*. Glencoe, Ill.: Free Press.

1965   "Introduction" and "Epilogue: Religion and Progress in Modern Asia." In *Religion and Progress in Modern Asia*, ed. Bellah, pp. ix-xxv and 168-229. New York: Free Press.

1970a   *Beyond Belief*. New York: Harper.

1970b   "Christianity and Symbolic Realism." *Journal for the Scientific Study of Religion* 9 (Summer):89-96.

1970c   "Response to Comments." *Journal for the Scientific Study of Religion* 9 (Summer):112-15.

1970d   "Confessions of a Former Establishment Fundamentalist." *Council on the Study of Religion Bulletin* 1 (December):3-6.

1975   *The Broken Covenant*. New York: Seabury Press.

1976   "The Revolution and the Civil Religion." In *Religion and the American Revolution*, ed. Jerald C. Brauer, pp. 55-73. Philadelphia: Fortress Press.

BELLAH, ROBERT N., AND PHILLIP E. HAMMOND

1980   *Varieties of Civil Religion*. San Francisco: Harper.

BERGER, PETER L.

1961a   *The Noise of Solemn Assemblies*. Garden City, N.Y.: Doubleday.

1961b   *The Precarious Vision*. Garden City, N.Y.: Doubleday.

---

[63]See Segal (1983a:97-98).

1969   *The Sacred Canopy.* Garden City, N.Y.: Doubleday Anchor Books.
        Original publ.: Garden City, N.Y.: Doubleday, 1967.

1970   *A Rumor of Angels.* Garden City, N.Y.: Doubleday Anchor Books.
        Original publ.: Garden City, N.Y.: Doubleday, 1969.

1980   *The Heretical Imperative.* Garden City, N.Y.: Doubleday Anchor Books.
        Original publ.: Garden City, N.Y.: Doubleday, 1979.

DOUGLAS, MARY
1970   *Purity and Danger.* Baltimore: Penguin Books. Original publ.: London:
        Routledge & Kegan Paul, 1966.

1973   *Natural Symbols.* Second ed.: New York: Vintage Books. Original publ.
        of first ed.: New York: Pantheon, 1970.

1975   *Implicit Meanings.* London and Boston: Routledge & Kegan Paul.

1982   *In the Active Voice.* London and Boston: Routledge & Kegan Paul.

1986   *How Institutions Think.* Syracuse, N.Y.: Syracuse University Press.

DURKHEIM, ÉMILE
1933   *The Division of Labor in Society.* Tr. George Simpson. New York:
        Macmillan.

1965   *The Elementary Forms of the Religious Life.* Tr. Joseph Ward Swain.
        New York: Free Press. Original publ. of tr.: London: Allen & Unwin,
        1915.

1975   "Individualism and the intellectuals." In *Durkheim on Religion,* ed. W.
        S. F. Pickering and trs. Jacqueline Redding and Pickering, pp. 59-73.
        London and Boston: Routledge & Kegan Paul.

DURKHEIM, ÉMILE, AND MARCEL MAUSS
1963   *Primitive Classification.* Ed. and tr. Rodney Needham. Chicago:
        University of Chicago Press.

ELIADE, MIRCEA
1959   *The Sacred and the Profane.* Tr. Willard R. Trask. New York: Harcourt,
        Brace.

FUSTEL DE COULANGES, NUMA DENIS
1873   *The Ancient City.* Tr. Willard Small. Boston: Lothrop, Lee.

GEERTZ, CLIFFORD
1960   *The Religion of Java.* Glencoe, Ill.: Free Press.

1968a   "Religion: Anthropological Study." In *International Encyclopedia of the
        Social Sciences* 12:398-406.

1968b   *Islam Observed.* New Haven, Conn.: Yale University Press.

1973   *The Interpretation of Cultures.* New York: Basic Books.

1983   *Local Knowledge.* New York: Basic Books.

MALINOWSKI, BRONISLAW

1925   "Magic, Science and Religion." In *Science, Religion and Reality*, ed. Joseph Needham, pp. 20-84. New York and London: Macmillan.

MARX, KARL, AND FRIEDRICH ENGELS

1957   *On Religion*. Moscow: Foreign Languages Publishing.

RADCLIFFE-BROWN, A. R.

1922   *The Andaman Islanders*. Cambridge, Eng.: Cambridge University Press.

1952   *Structure and Function in Primitive Society*. Glencoe, Ill.: Free Press.

1958   *Method in Social Anthropology*. Ed. M. N. Srinivas. Chicago: University of Chicago Press.

RICHARD, GASTON

1975   "Dogmatic atheism in the sociology of religion." In *Durkheim on Religion*, ed. W. S. F. Pickering and trs. Jacqueline Redding and Pickering, pp. 228-76. London and Boston: Routledge & Kegan Paul.

SEGAL, ROBERT A.

1976   "The First Sociologist of Religion: Fustel de Coulanges." *Journal for the Scientific Study of Religion* 15 (December):365-68. Reprinted in revised form in the present book as ch. 9.

1983a   "In Defense of Reductionism." *Journal of the American Academy of Religion* 51 (March):97-124. Reprinted in revised form in the present book as ch. 1.

1983b   "Victor Turner's Theory of Ritual." *Zygon* 18 (September):327-35. Reprinted in revised form in the present book as ch. 11.

1985   "Have the Social Sciences Been Converted?" *Journal for the Scientific Study of Religion* 24 (September):321-24. Reprinted in revised form in the present book as ch. 4.

1986   "Response to Blasi and Nelson." *Journal for the Scientific Study of Religion* 25 (September):369-72. Reprinted in revised form in the present book as ch. 6.

forth-   "Comment on Steven Kepnes' 'Bridging the Gap Between Understanding
coming   and Explanation Approaches to the Study of Religion'." *Journal for the Scientific Study of Religion*.

SWANSON, GUY E.

1960   *The Birth of the Gods*. Ann Arbor: University of Michigan Press.

1967   *Religion and Regime*. Ann Arbor: University of Michigan Press.

TURNER, VICTOR W.

1957   *Schism and Continuity in an African Society*. Manchester, Eng.: Manchester University Press.

1967   *The Forest of Symbols*. Ithaca, N.Y.: Cornell University Press.

1968   *The Drums of Affliction*. Oxford: Clarendon Press.

1969   *The Ritual Process.* Chicago: Aldine.

1974   *Dramas, Fields, and Metaphors.* Ithaca, N.Y.: Cornell University Press.

1975   *Revelation and Divination in Ndembu Ritual.* Ithaca, N.Y.: Cornell University Press.

1985   *On the Edge of the Bush.* Ed. Edith L. B. Turner. Tucson: University of Arizona Press.

TURNER, VICTOR, AND EDITH TURNER
1978   *Image and Pilgrimage in Christian Culture.* ACLS Lectures on the History of Religions, n.s., no. 11. New York: Columbia University Press.

TYLOR, EDWARD B.
1958   *Primitive Culture.* 2 vols. New York: Harper Torchbooks. Vol. I is retitled *The Origins of Culture* and vol. II retitled *Religion in Primitive Culture.* Original publ. of first ed.: London: Murray, 1871.

WEBER, MAX
1958   *The Protestant Ethic and the Spirit of Capitalism.* Tr. Talcott Parsons. New York: Scribner.

1963   *The Sociology of Religion.* Tr. Ephraim Fischoff. Boston: Beacon Press.

Chapter Eleven

Victor Turner's Theory of Ritual

Among contemporary anthropologists, few have devoted themselves more passionately to religion than Victor Turner, Clifford Geertz, and Mary Douglas. In turn, few contemporary anthropologists have been more enthusiastically received by "religionists" than they.

The three contend that religion functions above all to express beliefs, beliefs about the place of humans in the world. For them, not only religion but all of culture serves to express those beliefs. The three find those beliefs not only in obvious places like schools and politics but also in unexpected, seemingly random locales like color schemes (Turner), cockfights (Geertz), and diet (Douglas). In the case of religion all three focus not on myths or creeds but on rituals, which, as physical rather than mental activities, might seem unlikely sources of belief. Says Douglas: "Implicitly I find myself returning to Robertson Smith's idea that rites are prior and myths are secondary in the study of religion" (Douglas 1973:30). All three view rituals the way they do colors, cockfights, and diet: *as* mental activities, as expressions of belief.

The Social Scientific Study of Ritual

Within the social sciences there have been two main views of ritual, which here will mean religious ritual.[1] One view has considered it a matter of *feelings,* which ritual either implants or releases. This view, by far the more common one, is found above all in Émile Durkheim, A. R. Radcliffe-Brown, Bronislaw Malinowski, Karl Marx, and Sigmund Freud.[2] For Durkheim and Radcliffe-Brown, ritual creates feelings: for Durkheim, feelings of dependence on society and of possession by society; for Radcliffe-Brown, feelings of dependence on society and also of love and hatred toward phenomena which, respectively, help and hurt society. For Malinowski, Marx, and Freud, ritual discharges feelings:

---

[1]On the distinction between religious and secular rituals see Moore and Myerhoff (3-24). Certainly Turner, Geertz, and Douglas by no means consider all rituals religious.

[2]On their theories of ritual see Durkheim (esp. bk. 3), Radcliffe-Brown (esp. ch. 5), Malinowski (passim), Marx and Engels (passim), Freud (passim).

for Malinowski, feelings of helplessness before nature; for Marx, pent-up economic desires; for Freud, pent-up instinctual ones.

The other main view of ritual has deemed it fundamentally a matter of *belief*, which ritual applies. This view is found above all in Edward Tylor and James Frazer.[3] For both, ritual controls the world by applying prescientific beliefs about it.

Like Tylor and Frazer, Turner, Geertz, and Douglas regard ritual as belief.[4] Unlike them, the three regard ritual as the expression, not the application, of belief. Even more unlike them, they regard the belief expressed as other than primitive science. For Tylor and Frazer, ritual is the primitive equivalent of applied science: for the purpose of controlling the world, ritual puts into practice the primitive belief that personal gods rather than impersonal laws of nature regulate the world. For Tylor and especially Frazer, not just ritual but religion as a whole gives way to modern technology.

For Turner, Geertz, and Douglas, by contrast, ritual is a modern as well as primitive phenomenon. It can be modern exactly because even as part of religion it does not rival science and therefore does not get superseded by science. Rather than either explaining or controlling the world, ritual for all three describes the place of human beings in the world.

Ritual describes the place of humans in not only the cosmos but also society. It describes the place of humans vis-à-vis not only the physical world and god but also other humans. Ideally, the cosmic and social places are in harmony. Ideally, they parallel, if not mirror, each other – a point stressed by Geertz above all.

For Turner and Geertz, the need for a place is existential: a fixed, certain place makes life secure, fair, and tolerable. For Douglas, the need is more intellectual: a fixed, certain place makes life intelligible. Perhaps because Turner and Geertz deal with changing societies, they are more attentive to "existential" anxiety than Douglas, who, dealing with stable societies, is freer to concentrate on purely intellectual issues.

As concerned as Turner, Geertz, and Douglas are with the function of ritual for the individual, they also are concerned with its function for society. As resolutely as they reject Durkheim and Radcliffe-Brown for their "emotivist" view of ritual, they accept the view of Durkheim and Radcliffe-Brown that the function served by ritual is social, albeit individual as well. Turner, Geertz, and Douglas assert that ritual serves at once to uphold society and to give humans places in both it and the cosmos.

---

[3]On their theories of ritual see Tylor (esp. II:ch. 18), Frazer (passim).
[4]Because Turner, Geertz, and Douglas write almost entirely on ritual, for their theories of ritual see their works in general.

Turner's Theory of Ritual

The Drums of Affliction typifies Turner's approach to ritual. He begins by defining ritual as a process of communication: it serves "the highly important functions ... of storing and transmitting information" (Turner 1968:1). The function of ritual is thus less "instrumental" than "expressive." Ritual is expressive not because it, like an archaeological find, merely reflects beliefs but because it intentionally discloses them.

To say that *myth* conveys information is commonplace. To say that ritual does is not. Turner rejects the conventional split into nonverbal and verbal behavior: physical as well as verbal behavior conveys information.[5]

The information conveyed by ritual concerns both the present and the ideal place of the individual in both society and the cosmos: "We are not dealing with information about a new agricultural technique or a better judicial procedure: we are concerned here with the crucial values of the believing community, whether it is a religious community, a nation, a tribe, a secret society, or any other type of group whose ultimate unity resides in its orientation towards transcendental and invisible powers" (Turner 1968:2).

The Drums of Affliction focuses on Ndembu rituals of affliction: rituals performed on behalf of persons whose illnesses or misfortunes are believed to be the work of ancestors or witches. Symptoms of affliction include backache, fever, boils, and difficulties in childbirth and hunting. The ritual tries to placate the spirits responsible. Unlike rites of passage and other life-crisis rituals, which occur at regular times in the lives of individuals, rituals of affliction get performed only in times of stress. In the Ndembu village studied by Turner there loomed economic, political, and social decay in the wake of the colonial government's withdrawal of official recognition of the village chieftain. The loss of that recognition cost the village jobs, goods, and most of all clout. The village was also facing problems in hunting and farming.

The consequent frustration stirred previously suppressed tensions among individuals and among clans – tensions rooted ultimately in the clash between matrilineal descent and virilocal marriage. Because of both his particular lineage and his passive, effeminate personality one villager, Kamahasanyi, became the scapegoat. Overwhelmed by the scorn of his relatives and neighbors, he developed various physical ills, which he blamed on ancestors and witches. His ancestors, he claimed, were punishing him for the failure of his line to retain the chieftainship, and his relatives and neighbors were bewitching him out of frustration at their own plight.[6]

Kamahasanyi demanded and received ritual curing. During the rituals all the personal antagonisms, which had been less unrecognized than ignored, were

---

[5]For an argument that verbal and nonverbal behavior, or "word-meanings" and "action-meanings," are distinct see Papineau (97-105).
[6]On Kamahasanyi see also Turner (1967:ch. 10).

acknowledged and at least temporarily purged: "Ritual ... must give expression to the illicit drives, bring them into the open, as Ndembu say themselves, in order that they may be purged and exorcised" (Turner 1968:236). Kamahasanyi himself was vindicated, and his ailments ceased, though the underlying tensions were scarcely eliminated.

On the one hand Turner certainly says that ritual serves to alleviate *social* turmoil: "Ndembu ritual ... may be regarded as a magnificent instrument for expressing, maintaining, and periodically cleansing a secular order of society without strong political centralization and all too full of social conflict" (Turner 1968:21). On the other hand he says that ritual also serves to alleviate *existential* turmoil: "In the idiom of the rituals of affliction it is as though the Ndembu said: 'It is only when a person is reduced to misery by misfortune, and repents of the acts that caused him to be afflicted, that ritual expressing an underlying unity in diverse things may fittingly be enacted for him'.... It is as though he were stripped of all possessions, all status, all social connections, and *then* endowed with all the basic virtues and values of Ndembu society" (Turner 1968:22). If on the one hand ritual restores order to society, on the other hand it restores order to individuals' lives. Even though existential turmoil grows out of social turmoil,[7] it is more than an indirect expression of social turmoil.

Ritual alleviates both kinds of turmoil by acting out, by literally dramatizing, the situation it remedies. To use one of Turner's pet phrases, ritual is "social drama": "This notion of 'drama' is crucial to the understanding of ritual. Both in its plot and in its symbolism, a ritual is an epitome of the wider and spontaneous social process in which it is embodied and which ideally it controls" (Turner 1968:273-74). As drama, ritual is not merely a part of social life but the depiction of it. Where in the quotation ritual is itself social drama, elsewhere for Turner it is a response to a social drama: the drama thereby refers to the turmoil itself; the ritual, to the depiction of the turmoil. More precisely, ritual is the last stage *within* a social drama, which begins with the turmoil and ends with what Turner calls "redress." Ritual is only one form of redress. A law suit is another.

Ritual for Turner describes not only how things are but also how they should be. It thereby serves as a model for altering society: "Ritual is a periodic restatement of the terms in which men of a particular culture must interact if there is to be any kind of a *[sic]* coherent social life.... It has been more than once suggested that religious ritual is mainly 'expressive', that it portrays in symbolic form certain key values and cultural orientations. This is true as far as it goes, but it points to only one of many properties it possesses. More important is its creative function – it actually creates, or re-creates, the categories through which men perceive reality – the axioms underlying the structure of society and the laws of the natural and moral orders. It is not here a case of life

---

[7]See Turner (1968:89; 1975:25).

being an imitation of art, but of social life being an attempted imitation of models portrayed and animated by ritual" (Turner 1968:6-7).[8] In arguing that ritual not simply mirrors society but also forges it, Turner is much akin to Geertz.

Turner's effort is daring. He is claiming that ritual actually works, not merely is believed to work, and works by making sense of participants' experiences, not merely by releasing or redirecting their emotions. The individual ills treated by ritual are psychosomatic, and Turner often compares Ndembu rituals with psychoanalysis. By the comparison he does not, however, mean to be reducing the ills to feelings. Far from it, he means to be elevating them to thoughts, or beliefs. Ndembu rituals work precisely because, like psychoanalysis, they make conscious not only repressed or, here, suppressed feelings but also suppressed beliefs.

There are several senses in which ritual for Turner might be labeled "meaningful." First, ritual is undeniably meaningful in the sense of being intentionally rather than mechanically caused: participants perform a ritual for some conscious end. But who would deny that ritual is meaningful in this innocuous sense? The real issue is whether the conscious intent is the true or deepest source of ritual. Insofar as one function of ritual for Turner is the preservation of society, that end is surely not even unconsciously intentional: whatever the conscious or unconscious end for which participants perform ritual, it is surely not for the sake of society. Indeed, even the individual, existential function of ritual for Turner is as likely subconscious as conscious. Only insofar as some conscious intent, however superficial, impels participants to act is ritual for Turner meaningful in this first sense.

Second, ritual for Turner might be meaningful in the more technical sense of constituting the manifestation rather than the effect of an intent. Here the distinction is not that between an intended and an unintended cause, much less that between a consciously and an unconsciously intended one. Rather, it is that between intent *qua* meaning and intent *qua* cause. Ritual is meaningful insofar as it is the manifestation of an intent, conscious or unconscious, and is meaningless insofar as it is the effect of either an intent or a mechanism. The distinction between meaning and cause is that, in a strict sense, between interpretation and explanation.[9] Of the three contemporary theorists of ritual considered here, only Geertz is concerned with this distinction, and even he often effaces it.[10] Turner himself nowhere makes it. In this second sense, then, ritual for Turner is not meaningful.

Third, ritual for Turner might be meaningful in the sense of constituting a text, which therefore harbors a message, or "meaning." In different, looser senses

---

[8]See also Turner (1974:56; 1980:162-63).
[9]On this distinction see Segal (1986; forthcoming₁; forthcoming₂).
[10]See Segal (forthcoming₂).

of the terms ritual here must be not only "explained," or accounted for genetically, but also "interpreted," or translated into a coherent and intelligible script. Where the prior distinction makes explanation and interpretation incompatible – *both* seek to account for ritual – this third one does not: explanation alone seeks the origin and, secondarily, function of ritual; interpretation, the content.

Of the three contemporary theorists of ritual considered, Geertz is, again, the one most preoccupied with ritual as a text. In characterizing ritual as drama, or the depiction of the situation which triggers it, Turner is also clearly deeming ritual a text. He even follows Geertz's lead in characterizing ritual as a "metasocial commentary" on the situation it depicts.[11] To object that ritual is the *enactment* of a text rather than the text itself would be to miss the point: ritual not merely enacts the script, as for many myth ritualists, but is the script itself.

Still, ritual for Turner, unlike Geertz, serves also to sublimate anti-social emotions, not just to communicate meaning, or beliefs. In ritual "a transference of affective energy is made from socially negative to socially positive symbolism and behaviour" (Turner 1968:237). Put more succinctly: "... ritual action is akin to a sublimation process ..." (Turner 1974:56). Ritual is, then, more than a text.

Even more important, Turner, for all his concern with the communicating of meaning as well as the channelling of emotion, is concerned more with the communicating itself than with the meaning communicated. Where Geertz actually interprets the meaning of rituals, Turner takes their interpretation for granted and concentrates instead on the effect of the meaning on individuals and society.[12] In, then, the third sense of the term – as a text to be interpreted – ritual for Turner is only partly meaningful.

Fourth and last, ritual for Turner might be meaningful in the sense of serving an existential function: giving participants a secure place in society and the cosmos. Here what is meaningful is neither the *source* of ritual, as in the first two senses of the term, nor the *nature* of ritual, as in the third, but the *function* of ritual: ritual provides meaningful*ness*. Certainly ritual for Turner does not bestow on participants an *elevated* place in either society or the cosmos. Especially in primitive society ritual typically reinforces the existing place of participants. Nor does ritual justify the place of participants, though the fit between one's cosmic place and one's social place does bolster each. Rather, ritual for Turner gives participants a permanent place per se. Still, in this fourth and final sense ritual for Turner is fully meaningful.

---

[11] See Turner (1985:125, 193, 239).
[12] For differences between Geertz's and Turner's views of ritual see Geertz (1983:26-30) and Turner (1985:298-301).

Criticism

Again and again, Turner confuses the reality of a *need* for a meaningful world with the *reality* of a meaningful world. For example, he says that "after many years as an agnostic and monistic materialist I learned from the Ndembu that ritual and its symbolism are not merely epiphenomena or disguises of deeper social and psychological processes, but have ontological value ..." (Turner 1975:31). Turner is here claiming more than that the origin and function of ritual are existential rather than social or psychological. He is saying that the claims ritual makes about the world are true. More explicit is his statement that the social sciences dare not deny the *truth* of religion, as if their accounts of the origin and function of religion encroached on its truth: "... a strictly sociological explanation of the white symbolism we have been discussing would appear to be inadequate. One has to consider religious phenomena in terms of religious ideas and doctrines .... It was truly said by H. Butterfield ... 'that it might well be required of any religion that its truth should be open to the vision of the humble and poor ....' In studying religious symbols, the product of humble vision, we must ourselves be humble if we are to glimpse, if not fully to comprehend, the spiritual truths represented by them.... That is the reason why the attempts of such scholars and philosophers as James Fraser *[sic]* and Durkheim to explain away religious phenomena in naturalistic terms have been so obviously unsuccessful" (Turner 1975:195-96).

Because Turner conflates origin and function with truth, he argues that the existence of a need for a meaningful world somehow suggests, even if not entails, the existence of such a world. Denying that the wish for meaningfulness is reducible to a wish for material security, as he oddly takes the Freud of the last of the *New Introductory Lectures* to be saying, Turner proceeds to deny that the wish is delusory. There may, he says, be unity, which he equates with meaningfulness, amidst the apparent discreteness of things: "He [Freud] would have argued, as I have myself heard analysts argue, that the Ndembu wish that things and people, recognized in ordinary life as irrevocably divided, should be brought into harmony, and that this wish engenders the belief that in ritual action there is some inherent efficacy that brings about this miracle of unification. He would also have doubtless argued that behind this wish stands the recognition of the need for social and economic security, and that in fact material interest is its prime mover.... But to my mind it seems just as feasible to argue that 'the wish to gain control of the sensory world' may proceed from something else – a deep intuition of a real and spiritual unity in all things" (Turner 1968:21).

While denying on independent, nonsocial scientific grounds that the world is harmonious or unified, Freud does not deny that humans *wish* it so. Contrary to Turner, he grants both the existence and the strength of the wish. In jumping backwards from Freud's denial of the fulfillment of the wish to Freud's purported denial of the wish itself, and in jumping forward from the existence of the wish to even the possibility of its fulfillment, Turner jumps – or leaps – from social scientist to would-be believer.

Periodization

Turner's writings are classifiable into three periods. In the 1950's, the period of *Schism and Continuity in an African Society,* Turner was concerned with only the social function of ritual. Yet even here he broke with mainstream social functionalists: where Radcliffe-Brown, for example, compares society with a perfectly integrated, smoothly operating body – something static and mechanical, even if alive – Turner compares it with, once again, an endless series of dramas, in which clashes produce crises requiring resolution. Still, the function of ritual here is entirely social: like culture generally, ritual serves to restore order to *society* and only coincidentally, if at all, to individuals' lives.

In the 1960's, in works like *The Forest of Symbols, The Drums of Affliction,* and *The Ritual Process,* Turner turned from the social function of ritual, a function that he nevertheless continued to acknowledge, to the individual, existential one. In the1970's, in such works as *Dramas, Fields, and Metaphors* and *Image and Pilgrimage in Christian Culture,* he turned from primitive to modern society. In static, primitive society ritual serves to reinforce both existing society and the existing places of humans in both society and the cosmos. In dynamic, modern society ritual serves to alter both society itself and the places of humans in both society and the cosmos. Ritual challenges, not supports, society.

REFERENCES

DOUGLAS, MARY

1970   *Purity and Danger.* Baltimore: Penguin Books. Original publ.: London: Routledge & Kegan Paul, 1966.

1973   *Natural Symbols.* Second ed. New York: Vintage Books. Original publ. of first ed.: New York: Pantheon, 1970.

1975   *Implicit Meanings.* London and Boston: Routledge & Kegan Paul.

1982   *In the Active Voice.* London and Boston: Routledge & Kegan Paul.

1986   *How Institutions Think.* Syracuse, N.Y.: Syracuse University Press.

DURKHEIM, ÉMILE

1915   *The Elementary Forms of the Religious Life.* Tr. Joseph Ward Swain. London: Allen & Unwin.

FRAZER, JAMES G.

1911-15 *The Golden Bough.* 3rd ed. 12 vols. London: Macmillan.

FREUD, SIGMUND

1950   *Totem and Taboo.* Tr. James Strachey. New York: Norton.

1964   *New Introductory Lectures on Psychoanalysis.* Tr. James Strachey. New York: Norton.

GEERTZ, CLIFFORD

1960   *The Religion of Java.* Glencoe, Ill.: Free Press.

1968   *Islam Observed.* New Haven, Conn.: Yale University Press.

1973   *The Interpretation of Cultures.* New York: Basic Books.

1983   *Local Knowledge.* New York: Basic Books.

MALINOWSKI, BRONISLAW

1925   "Magic, Science and Religion." In *Science, Religion and Reality,* ed. Joseph Needham, pp. 20-84. New York and London: Macmillan.

MARX, KARL, AND FRIEDRICH ENGELS

1957   *On Religion.* Moscow: Foreign Languages Publishing.

MOORE, SALLY FALK, AND BARBARA G. MYERHOFF, EDS.

1977   *Secular Ritual.* Assen, The Netherlands: Van Gorcum.

PAPINEAU, DAVID

1979   *For Science in the Social Sciences.* New York: St. Martin's Press.

RADCLIFFE-BROWN, A. R.

1922   *The Andaman Islanders.* Cambridge, Eng.: Cambridge University Press.

SEGAL, ROBERT A.

1986   "Response to Blasi and Nelson." *Journal for the Scientific Study of Religion* 25 (September):369-72. Reprinted in revised form in the present book as ch. 6.

forth-   "Comment on Steven Kepnes' 'Bridging the Gap Between Understanding
coming₁   and Explanation Approaches to the Study of Religion'." *Journal for the Scientific Study of Religion.*

forth-   "Interpreting and Explaining Religion: Geertz and Durkheim."
coming₂   *Soundings.*

TURNER, VICTOR W.

1957   *Schism and Continuity in an African Society.* Manchester, Eng.: Manchester University Press.

1967   *The Forest of Symbols.* Ithaca, N.Y.: Cornell University Press.

1968   *The Drums of Affliction.* Oxford: Clarendon Press.

1969   *The Ritual Process.* Chicago: Aldine.

1974   *Dramas, Fields, and Metaphors.* Ithaca, N.Y.: Cornell University Press.

1975   *Revelation and Divination in Ndembu Ritual.* Ithaca, N.Y.: Cornell University Press.

1978   "Encounter with Freud: The Making of a Comparative Symbolist." In *The Making of Psychological Anthropology,* ed. George D. Spindler, pp. 556-83. Berkeley: University of California Press.

1979   *Process, Performance and Pilgrimage.* Ranchi Anthropology Series, vol. I. New Delhi: Concept Publishing.

1980   "Social Dramas and Stories about Them." *Critical Inquiry* 7 (Autumn):141-68.

1982   *From Ritual to Theatre.* New York: Performing Arts Journal Publications.

1985   *On the Edge of the Bush.* Ed. Edith L. B. Turner. Tucson: University of Arizona Press.

TURNER, VICTOR, AND EDITH TURNER
1978   *Image and Pilgrimage in Christian Culture.* ACLS Lectures on the History of Religions, n.s., no. 11. New York: Columbia University Press.

TYLOR, EDWARD B.
1958   *Primitive Culture.* 2 vols. New York: Harper Torchbooks. Vol. I is retitled *The Origins of Culture* and vol. II retitled *Religion in Primitive Culture.* Original publ. of first ed.: London: Murray, 1871.

Chapter Twelve

Symbolic Anthropology Applied to Religions of the Greco-Roman World

The Contemporary Social Scientific Study of Religion

Rightly or wrongly, the social sciences have long been considered hostile to religion. Within the last few decades, however, there have emerged various movements in the social sciences which have proved particularly sympathetic to religion and to which, not coincidentally, "religionists" have proved particularly sympathetic in turn. These movements span the social sciences most concerned with religion: psychology, sociology, and anthropology. The most notable movements among them are humanistic and existential psychology, symbolic interactionism and ethnomethodology, and cognitive and symbolic anthropology.

The difference between these movements and their predecessors is not, first, over the truth of religion. On the one hand the social sciences by nature usually deal with only the origin, function, and meaning of religion, not the truth of it. To invoke either the origin or the function of religion to assess its truth is to commit the genetic fallacy or its functionalist equivalent.[1]

On the other hand the contemporary movements sympathetic to religion do not themselves assert its truth – their inability to do so aside. Earlier social scientists often assumed the falsity of religion, and their convictions often affected their theorizing. Most blatantly, James Frazer (1922) says unabashedly that religion and magic fail to provide basic necessities because the two presuppose false explanations of the physical world.[2] Yet rather than, by contrast, proclaiming religion true, contemporary theorists are almost uniformly mute about the issue.[3]

The difference between contemporary theorists and their predecessors is not, second, over the importance of religion. Since the beginnings of their disciplines sociology, anthropology, and psychology have been preoccupied with religion.

---

[1] See Segal (1980).
[2] See Frazer (esp. 13, 22, 43, 52-53, 55, 57, 65).
[3] The boldest exceptions are Peter Berger (1970:52-97; 1980:58-60, ch. 5) and Mary Douglas (1975:ix-xxi; 1979).

Among classical social scientists, Frazer, Edward Tylor (1958), Émile Durkheim (1965), A. R. Radcliffe-Brown (1922), Bronislaw Malinowski (1925), Karl Marx (1957), Sigmund Freud (1950), and Carl Jung (1938) consider religion at least as important as any of their contemporary counterparts do. For all of these classical theorists, religion serves, at the least, an exceedingly important function.

For Tylor, Frazer, Durkheim, Radcliffe-Brown, and Malinowski, religion serves an outright indispensable function. In explaining the world, religion for Tylor fulfills an indispensable individual need: humans will not die without an explanation, but *qua* humans they seek one. In purporting to provide food and other necessities, religion for Frazer clearly fulfills an indispensable individual need. In preserving society, religion for Durkheim, Radcliffe-Brown, and Malinowski serves an indispensable need on the part of society itself.

For Marx, by contrast, the need religion serves is indispensable not to any society but to only an economically oppressed one: the need either to maintain that oppression or to compensate for it. As soon as society ceases to be economically oppressed, the need for religion will dissolve. For the Freud of *Totem and Taboo,* the need religion serves is similarly indispensable to only a sexually repressed society: the need to maintain that repression. As society becomes less sexually repressed, the need for religion will disappear. Likewise for Jung the need religion serves is indispensable to only a psychologically unrealized humanity: to realize the collective unconscious unconsciously rather than consciously. Once humanity becomes conscious of the collective unconscious, the need for religion, though not for myth, will end.

There is a difference between the indispensability of the function served by religion and the indispensability of religion itself. Few who consider the function served by religion indispensable consider religion indispensable to the serving of it. For Tylor and Frazer, modern science serves the same function as religion: for Tylor, religion may serve its function nearly as well as science, but for Frazer science alone serves the function religion claims to serve. For Radcliffe-Brown and Malinowski, secular ideology likely serves its same function far *less* potently than religion, but neither Radcliffe-Brown nor Malinowski thereby advocates the retention of religion. Only Durkheim, among classical social scientists, does. For him alone is religion itself indispensable: to survive, society needs religion itself, not merely some functional equivalent. No contemporary social scientist, however, goes as far as he. At most, "contemporaries" are like Tylor, Frazer, Radcliffe-Brown, and Malinowski: however effective religion is, only the function it serves, not it itself, is indispensable.

The difference between contemporary social scientists and classical ones is not, third, over the "positiveness" of the function religion serves. Marx and the Freud of *Totem and Taboo* may deem religion harmful to either individuals or society, but all of the other classical social scientists noted deem it helpful. Indeed, they deem it at least as beneficial as contemporary social scientists do.

The true difference between contemporary social scientists and their predecessors is over the eternality of religion. With the conspicuous exception of Durkheim all of the classical social scientists mentioned deem religion either primitive or pre-modern. For none of them does religion or will religion serve its function for moderns. Even Durkheim must find a distinctively modern variety of religion. Contemporary social scientists, by contrast, deem religion compatible with modernity. They assume not that everyone either is religious or, in light of the dispensability of religion, need be religious but rather that everyone *can* be religious.

Symbolic Anthropology

Among the contemporary movements sympathetic to religion, the one most enthusiastic about religion and the one about which "religionists" are most enthusiastic in turn is symbolic anthropology, of which there are two strains. One strain, which goes back at least to Edward Evans-Pritchard (1937; 1951; 1956; 1962; 1965; 1981),[4] is represented above all by Mary Douglas (1970; 1973; 1975; 1982; 1986), Victor Turner (1957; 1967; 1968; 1969; 1974; 1975; 1985; Turner and Turner), and Clifford Geertz (1960; 1968; 1973; 1983).[5] The other strain, which has more complicated, "extra-anthropological" roots, is represented above all by Claude Lévi-Strauss (1963-76; 1966; 1967; 1969-81; 1978). To be sure, the term "symbolic anthropology" sometimes gets confined to the first strain, which is then contrasted to "structuralism," but the term will be used here to cover both movements.

Ironically, in the conventional sense of the term "symbol," in which a symbol stands for something else, neither branch of symbolic anthropology deals with symbols. More accurately, for Lévi-Strauss symbols *collectively* stand for something else, but *individually* they do not. The *relationships* among individual symbols give them their symbolic meaning. Individually, symbols mean nothing. For Douglas, Turner, and Geertz, who in this respect are more radical, even collectively symbols do not necessarily stand for anything. Rather than *representations* of the symbolized, symbols are *expressions*, or *manifestations*, of it.

For both groups of symbolic anthropologists, the symbolized is beliefs, beliefs about the place of humans in the world. All of culture expresses those beliefs.

For Douglas, the expressions are to be found not only in conventional domains of belief like religion and ideology but above all in seemingly meaningless, rote, random, or trivial ones like the kinds of food one does and does not eat; the kinds of clothes one does and does not wear; the way one

---

[4]On Evans-Pritchard see Segal (1981).
[5]Although Douglas alone was Evans-Pritchard's student, Turner and Geertz are part of the same broad movement of which he was a founder.

categorizes animals, time, and space; and one's attitude toward one's body. For Douglas, these expressions of belief take the form of either classifications – for example, into permitted and forbidden food – or attitude – for example, one's attitude toward one's body.

All of culture for Douglas not merely unintentionally reflects beliefs but outright propounds them. To eat only certain food is not just coincidentally to evince one's convictions about one's place in the world but, consciously or not, to proclaim those convictions. It is to make a statement.

Yet even as a declaration of beliefs culture does not symbolize the beliefs. It articulates them. Put another way, culture spreads rather than symbolizes beliefs. The way one classifies food parallels, not represents, the way one classifies clothes. The way one treats one's body parallels, not represents, the way one treats others or others one. The same set of beliefs, formulated as either classifications or attitudes, pervades all of culture.

Though Geertz as well as Douglas examines unexpected domains of belief – notably, cockfights, funerals, and sheep raids[6] – he, in contrast to her, is equally concerned with conventional domains like religion, ideology, common sense, and art. Still, he, like her, argues unconventionally that the beliefs expressed in even the most conventional domains concern neither the world itself, as religion is often taken to do, nor the domain itself, as art taken as irreducibly aesthetic is assumed to do. Rather, the beliefs concern the place of humans in the world. At the same time Geertz is far less concerned than Douglas with classification as a form of expression. He is also far less concerned with parallels between one cultural domain and another, though at times he draws them.[7] Perhaps because he usually considers much broader domains,[8] each of which can seemingly constitute the whole of one's culture, he is less concerned with showing the linkage of beliefs across domains.

Yet Geertz is concerned, indeed preoccupied, with paralleling beliefs about one's place in the cosmos – what in the case of at least religion he calls the "world view" – with beliefs about one's place in society – what in the case of at least religion he calls the "ethos." He stresses the need for a fit between the world view and the ethos. Where there is a fit, the two reinforce each other: the world view makes the ethos natural rather than arbitrary by rooting it in the nature of things, and the ethos makes the world view germane rather than irrelevant by constituting a concrete instance of it. In even the tightest fit, however, each domain still only reflects, not represents, the other.

Turner[9] is closer to Geertz than to Douglas. He, too, is less concerned than she with unexpected domains of beliefs yet at the same time explores some –

---

[6]See Geertz (1973:chs. 15 [on cockfights], 6 [on funerals], 1 [on sheep raids]).
[7]See esp. Geertz (1973:ch. 14).
[8]But not always: see, e.g., Geertz (1973:ch. 14).
[9]On Turner see Segal (1983).

especially colors and trees.[10] Again like Geertz, Turner usually considers not only conventional domains but also broad ones. Unlike Geertz, he concentrates overwhelmingly on the domain of religion. Although Turner sees colors and trees as systems of classification, he, like Geertz, does not regard classification as the prime form of expression.

Turner and Geertz alike stress the difficulty of establishing and maintaining a secure sense of place. Dealing with changing societies rather than, like Douglas, stable ones, both are far more attentive than she to threats to a secure place. Douglas herself stresses the need to forge one's place, but she is much less worried than they about threats to the place forged.

If for Geertz the prime threat to a secure place comes from the disparity between one's place in the cosmos and one's place in society, for Turner it comes from the precariousness of one's place in society itself. Turner hardly denies the need for a fit between one's cosmic and one's social place. Indeed, Douglas hardly denies the need either: she simply takes its fulfillment for granted. Turner refuses to take for granted one of the parts: one's social place. Where the disparity on which Geertz focuses is that between the way the *cosmos* purportedly is – the world view – and the way *society* purportedly is – the ethos – the disparity on which Turner focuses is that between the way society *purportedly* is and the way society *actually* is.

For Douglas, one's purported place in the cosmos mirrors one's purported place in society, which mirrors in turn one's actual place. Indeed, Douglas does not really distinguish between one's ideal place and one's actual place. For Turner as well, one's purported place in the cosmos mirrors one's purported place in society, but one's purported place in society by no means mirrors in turn one's actual place. Turner, like Geertz, allows for far more creativity. In forms that he calls "anti-structure," "liminality," and "communitas," culture offers a sharp alternative to one's actual place. That alternative can even serve as a model for creating a new "actual" place.[11] For Geertz, one's purported place in the cosmos can likewise serve as a model for creating an ideal and in turn actual place in society.

For Douglas, too, culture is creative: it *creates* one's sense of place. But that place is created out of one's actual social place rather than, as for Turner and Geertz, out of the imagination. Without that place humans for all three would be lost – cognitively for Douglas, existentially for Turner and Geertz.

The place that culture gives one is for all three the symbolized. It is the subject matter of culture. But once again, culture expresses, not symbolizes, that

---

[10]See Turner (1967:chs. 3 [on colors], 1-2 [on trees]).

[11]Turner even suggests that the classification of bodily emissions is the source rather than, as for Douglas, the expression of socialization, or of one's actual place in society (1967:ch. 3).

"symbolized," in which case none of the three, despite the collective label given them, is, strictly, concerned with symbols.

For Lévi-Strauss, in contrast to the three, symbols do not serve to establish the place of humans in either society or the cosmos. Rather, they presuppose the establishment of the places of humans in both and serve entirely to harmonize those places. Like Geertz, Lévi-Strauss is preoccupied with the tension between one's place in society and one's place in the cosmos. That tension is, as for Douglas, cognitive rather than existential, but it is still, as for Geertz, a tension between one's social and one's cosmic place.

What Lévi-Strauss would mean by both "society" and "cosmos" is, however, different from what Geertz means. For Geertz, the "cosmos" means the entire external world, everything beyond humans. "Society" means the human world. For Lévi-Strauss, the "cosmos," for which he uses the term "nature," means the animal world and, even more specifically, the animal side of humans. "Society," for which he uses the term "culture," means the human world – more precisely, the civilized side of humans. Even more confusing is the distinction rigidly drawn by Geertz and others between "social structure" and "culture." Vis-à-vis "cosmos," "society" does not mean social structure. It means ethos, which, like world view, falls under "culture."

For Geertz, there is no inherent tension between one's cosmic and one's social one. Whatever tension exists stems from the disparity between what one happens to believe about the world as a whole – for example, that it is just – and what one actually experiences in society. For Lévi-Strauss, by contrast, there is an inherently irresolvable tension between, in his terms, "nature" and "culture": between one's anti-social, instinctual side and one's socialized, sublimated side. The conflict is not, as for Geertz, between what one is taught and what one experiences. It is between one's experience of oneself as part of nature and one's experience of oneself as part of civilization. Still, the conflict may well coincide with the difference between what one is taught about human nature and what one experiences.

In any case the conflict cannot be overcome. There can never, as for Geertz, be a fit between culture and nature. But the conflict can be alleviated. Symbols alleviate it in various ways: by juxtaposing to a case of the clash a kindred case which is somehow more easily tolerated, by citing phenomena which manage to encompass aspects of both culture and nature, and by demonstrating that capitulation to either side would prove worse than endurance of the tension between them.

Like Douglas, Lévi-Strauss is intent on showing the pervasiveness of beliefs. For him, as for her, beliefs are everywhere. Cooking, music, art, literature, dress, etiquette, marriage, and economics are among the areas he has analyzed. He considers these areas both in their own right and as topics in myths – for example, the cooking done by mythic characters.

Unlike Douglas, Geertz, and Turner, Lévi-Strauss deems these expressions of belief not mere expressions but also actual symbols. At times he implies that the symbolized is always the opposition between culture and nature, but some of the oppositions surely fall either entirely within culture – matrilineal versus patrilocal kinship – or entirely within nature – life versus death. Still, the prime opposition is that between culture and nature – for Geertz, between society and cosmos. For Turner, the prime, if not sole, opposition is within culture, or society. Douglas, again, does not deal with opposition.

Like Turner, Lévi-Strauss stresses the way symbols not only explicate tensions but also overcome or at least allay them. For Turner, "symbols" – here used loosely for sheer expressions of belief – allay tensions by either the sheer explication of the tensions or the presentation of a better alternative. For Lévi-Strauss, symbols allay tensions only secondarily by the explication of them. Primarily, symbols either present a *worse* alternative, which thereby makes the existing situation preferable by default, or else partially resolve existing tensions by showing them to be less severe and therefore more manageable than they seem. Lévi-Strauss is here like both Geertz and Turner: symbols do not merely reflect the existing situation but create a new one.

As concerned as symbolic anthropologists of both camps are with what symbols do for individuals – namely, order their world – they also are concerned with what symbols do for society. Yet the interest of most of them in the social function of symbols declines. Geertz is far more concerned with the effect of religion on society in his earlier writings than in his later ones, when he becomes much more concerned with the effect of religion on individuals.[12] Turner's focus likewise shifts from society to the individual.[13] Still, both remain concerned with the effect of religion on society. Lévi-Strauss, by contrast, becomes almost indifferent to that effect.[14] Conversely, Douglas' interest in the social effect of religion never wanes.

Because for Douglas the ideal cosmic and social places, which symbols provide, mirror one's actual social place, symbols automatically serve to reinforce that place. Because for Geertz the cosmic place ideally parallels the social one, the cosmic place ideally makes the social one appear natural and thereby reinforces it. In addition, symbols help create the social place itself.

Sometimes symbols for Turner merely depict existing society. Because social conflict is otherwise either missed or ignored, the depiction itself is

---

[12]Of Geertz's earlier writings see esp. Geertz (1960; 1968; 1973:ch. 6, originally published in 1959); of his later ones, Geertz (1973:esp. ch. 4; 1983). Still, he is concerned with the fate of the individual in some of his earliest works: see Geertz (1973:ch. 5, originally published in 1957).

[13]Of Turner's earlier writings see esp. Turner (1957); of his later ones, Turner (1967; 1968; 1969; 1974; 1975; Turner and Turner).

[14]Of Lévi-Strauss' earlier writings see esp. Lévi-Strauss (1967); of his later ones, Lévi-Strauss (1963-76; 1969-81).

efficacious: it compels members of society to recognize the conflict. Where for Douglas symbols articulate existing society in order to *perpetuate* it, for Turner they do so in order to *remedy* it. Other times symbols for Turner present an alternative society – one not necessarily worse than the present one, as for Lévi-Strauss, but simply contrary to it. The alternative society usually gets depicted merely to make the present one clearer by the contrast, not to spur its rejection.

Symbolic Anthropology and Other Approaches to Religion

The approach of symbolic anthropology to religion differs, first, from an irreducibly religious one – the approach of Mircea Eliade (1959) above all. Approached irreducibly religiously, the origin and function of religion are transcendent: religion originates and functions to establish and maintain the relationship of humans to the sacred. The relationships of humans to society and the cosmos either are independent of their relationship to the sacred or else result from that relationship.

For symbolic anthropologists, by contrast, the origin and function of religion are secular: religion originates and functions either to maintain or outright to establish the relationships of humans to society and the cosmos themselves. The establishment and maintenance of a relationship to the sacred are only one means to that end. Even if religion proved the sole means, the end achieved would remain secular. Moreover, that secular end is social as well as individual: religion serves society itself as well as the individual.

The approach of symbolic anthropology differs, second, from an exclusively intellectualist one – the approach of, notably, Tylor (1958). Approached wholly intellectually, the origin and function of religion are proto-scientific: religion originates and functions to explain the cosmos. Even though the explanation provided is supernatural, the need fulfilled is still secular. Even if religion provided the only explanation, the need it fulfilled would remain secular. Moreover, religion here deals entirely with the cosmos, not with society, and deals with the cosmos itself, not with the relationship of humans to it: the explanation provided is of the cosmos itself, not of the place of humans in it.

For symbolic anthropologists, by contrast, the function, not to say origin, of religion is social as well as individual: religion abets society as well as the individual. In dealing with the cosmos, religion deals not with it in itself but with the relationship of humans to it. For Douglas, Geertz, and Turner, religion serves, furthermore, not only to explain that relationship but, even more, to establish it in the first place.

The approach of symbolic anthropologists differs, third, from an exclusively social functionalist one – the approach, to varying degrees, of Durkheim (1965), Radcliffe-Brown (1922), Malinowski (1925), and, taken negatively, Marx (1957) and Freud (1950). Approached functionally, the origin and function of religion are entirely social: religion originates and functions to preserve society. More precisely, religion either originates to preserve society or, whatever its origin, simply effects the preservation of society. If "social function" is taken to mean intended social effect, none of the figures cited save perhaps the Freud of *Totem and Taboo* qualifies as a social functionalist. If, more typically, "social function" is taken to mean sheer effect, Durkheim, Radcliffe-Brown, Malinowski, and perhaps Marx also qualify as functionalists. Indeed, Durkheim, Radcliffe-Brown, and Malinowski are the founders of the "functionalist" school.

Approving of existing society, Durkheim, Radcliffe-Brown, and Malinowski approve of the role religion plays in maintaining it. Disapproving of existing society, Marx and Freud disapprove of that same role. For both groups, religion may well explain and justify the relationships of humans to society and the cosmos, but it serves only to keep humans in their social place. Rather than, moreover, first creating that place, religion presupposes it and simply reinforces it. The place of humans in the cosmos serves simply to legitimate their place in society.

For symbolic anthropologists, by contrast, the origin and function of religion are, once again, individual as well as social: religion serves to abet the individual at least as much as society itself. Religion upholds the place of humans in the cosmos as well as in society and upholds both places as an end in itself, not merely as a means to a social end. For Douglas, Geertz, and Turner, religion creates those places in the first place.

Symbolic anthropologists find symbols in far more domains than religion. Most of human life is for them symbolic. They focus on religion because it provides so strong a case for their fundamental tenet: that human behavior is motivated by beliefs. Where other areas of life like kinship and economics presuppose beliefs, religion appears to be fundamentally a set of beliefs themselves. Religious belief, moreover, appears to be the most deeply held of all beliefs. Because it matters so much to humans, it demonstrates the power of belief for them.

Symbolic anthropologists find religious symbols in far more domains than creeds and other conventional expressions of belief. Lévi-Strauss finds them in myths. More strikingly, Douglas, Turner, and Geertz find them in rituals, which, as physical activities, might seem to be the least likely expressions of belief. The three nevertheless interpret rituals as mental activities, as statements of belief.

Recently, there have appeared three works applying the tenets of symbolic anthropology to the religions of the Greco-Roman world: Christianity, Judaism, and paganism. In *The Lord's Table* Gillian Feeley-Harnik applies the theory of Douglas to the Last Supper. In *The Passover Seder* Ruth Fredman applies the theory of Lévi-Strauss to the Seder. In *The Meaning of Aphrodite* Paul Friedrich applies the theory of Turner to the goddess Aphrodite. No work has appeared so far which applies the theory of Geertz to any Greco-Roman religion. The work which best applies Geertz's theory to religion of any kind is Sherry Ortner's *Sherpas through their Rituals*.

The Last Supper

Following Douglas' study of Leviticus 11, Feeley-Harnik focuses on dietary laws as the key element of Jewish life in the Greco-Roman era. At first glance, she seems to be a sheer social functionalist. She asserts that dietary laws were a means of maintaining group membership: they determined with whom, not just what, one could eat. They served to give Jews a place in society – more precisely, to do so for the purpose of controlling both the membership and the behavior of the group. Were Feeley-Harnik to assert that dietary laws served to give Jews a place in society for its own sake as well, she would be a symbolic anthropologist. For the purpose of the laws would then have been not only social but also individual. But at first glance she deems their sole purpose social. Ironically, Douglas herself is least functionalist in analyzing Jewish dietary laws, which she explicitly denies were *intended* to keep Jews apart from others.[15]

Early Christians as well, continues Feeley-Harnik, used dietary laws for wholly social ends: to win converts and to rule the converted. Christians appealed to Jesus' violation of those laws as justification for their break with Judaism and so for their freedom from its control. Jesus, notes Feeley-Harnik, gathered food on the Sabbath, ate without washing, ate anything, and ate with anyone. At the Last Supper Christians themselves ate not an animal but a human being, and in consuming his body and blood violated the prohibition of their mixing. The Crucifixion violated the Passover in various ways: it occurred not at midnight but at midday, occurred not at the Temple but outside it, affected not only Jews but all humanity, and was not the sacrifice of a scapegoat but self-sacrifice.

Feeley-Harnik does not deny that Hellenistic Jews and early Christians genuinely believed in God. She does not deny that they were consciously observing or violating dietary laws for religious reasons: to maintain, if not outright establish, their relationship to God. She is simply asserting that their primary reasons were social: to maintain their relationship to their own group – not, again, in order to have a place in society but in order to be kept in that place. Religion was a means to this end, not the end itself. Alternatively, she may, as a social functionalist, be asserting only that the *effect* of the observance or violation of dietary laws was "social solidarity," not that that effect was even unconsciously intended.

In actuality, Feeley-Harnik is more than a social functionalist. She is a symbolic anthropologist. She contends that the function of dietary laws was not

---

[15]See Douglas (1970:61-62, 71).

only social but also individual: the laws served to give individual Jews a place in society for its own sake as well as for the sake of controlling them. Furthermore, the laws served to establish, not simply reinforce, the social place of Hellenistic Jews and early Christians. The observance of the laws defined, not merely bolstered, relations among Jews, and their violation defined, not merely bolstered, relations among Christians. At the same time religion was only a means to a secular end: a place per se, not a religious place in particular.

As preoccupied as Feeley-Harnik is with the place of Jews in society, she is also concerned with their place in the cosmos. Dietary laws, she argues, prescribed the relationship of Jews to the physical world as well as to one another. The laws determined what, not just with whom, one could eat.

Here, too, the laws served not simply to explain the existing place of humans in the cosmos but also to establish that place altogether. They served not only to explain why some food was edible and some not but, more, to determine what food was edible and what not. They shaped, not merely explained, Jews' experience of the physical world in the form of food.

Again, Feeley-Harnik is hardly denying that Jews were consciously observing dietary laws for religious reasons: to link themselves to God. She is simply asserting that their primary reasons were to link themselves to both society and the cosmos. Indeed, at times she emphasizes the religious reasons *over* the secular ones.

How does Feeley-Harnik prove that the reasons for upholding or violating dietary laws were at all secular and not exclusively religious? She cannot, and does not, appeal to any statements of Jews or Christians, for their explicit reasons are entirely religious. Any secular reasons must therefore be implicit. Nor does she appeal to the incorrectness of a religious explanation. For her, as for Douglas, dietary laws did serve a religious function. They simply served secular functions as well.

Like Douglas, Feeley-Harnik appeals instead to the inadequacy of a religious explanation: to its inability to explain all aspects of the observance or violation of dietary laws. Unlike Douglas, she also appeals to the sheer compatibility of secular explanations with a religious one.

Feeley-Harnik justifies neither appeal. To take them in reverse order: rather than demonstrating that a secular explanation of dietary laws is compatible with a religious one, she simply takes their compatibility for granted. There are many arguments she could muster. First, she could argue that dietary laws, like any other phenomenon, can have multiple origins and, even more, functions, so that the existence of a religious origin or function would not preclude a secular one. Second, she could argue that the specific secular origins and functions she proposes do not challenge the truth of religion and could therefore have been accepted by Jews and Christians themselves. Third, she could argue that those secular origins and functions were in fact unconscious and therefore need not have been acceptable to believers. Fourth, she could argue that those functions were only unintended consequences, in which case as well they need not have been acceptable to believers. Feeley-Harnik herself provides no arguments for the compatibility of a secular explanation with a religious one.

Nor does she provide any arguments for the inadequacy of a religious explanation. She does tacitly argue that a religious explanation cannot explain the secular aspects of dietary laws, but she thereby takes for granted exactly what she must prove: the existence of those aspects in the first place. Whether Jewish dietary laws were observed or violated for overtly religious reasons is not, again, the issue. Whether they were observed or violated for any other reasons is.

On the one hand historians of religions who follow Eliade would dogmatically deny the possibility. They would claim *a priori* that secular reasons did not exist; were secondary if they did; and, if important, had nothing to do with religion: for Eliade, only a religious origin can yield religion. The dogmatism lies not in the appeal itself to these claims in even every case but in the *unsupported* appeal to them. Their cogency is assumed rather than proved.

On the other hand Feeley-Harnik, for her part, is seemingly no less dogmatic. Although she does not, like Eliade, presume to generalize to all cases of religion, she does not, like Marx, Freud, and other *nondogmatic* social scientists, *argue* for the inadequacy of an exclusively religious explanation of religion. It is not enough for her to say that a secular explanation is *possible*. Many things are possible. It is necessary for her to *show* that a secular explanation is *probable* – by showing the inadequacy of an exclusively religious one.

Feeley-Harnik could, most readily, argue for merely the secular effects, not origins, of the observation or violation of dietary laws. But she herself assumes that those effects were *intended*, consciously or otherwise. She is claiming not merely that the practice or rejection of dietary laws had secular consequences but also that those consequences were sought. To prove them intentional, however, she must appeal to their importance for believers, but that importance is what she must first prove. She must first prove that Hellenistic Jews and early Christians cared about the secular effects of dietary laws *before* appealing to their caring as evidence of the intendedness and therefore importance of those effects. In short, Feeley-Harnik fails to prove that dietary laws served significant social or intellectual, not merely religious, functions.

The Seder

Fredman applies Lévi-Strauss' analysis of myth to the *ritual* of the Passover Seder. She argues that the Seder constitutes a means of communicating information, as myth and ritual do for Douglas, Geertz, and Turner as well: to say that culture expresses beliefs is to say that it conveys them. In distinctively structuralist fashion the Seder message gets presented redundantly in order to insure its getting understood. That message is, as for Lévi-Strauss, the presentation and alleviation of the contradiction humans experience between themselves as part of nature and themselves as part of culture. But where for Lévi-Strauss myths alleviate the contradiction by partially reconciling nature with culture, for Fredman, who herself misses the difference, the Seder alleviates it by transforming nature into culture. Where for Lévi-Strauss "nature" means humans' animal side, which "coexists" with their civilized side, for Fredman it means humans' animal state before its transformation into civilization.

For Fredman, as for Feeley-Harnik, religion serves multiple functions. Even more than for Feeley-Harnik, religion for Fredman functions primarily to give individuals a sense of place – in society, the cosmos, and even heaven. In all three locales it transports Jews from a state of nature to one of culture. Socially, the move from nature to culture is from an assimilated Jewry to a separate one. "Cosmically," the move is from undifferentiated participation in the world – one can eat anything – to differentiated participation – one can eat only certain things. Religiously, the move is from sinfulness to salvation.

Like dietary laws for Feeley-Harnik, the Seder for Fredman is creative as well as supportive. It does not simply bolster Jews' experiences of society, the cosmos, and God but also helps fashion them. Even more than dietary laws for Feeley-Harnik, the Seder does so by categorizing phenomena. It gives Jews their social place exactly by distinguishing them from Gentiles. It gives Jews their cosmic place by distinguishing the parts of nature they can eat from the parts they cannot. It gives Jews their religious place by distinguishing obedience to God from disobedience. Without these distinctions Jews would lack not just reinforcement for their places but the places themselves. Without the distinctions Jews would live not, for example, in an unexplained Jewish society but in none at all.

For Fredman, the Seder functions socially as well as individually. The move from an assimilated to a separate Jewry serves not only to give Jews a place in society but also to keep them in it. Like dietary laws for Feeley-Harnik, the Seder for Fredman thus serves to maintain the identification of Jews as Jews. The Seder functions religiously as well. The move from a sinful to a saved Jewry serves not only to give Jews a place in heaven but also to keep them in it. Like, again, dietary laws for Feeley-Harnik, the Seder for Fredman serves to maintain the devotion of Jews to God.

Fredman's main argument for secular, not merely religious, explanations of the Seder is like Feeley-Harnik's. She appeals not to the incorrectness but, like Lévi-Strauss himself, to the inadequacy of a religious explanation. She tacitly argues that a religious explanation cannot explain precisely the secular dimensions of the Seder. But she, no less than Feeley-Harnik, fails to prove either that those dimensions exist in the first place or that, even if they do, they are more than coincidental. To prove them intentional, as she claims they are, she, too, must presuppose exactly what she is seeking to prove: that those aspects are too important to believers to have been unintended.

Aphrodite

Friedrich applies Turner's theory of ritual and, secondarily, Lévi-Strauss' theory of myth to Aphrodite. Examining the behavior, if not quite the rituals, of the goddess described in myths, he argues that she symbolizes at once both sides of one contradiction and only one side of another.

Friedrich argues first that Aphrodite embraces both sides of the fundamental, Lévi-Straussian contradiction between nature and culture. She is, notably, (1) a goddess with whom mortals dare have sex, (2) a goddess whom mortals dare see naked, (3) a female who can have extramarital sex without becoming polluted, (4) a female who takes the initiative sexually, (5) a female who is both lover and mother, and (6) a female whose love making is both instinctual and refined.

It is hardly clear how all of these contradictions, like many of Lévi-Strauss' own, are between nature and culture, at least when nature means the animal-like side of humans and culture their civilized side. At best, only the last two fit these definitions. In the other cases, and likely in the last two as well, the contradictions lie not between nature and culture but within culture itself.

In some of these cases females are barred from activities open to males: engaging in extramarital sex, taking the initiative in sex, and, on the part of goddesses, engaging in sex with mortals and appearing naked before them. The contradiction here is between femininity and sexuality. In other cases females are barred from dual activities either open or irrelevant to males: being both lover and parent and practicing both instinctual and refined love. The contradiction here is between one aspect of femininity and another.

Yet because nature finds compatible activities which culture deems contradictory, there does result a contradiction between nature and culture, even if it stems from contradictions within culture itself. Conversely, culture considers these contradictions to lie between it and nature: for females to violate the civilized, or cultural, taboo against extramarital sex, for example, is animal-like, or natural.

To the extent that the contradictions are between nature and culture, as Friedrich says they are, he is following Lévi-Strauss. To the extent that they are within culture, or society, itself, as is in fact more probable, he is following Turner. To the extent that they are contradictions, as they certainly are, he is following either Turner or Lévi-Strauss rather than either Douglas or Geertz.

Turner considers humans anti-social. Symbols are therefore necessary not only to give them a place in society but also to reconcile them to it. By contrast, Douglas and Geertz consider humans merely asocial. Symbols are necessary only to wed, not reconcile, them to society. Lévi-Strauss deems contradictory humans' social and cosmic places themselves. Symbols must therefore reconcile, not merely link, them. By contrast, Douglas and Geertz deem those places merely independent, not contradictory, so that symbols need only link, not reconcile, them.

If for Friedrich the contradictions Aphrodite resolves are between nature and culture, or cosmos and society, the contradictions are, as for Lévi-Strauss, between the cosmic and the social places of humans. If, as is more likely, the contradictions are within culture, or society, itself, they are, as for Turner, between humans and their social place.

In explaining how Aphrodite resolves contradictions, wherever they lie, Friedrich follows Turner rather than Lévi-Strauss. For Lévi-Strauss, a single symbol harbors only one side of a contradiction, the representation of which requires a pair of symbols. The resolution of the contradiction requires an additional symbol or pair of symbols to bridge it. For Turner, a single symbol harbors both sides of the contradiction and bridges it by its containment of both. As a single symbol embracing both halves of the contradictions she resolves, Aphrodite for Friedrich thus functions like symbols for Turner rather than for Lévi-Strauss.

For symbolic anthropologists, a symbol *can* be the representation of the symbolized. It simply need not be. It can be either the literal place of humans in society and the cosmos or the representation of that place. What counts is that a symbol serve individual as well as social ends.

For Friedrich, it does. Aphrodite served to give Greek women places in both society and the cosmos. In structuralist fashion their social place got defined vis-à-vis that of men: women were those humans barred from various activities either open or irrelevant to men. Women's participation in them was therefore, in contrast to men's, contradictory. Women and men constituted a contradiction in turn. In resolving the contradictions in the social place of women, Aphrodite thus helped resolve the contradiction between their social place and that of men: the resolution of contradictions imposed exclusively on women left women more like men.

The cosmic place of women got defined vis-à-vis that of goddesses. On the one hand women were females barred from various male activities open to their divine counterparts: engaging in extramarital sex and taking the initiative in sex. On the other hand women were females even the divine counterparts of whom were barred from various activities open to males: having sex with mortals and appearing naked before them. On the one hand only goddesses were free of some of the restrictions, or contradictions, imposed on females. On the other hand not even they were free of others.

Like symbols for not only Turner but also Douglas and Geertz, Aphrodite for Friedrich functioned to establish, not merely reinforce, the social and cosmic places of Greek women. She also served to link those places. She did so the way symbols link the two for Geertz above all. As a divinity, Aphrodite bestowed cosmic sanction on the social place of her human "sisters": her place in Olympian society explained and justified their restricted place in human society. In turn, the place of women in human society evinced and thereby confirmed the cosmic place of females: the actual, daily submission of women to the restrictions imposed on all females made those restrictions real.

Providing cosmic sanction for social norms and social expression for cosmic ones presupposes the compatibility of the social and cosmic places of human beings. The contradiction resolved by Aphrodite must therefore be, as for Turner, between humans and their social place. Were it to be between the social and the cosmic places of humans, other, Lévi-Straussian means of reconciling them would be necessary.

For Friedrich, Aphrodite functioned socially as well as individually. If individually she served to give Greek women places in society and the cosmos, socially she served to keep them in their social place. In sanctioning their social place, Aphrodite was serving to keep them in it.

Since, however, Aphrodite functioned to resolve, not perpetuate, contradictions in Greek society, her true function was revolutionary: in resolving contradictions imposed on Greek women by culture, she was freeing women of them. Individually, she was freeing women, if not also men, of the restrictions those contradictions imposed on the definitions of women's social and cosmic places. Socially, she was freeing women, if not also men, of the restrictions those contradictions imposed on women's social place. In emphasizing the rebelliousness of Aphrodite, Friedrich is following Turner, who is especially concerned with the anti-social as well as social consequences of ritualistic behavior.

Unlike both Feeley-Harnik and Fredman, Friedrich ignores any religious function. He nowhere *denies* that Aphrodite served either to establish or to maintain the relationship of Greek women to the gods. He simply concentrates entirely on her serving to establish and maintain their relationships to society and the cosmos, whether as an end in itself or as a means to a social end.

Because Friedrich never denies that Aphrodite served a religious function, a religious explanation must for him be merely inadequate, not incorrect. To prove it inadequate he, like Feeley-Harnik and Fredman, must prove the existence of the additional, nonreligious functions he cites. But because he, too, seeks to prove the importance, not merely the existence, of those functions, he faces the same predicament as they. Aphrodite's secular functions were important only if important to Greek women, who must therefore have intended them, but the evidence of their intent is the importance of those functions to them.

Having argued that Aphrodite symbolizes and thereby reconciles both sides of various contradictions in females, Friedrich asserts that she also symbolizes only one side of another uniquely female contradiction: that between females as lovers and females as mothers. Inexplicably, Friedrich earlier deemed this contradiction one of the ones symbolized by Aphrodite alone. Now she somehow symbolizes only the erotic side of females. Demeter symbolizes the maternal side. Like the contradictions symbolized by Aphrodite alone, this one is seemingly between culture and nature but is in fact within culture itself, which creates it. Like the contradictions symbolized by Aphrodite alone as well, this one restricts females, who cannot simultaneously love and mother.

Unlike the contradictions symbolized wholly by Aphrodite, this one never gets reconciled. Friedrich's explanation, that the contradiction is too deeply embedded in culture to be resolvable, begs the question. His evidence that the contradiction goes unresolved is its representation by two symbols, Aphrodite and Demeter, rather than one. For him, as for Turner, the resolution of a contradiction requires a single, all-encompassing symbol. Friedrich no more proves the existence of this unresolved contradiction than he does that of the resolved ones. Admittedly, he need prove that Aphrodite and Demeter only present, not resolve, this contradiction, but his tacit proof involves the same circular argument that his proof of the existence of the resolved contradictions does.

REFERENCES

BERGER, PETER L.

1970   *A Rumor of Angels*. Garden City, N.Y.: Doubleday Anchor Books. Original publ.: Garden City, N.Y.: Doubleday, 1969.

1980   *The Heretical Imperative*. Garden City, N.Y.: Doubleday Anchor Books. Original publ.: Garden City, N.Y.: Doubleday, 1979.

DOUGLAS, MARY

1970   *Purity and Danger*. Baltimore: Penguin Books. Original publ.: London: Routledge & Kegan Paul, 1966.

1973   *Natural Symbols*. Second ed. New York: Vintage Books. Original publ. of first ed.: New York: Pantheon, 1970.

1975   *Implicit Meanings*. London and Boston: Routledge & Kegan Paul.

1979   "World View and the Core." In *Philosophical Disputes in the Social Sciences,* ed. S. C. Brown, pp. 177-87. Sussex, Eng.: Harvester Press; Atlantic Highlands, N.J.: Humanities Press.

1982   *In the Active Voice*. London and Boston: Routledge & Kegan Paul.

1986   *How Institutions Think*. Syracuse, N.Y.: Syracuse University Press.

DURKHEIM, ÉMILE

1965   *The Elementary Forms of the Religious Life*. Tr. Joseph Ward Swain. New York: Free Press. Original publ. of tr.: London: Allen & Unwin, 1915.

ELIADE, MIRCEA

1959   *The Sacred and the Profane.* Tr. Willard R. Trask. New York: Harcourt, Brace.

EVANS-PRITCHARD, E. E.

1937   *Witchcraft, Oracles and Magic among the Azande.* Oxford: Clarendon Press.

1951   *Social Anthropology.* London: Cohen & West.

1956   *Nuer Religion.* Oxford: Clarendon Press.

1962   *Essays in Social Anthropology.* London: Faber & Faber.

1965   *Theories of Primitive Religion.* Oxford: Clarendon.

1981   *A History of Anthropological Thought.* Ed. André Singer. Basic Books.

FEELEY-HARNIK, GILLIAN

1981   *The Lord's Table.* Philadelphia: University of Pennsylvania Press.

FRAZER, JAMES G.

1922   *The Golden Bough.* One-vol. abridgment. London: Macmillan.

FREDMAN, RUTH GRUBER

1981   *The Passover Seder.* Philadelphia: University of Pennsylvania Press.

FREUD, SIGMUND

1950   *Totem and Taboo.* Tr. James Strachey. New York: Norton.

FRIEDRICH, PAUL

1978   *The Meaning of Aphrodite.* Chicago: University of Chicago Press.

GEERTZ, CLIFFORD

1960   *The Religion of Java.* Glencoe, Ill.: Free Press.

1968   *Islam Observed.* New Haven, Conn.: Yale University Press.

1973   *The Interpretation of Cultures.* New York: Basic Books.

1983   *Local Knowledge.* New York: Basic Books.

JUNG, CARL G.

1938   *Psychology and Religion.* New Haven, Conn.: Yale University Press.

LÉVI-STRAUSS, CLAUDE

1963-76 *Structural Anthropology.* 2 vols. Trs. Claire Jacobson and Brooke Grundfest Schoepf (vol. I) and Monique Layton (vol. II). New York: Basic Books.

1966   *The Savage Mind.* Tr. not given. Chicago: University of Chicago Press.

1967   "The Story of Asdiwal." In *The Structural Study of Myth and Totemism,* ed. Edmund Leach, pp. 1-47. A. S. A. Monographs, No. 5. London: Tavistock.

1969-81   *Introduction to a Science of Mythology.* 4 vols. Trs. John and Doreen Weightman. New York: Harper.

1978   *Myth and Meaning.* Toronto: University of Toronto Press.

MALINOWSKI, BRONISLAW
1925   "Magic, Science and Religion." In *Science, Religion and Reality,* ed. Joseph Needham, pp. 20-84. New York and London: Macmillan.

MARX, KARL, AND FRIEDRICH ENGELS
1957   *On Religion.* Moscow: Foreign Languages Publishing.

ORTNER, SHERRY
1978   *Sherpas through their Rituals.* Cambridge, Eng.: Cambridge University Press.

RADCLIFFE-BROWN, A. R.
1922   *The Andaman Islanders.* Cambridge, Eng.: Cambridge University Press.

SEGAL, ROBERT A.
1980   "The Social Sciences and the Truth of Religious Belief." *Journal of the American Academy of Religion* 48 (September):403-13. Reprinted in revised form in the present book as ch. 7.

1981   "Sir Edward Evans-Pritchard, *A History of Anthropological Thought.*" *Annals of Scholarship* 2 (Winter):119-28.

1983   "Victor Turner's Theory of Ritual." *Zygon* 18 (September):327-35. Reprinted in revised form in the present book as ch. 11.

TURNER, VICTOR W.
1957   *Schism and Continuity in an African Society.* Manchester, Eng.: Manchester University Press.

1967   *The Forest of Symbols.* Ithaca, N.Y.: Cornell University Press.

1968   *The Drums of Affliction.* Oxford: Clarendon Press.

1969   *The Ritual Process.* Chicago: Aldine.

1974   *Dramas, Fields, and Metaphors.* Ithaca, N.Y.: Cornell University Press.

1975   *Revelation and Divination in Ndembu Ritual.* Ithaca, N.Y.: Cornell University Press.

1985   *On the Edge of the Bush.* Ed. Edith L. B. Turner. Tucson: University of Arizona Press.

TURNER, VICTOR, AND EDITH TURNER
1978   *Image and Pilgrimage in Christian Culture.* ACLS Lectures on the History of Religions, n.s., no. 11. New York: Columbia University Press.

TYLOR, EDWARD B.
1958   *Primitive Culture*. 2 vols. New York: Harper Torchbooks. Vol. I is retitled *The Origins of Culture* and vol. II retitled *Religion in Primitive Culture*. Original publ. of first ed. London: Murray, 1871.

Chapter Thirteen

Relativism and Rationality in the Social Sciences: A Review Essay of Lucien Lévy-Bruhl's *How Natives Think*

Lucien Lévy-Bruhl, a philosopher who became an armchair anthropologist, continues to be of interest to both anthropologists and philosophers. His first and most important anthropological work, *How Natives Think*, was originally published in 1910 and translated into English only in 1926 – three years after the translation of his second and next most important anthropological work: *Primitive Mentality*, originally published in 1922. For a reprint of *How Natives Think*[1] anthropologist C. Scott Littleton has written a provocative fifty-page introduction. He argues that Lévy-Bruhl has been both less reviled (xxi-xxvii) and more influential (xxvii-xlii) among anthropologists than is recognized. Lévy-Bruhl, he claims, "anticipated," whether or not abetted, the trend in anthropology toward "cognitive relativity."

Relativism

There are various kinds of relativism. Moral relativism denies that objective criteria exist for evaluating the undeniable diversity of *values* and *practices*. Conceptual relativism, to which Littleton is referring, denies the existence of objective criteria for assessing the diversity of *beliefs* about the world. Perceptual relativism, which is more radical, denies the possibility of evaluating objectively the diversity of *experiences* of the world. Conceptual relativism allows for common experiences that simply get interpreted differently. Perceptual relativism, which entails but also reflects its conceptual counterpart, maintains that experiences themselves differ. People "occupy" different worlds altogether – with no way to judge the differences.

Most modern anthropologists are relativists. The staunchest ones have been Franz Boas and his students, especially Ruth Benedict and Melville Herskovits.[2] Says Herskovits of perception, for example: "Even the facts of the physical world are discerned through the enculturative screen, so that the perception of

---

[1] All unidentified references in the chapter are to this edition of this book.
[2] See Benedict (esp. 278), Herskovits (ch. 5).

time, distance, weight, size, and other 'realities' is mediated by the conventions of any given group" (Herskovits, 64). Anthropological nonrelativists are invariably "universalists" rather than "absolutists": they argue that cultures are the same, not that one is superior to the others.[3] Both sides typically commit the naturalistic fallacy: jumping from the *fact* of either diversity or uniformity to the *norm* of it.

The most prominent contemporary relativist is Clifford Geertz.[4] In stressing religion and other cultural systems as attempts to make experience meaningful, he is seemingly only a conceptual relativist: the cultural systems of each society are responses to the same kinds of inexplicable, unendurable, or unjustifiable experiences.[5] But in describing those cultural systems, Geertz presents the differing concepts of person, time, and social behavior that shape, not merely reflect, each people's experiences.[6] Yet if, then, he is a perceptual as well as conceptual relativist, he is no moral one: he is content with understanding, not evaluating, alien values.

Littleton makes the extraordinary claim that Lévy-Bruhl, the nemesis of anthropological relativists, is himself an even greater one: "What his critics failed to realize, of course, was that Lévy-Bruhl was as much, if not more, of a relativist than they were" (xx). In part Littleton is certainly right: in the name of relativism the "Boasians" and others take for granted that other cultures, grasped in their own terms, are rational. Lévy-Bruhl's claim that other cultures see themselves otherwise makes the assumption of universal rationality parochial. Says Littleton: "... the logical rules [the Boasians] implicitly assumed to be universal were in fact themselves cultural artifacts" (xx).[7]

But Lévy-Bruhl is in actuality no relativist. He is an absolutist. His stress on the different ways primitives both perceive and conceptualize the world does not mean, as Littleton assumes, that those ways are for him correct. Littleton rightly emphasizes that Lévy-Bruhl never says, as he is accused, that primitives are inferior to moderns. Ironically, he means to be defending primitives *against* this charge, one made above all by Edward Tylor and James Frazer: "... let us abandon the attempt to refer their mental activity to an inferior variety of our

---

[3]See Linton, Kluckhohn (1962:chs. 16-17; 1949:41-42), Bidney (1953a:423-29; 1953b; 1968), Spiro (1978; 1982:ch. 6; 1984; 1986).
[4]See Geertz (1984). Yet far more radical is Douglas, who at times (1975:ix-xxi) is an uncompromising relativist over not only, like Geertz, empirical claims — what is a true conception or perception — but even logical ones — what constitutes truth, meaning, evidence, argument, and rationality.
[5]See Geertz (1968; 1973:chs. 4, 8; 1983:ch. 4).
[6]See Geertz (1973:ch. 14; 1983:ch. 3). To be sure, Geertz (1973:ch. 2) opposes not the claim of cultural universals but only the consequent dismissal of cultural differences.
[7]But Littleton also says inconsistently that, as relativists, the Boasians themselves never presupposed that "a particular culture has evolved the rule of non-contradiction" (xvi).

own" (76). For Tylor and Frazer, primitive thinking differs only in degree from modern, with which it can therefore be compared: primitives think less rigorously than moderns. For Lévy-Bruhl, primitive thinking differs in kind from modern and therefore runs askew to it. The reason is not, however, that primitives' minds differ but that their "collective representations," or group beliefs, do: "Undoubtedly they [primitives] have the same senses as ours ... and their cerebral structure is like our own. But we have to bear in mind that which their collective representations instil *[sic]* into all their perceptions" (43). Primitive conceptions shape their perceptions, or experiences (43-45, 106).

Prelogical Mentality

Primitives believe not, as for Tylor,[8] that all natural phenomena possess individual, human-like spirits but that all phenomena, including humans and their artifacts, are part of an impersonal sacred, or "mystic," realm pervading the natural one: "Primitive man, therefore, lives and acts in an environment of beings and objects, all of which, in addition to the [observable] properties that we recognize them to possess, are endued with mystic attributes" (65). Primitives believe, further, that the "participation" of all things in this mystic reality enables phenomena not only to affect one another magically (77-78) but also to become one another yet remain what they are: "... phenomena can be ... both themselves and something other than themselves" (76). The Bororo of Brazil declare themselves red parakeets: "This does not merely signify that after their death they become araras [parakeets], nor that araras are metamorphosed Bororos .... It is not a name they give themselves, nor a relationship that they claim. What they desire to express by it is actual identity" (77).

Lévy-Bruhl calls this belief "prelogical" because it violates the law of noncontradiction: the notion that something can simultaneously be both itself and something else. Primitives believe that all things are at once not simply mystically one, itself not contradictory, but also distinct. The Bororo believe that a human is really a parakeet yet still really a human. Lévy-Bruhl concludes not, as is conventionally said of him,[9] that primitives cannot think logically but that, ruled by their collective representations, they regularly suspend the practice of logic: primitive thought "is not *antilogical;* it is not *alogical* either. By designating it 'prelogical' I merely wish to state that it does not bind itself down, as our thought does, to avoiding contradiction" (78).

In arguing relentlessly that primitive thinking differs in kind from modern thinking, Lévy-Bruhl is not, however, arguing that it is equally true. In asserting that, as Littleton puts it, primitive thinking "must be understood *on its own*

---

[8] See Tylor (esp. II:chs. 11, 14). For other differences between Lévy-Bruhl and Tylor see Segal (1980:22-26).

[9] See, for example, Radin (13-15). Ironically, Radin's alternative to Lévy-Bruhl is in fact nearly identical with Lévy-Bruhl's own view.

terms" (xiv), he is not asserting that it must be *judged* on those terms. Primitive thinking does make sense in light of its premises, but its premises are false.

Even though moderns as well as primitives have collective representations, primitive ones alone come between them and direct experience of the world. Modern ones shape conceptions, not perceptions, which are not "theory-laden" (375-76). In a section entitled "The Transition to the Higher Mental Types" (361-86) Lévy-Bruhl speaks of "progress" and "evolution" in cognition, which requires the filtering out of the emotional elements that color primitive perceptions (380-81). Only modern representations are subject to "the test of experience" (380-81).

Many others no less absolutist than Lévy-Bruhl have been criticized far less severely. The reason, disputed by Littleton (xix-xx), is that, despite his undeniably neutral intent, Lévy-Bruhl in fact characterizes primitive mentality far more negatively than even Tylor and Frazer do: as outright "prelogical" rather than merely less logical. Other absolutists grant that primitives recognize not only the law of noncontradiction but most "modern" distinctions as well: between appearance and reality, subjectivity and objectivity, supernatural and natural, human and nonhuman, living and dead, literal and symbolic, part and whole, individual and group, one time and another, and one space and another. Lévy-Bruhl contends that primitives usually recognize none of these distinctions.[10] He is therefore really saying not simply that primitives think less acutely than moderns but that, by modern criteria, they scarcely think at all.

For example, the efficacy of magic for Frazer[11] does presuppose the dissolution of the distinctions between the literal and the symbolic – otherwise a voodoo doll would merely symbolize, not affect, a person – and between a part and the whole – otherwise a severed strand of hair would merely have once been part of a person, not still affect him. Yet Frazer never assumes that primitives in even the earliest, magical stage are oblivious to the distinctions between appearance and reality, subjectivity and objectivity, and supernatural and natural. Moreover, these distinctions involve not just conception but also perception, which Frazer, together with Tylor, considers invariant.[12] For Frazer and Tylor, primitives merely believe, not perceive, the identity of a voodoo doll with a person. In Frazer's stages of magic and religion alike primitives may get angry at a stone over which they stumble, as if the stone had tripped them, but they still

---

[10]But at least once Lévy-Bruhl does say that primitives recognize, even if blur, the difference between supernatural and natural (1935:34).

[11]See Tylor (I:112-41), Frazer (chs. 3-4).

[12]To be sure, Tylor does say that in dreams, visions, and other abnormal states primitive perceptions differ from modern ones, but then they differ from normal primitive ones as well (I:286, 297, 305-6ff.; II:29-31, 62, 83-84, 275, 280, 442).

experience it as a stone.[13] Both Frazer and Tylor are conceptual absolutists – pre-scientific beliefs are false – but perceptual universalists – all perceptions are the same.

In above all *How Natives Think* Lévy-Bruhl explicitly follows Émile Durkheim's fundamental principle that primitive beliefs not only are social, or "collective," rather than individual but also must therefore be explained socially rather than, as for Tylor and Frazer, individually: "Collective representations are social phenomena .... [S]ocial phenomena have their own laws, and laws which the analysis of the individual *qua* individual could never reveal" (23). For Lévy-Bruhl, following Durkheim,[14] moderns as well as primitives have collective representations; representations are primarily categorizations; without representations individuals would have no thoughts rather than merely private ones; primitive representations shape perception as well as conception; primitive representations are more emotion-laden than modern ones; primitive representations constitute religion, modern ones science; science succeeds religion as the explanation of the world; religion is false, science true.

Yet Durkheim severely criticizes Lévy-Bruhl[15] for exaggerating the differences between primitives and moderns. For Durkheim, primitives recognize the same categories as moderns and are therefore not prelogical.[16] Indeed, science inherits these categories from primitive religion. Without primitive religion there would be no science, even though science subsequently rivals religion. Admittedly, science is more nearly objective than religion. It is critical, unemotional, and testable. But it differs from religion in degree only.[17]

Durkheim does acknowledge that at least primitive religion, by personifying the world, blurs the line between the human and the nonhuman. Clan members, for example, identify themselves with their animal or plant totem. But Durkheim then argues that these connections, though false, spur the search for others and so even here spur the rise of science.[18]

Mary Douglas shares Lévy-Bruhl's preoccupation with categorizations yet is sharply critical of him.[19] She argues, first, that primitive religion, even when used for practical ends, does not work magically. A rain dance, for example, presumably serves to ask god for rain, not to imitate god's bringing it. She

---

[13]On the differences between primitives and moderns as conceptual rather than perceptual see Tylor (II:51-64, 246-53ff.).

[14]See Durkheim (1965:21-33, 267-72, 476-96; Durkheim and Mauss).

[15]See Durkheim (1965:267-72; 1975:169-73).

[16]But Durkheim does say, most surprisingly, that primitives often violate the law of noncontradiction (1965:25).

[17]See Durkheim (1965:270, 477, 486, 493; 1975:171). Though Durkheim also stresses the social role of majority opinion in determining objectivity, he never dismisses testing as an objective measure (1965:486-87).

[18]See Durkheim (1965:269-72).

[19]See Douglas (1970a:92-94; 1980:chs. 2-3).

argues, second, that primitive religion not only presupposes the distinction between the literal and the symbolic but itself often serves to symbolize other categorizations that, contrary to Lévy-Bruhl, primitives make – for example, distinctions in time and space. A rain dance may symbolize the difference between the rainy and the dry season. Douglas also argues that categories like pollution and cleanness, foods, animals, and parts of the body not only reflect but also serve to symbolize an individual's relationship to society, which one's relationship to the cosmos reflects and symbolizes in turn.[20] Taking for granted rather than, like Douglas, seeking to establish the primitive's capacity to symbolize and to categorize, Victor Turner similarly examines the use of categories like colors, trees, and bodily emissions to symbolize the same, but by creating as well as reflecting an individual's relationship to society and in turn the cosmos.[21] Although a fellow symbolic anthropologist, Geertz is concerned far less than Douglas or even Turner with categorizations as either symbols or the symbolized.

Against Lévy-Bruhl, Claude Lévi-Strauss[22] argues that primitives think no differently from moderns. They merely focus on the observable, qualitative aspects of phenomena rather than, like moderns, on the unobservable, quantitative ones: colors and sounds, not mass and length, faze them. Primitives secure a scientific knowledge of the world. Theirs is simply a "science of the concrete" rather than of the abstract. Indeed, even if they do not, like moderns, separate abstractions from concrete cases, they do express abstractions through concrete cases.

Moreover, their knowledge is basically taxonomic, so that primitives are quite capable of categorizing. In fact, their taxonomies take the form of oppositions, which, as the equivalent for Lévi-Strauss of contradictions, make primitives not only aware of contradictions but also intent on resolving them. Myths above all evince the austere, rigorous, logic-chopping nature of primitive thinking, which proves to be identical with that of nonmythic moderns. Where for Turner categorizing serves the existential end of "coping" with the world, for Douglas and especially Lévi-Strauss it serves the purely intellectual end of construing the world.[23]

The chief defender of Lévy-Bruhl against unfair charges, Edward Evans-Pritchard[24] nevertheless faults him for deeming primitive thinking "prelogical."

---

[20]On pollution and cleanness see Douglas (1970a; 1975:ch. 3); on foods, Douglas (1970a:ch. 3; 1973:ch. 3; 1975:ch. 16; 1982:ch. 4); on animals, Douglas (1970a:ch. 3; 1975:chs. 1-2, 16); on parts of the body, Douglas (1970a:ch. 7; 1973; 1975:chs. 4, 6).
[21]On colors see Turner (ch. 3); on trees, Turner (chs. 1-2); on bodily emissions, Turner (ch. 3).
[22]See Lévi-Strauss (1966:esp. ch. 1; 1955; 1970:Overture; 1978).
[23]On this difference see Segal (1984).
[24]See Evans-Pritchard (1934; 1937; 1956).

Where for Lévy-Bruhl primitive magic takes the place of science, for Evans-Pritchard it supplements proto-science: magic and proto-science coexist. To the Azande, the sheer physical features of a tree explain its ordinary, natural "behavior." Witchcraft, Evans-Pritchard's most famous example of supernatural causality, explains only unfortunate events involving the tree: why one day it falls on one person. For Lévy-Bruhl, by contrast, even events so regular and therefore so seemingly natural as birth, disease, and death get attributed to magic, a term that he, unlike Evans-Pritchard and others, uses broadly to encompass all supernatural causes (293-98).[25] While not oblivious to natural processes like pregnancy before birth and old age before death, primitives for Lévy-Bruhl deem them merely the means used by magicians to effect their ends.[26] Primitives do seek to explain only unusual events – fortunate as well as, like witchcraft for Evans-Pritchard, unfortunate – but they attribute all events to magic.[27] No room remains for chance.[28]

Lévy-Bruhl's claim that for primitives all causes are supernatural is more radical than even Tylor's or Frazer's. For Frazer and perhaps Tylor, the magician manipulates wholly natural laws, which operate on their own in his absence. Lévy-Bruhl seems closer to Frazer and Tylor on religion, in which there are no natural laws, only the decisions of gods. But for Lévy-Bruhl primitives initially believe in neither gods nor natural laws, just magicians.

Lévy-Bruhl grants that primitives must have practical, worldly skills to survive.[29] He simply distinguishes their quasi-scientific techniques from a scientific explanation of them. Primitives *explain* the efficacy of their practices either mystically or not at all.[30]

Shifting from the Azande to the Nuer, Evans-Pritchard contests Lévy-Bruhl's most striking evidence of prelogical mentality: statements that, for example, a cucumber is an ox and twins birds.[31] Lévy-Bruhl maintains that mystical representations override the senses, so that primitives somehow actually perceive, not just conceive, a cucumber as an ox. Evans-Pritchard denies that they do either. The Nuer, he asserts, are speaking only metaphorically: they are

---

[25]Though Tylor scarcely generalizes from the example, he, too, cites primitive peoples who attribute death to witchcraft exclusively (I:138).

[26]See Lévy-Bruhl (1985:263-87; 1923:ch. 1, 415-16, ch. 14; 1983:109, 139). Contrary to Douglas (1970b:xvi), Evans-Pritchard does not, like Lévy-Bruhl, say that the Azande attribute *all* deaths to witchcraft rather than to natural causes (1937:26, 77).

[27]See Lévy-Bruhl (1985:45, 67-68, 228-29, 245, 263-64, 293; 1923:437-38; 1983:16, 59-60).

[28]See Lévy-Bruhl (1923:43-50; 1935:56-58). For Evans-Pritchard, no room remains for chance in the case of only unfortunate events.

[29]See Lévy-Bruhl (1935:24, 92).

[30]See Lévy-Bruhl (1985:228-29; 1923:442-44; 1928:19-20).

[31]See Evans-Pritchard (1956:ch. 5). The example is Evans-Pritchard's, not Lévy-Bruhl's, but it is still apropos.

saying that a cucumber is sufficiently like an ox to serve as a substitute for it. Assuming that primitives never symbolize, Lévy-Bruhl wrongly takes their statements literally.

Rationality

Evans-Pritchard's responses to Lévy-Bruhl have inspired a continuing debate on "rationality" – a debate less in anthropology, where either relativism or universalism smugly reigns, than in philosophy. Notoriously hard to define,[32] the term gets raised about both beliefs and practices. Applied to beliefs, including values, "rational" usually means noncontradictory. Applied to practices, especially rituals, it typically means efficacious – more precisely, seemingly efficacious in the wake of the beliefs underlying the practices. Rationality has nothing to do with *truth*, as Evans-Pritchard's characterization of Azande witchcraft as rational yet false attests. Nor has it anything to do with *origin*, on which Lévy-Bruhl himself simply defers to Durkheim. Rationality does not, strictly, deal even with *function*. It deals instead with the *meaning* of beliefs and practices. As the terms *sometimes* get used, rationality is a matter of *interpretation*, not *explanation*.[33] To be rational is to be intelligible and coherent.

Since Lévy-Bruhl never says that primitive beliefs and practices are, on the basis of their mystical and prelogical premises, either unintelligible or incoherent, there might seem to be no debate. Yet his characterization of primitives as not merely mystical, itself neutral, but also prelogical seems absolutist: he seems to be judging them by modern standards.

Praising Evans-Pritchard for rejecting Lévy-Bruhl's assessment of primitives as prelogical, Peter Winch[34] castigates him for nevertheless deeming Azande witchcraft both false and at least partly irrational.[35] The issue of truth is not germane here, and Winch himself coincidentally drops it. As for rationality, Evans-Pritchard does note, for example, that despite their belief in an inherited "witchcraft-substance," the Azande rarely invoke heredity either to convict or to clear the accused. He concludes not, however, that they are illogical but that they fail to pursue the contradiction either between conviction and the innocence of one's kin or between acquittal and the guilt of one's kin.[36]

---

[32]See Lukes (207-8).

[33]For other uses of these confusing terms see Segal (1986; forthcoming₁; forthcoming₂).

[34]See Winch (1964).

[35]Most confusingly, Winch (1964) considers only *Witchcraft, Oracles and Magic among the Azande* (Evans-Pritchard [1937]), not *Nuer Religion* (Evans-Pritchard [1956]), in which Evans-Pritchard comes close to Winch.

[36]See Evans-Pritchard (1937:24-26, 127-28). Evans-Pritchard's other example of irrationality is the contradictoriness of the oracle, which is used to determine the presence of either witchcraft or sorcery: the oracle often either gives contradictory

Like the Boasians, Winch deems ethnocentric not the assumption of rationality worldwide but, on the contrary, the denial of it. Winch takes for granted that Azande witchcraft is, in its own terms, rational. He faults Evans-Pritchard for assuming that witchcraft is meant to be an explanation of unfortunate events. Understanding it in its own terms means grasping not just, as Evans-Pritchard does, its logic, or rules, but also the point of those rules. Doing so requires grasping what kind of activity, or Wittgensteinian "form of life," witchcraft is. Winch proposes that witchcraft is an existential rather than explanatory or even technological activity and that its point is therefore less to explain or even control events than to express, for example, powerlessness over one's life.[37]

Winch's denial that external criteria exist for judging Azande witchcraft seemingly makes him a relativist. But he vehemently denies that he is: both on the grounds that he acknowledges some external criteria[38] and, even more, on the grounds, not really germane, that the form of life exemplified by witchcraft is itself universal.[39] The criteria that make witchcraft rational are therefore not just idiosyncratic Azande ones, but they are still Azande ones.

Winch's writings have spawned an enormous debate over not the definition but the criteria of rationality.[40] For the absolutists, who consider the criteria entirely external and objective, primitive beliefs and practices invariably prove wholly irrational (Lévy-Bruhl), considerably less rational than modern ones but still rational (Tylor, Frazer, Evans-Pritchard [1937], Alasdair MacIntyre, Ernest Gellner, I. C. Jarvie, Joseph Agassi), or nearly as rational as modern ones (Durkheim, Robin Horton). For the relativists, who deem the criteria largely or entirely internal and "context dependent," primitive beliefs and practices invariably prove as fully rational as modern ones (Boas, Benedict, Herskovits, Evans-Pritchard [1956], Winch, Douglas [1975; 1979]). For those who consider

---

answers as to who is a witch or sorcerer or else gives noncontradictory answers contradicted by subsequent experience (1937:329-45). Yet contrary to Winch, Evans-Pritchard simultaneously cites rationalizations formulated by the Azande to resolve, not merely circumvent, contradictions.

[37]The example is mine, not Winch's. Most confusingly, Winch (1964), in switching his target from Evans-Pritchard to MacIntyre, switches from witchcraft to magic: where witchcraft deals with harm done by others, magic deals with controlling the forces of nature. Winch surely grants that Evans-Pritchard, as a pioneering social functionalist, recognizes the social function and therefore context of witchcraft. Winch must be criticizing Evans-Pritchard for missing the existential function and context, not for limiting himself to the explanatory function.

[38]See Winch (1964:308, 318). But see also Winch (1964:315, 317). See also Lukes (1973:233).

[39]See Winch (1964:322).

[40]On the rationality debate see, for example, Wilson, Borger and Cioffi (167-230), Horton and Finnegan (230-305), Benn and Mortimore, Dallmayr and McCarthy, Hollis and Lukes.

the criteria both external and internal, primitive beliefs and practices prove more rational than irrational (Steven Lukes). Finally, for the noncognitivists the issue of rationality is irrelevant: primitive beliefs and practices, like their modern religious counterparts, are primarily expressions of the meaningfulness of life rather than efforts either to explain or to control the world (Edmund Leach, Raymond Firth, John Beattie, Douglas [1970a; 1973], Susanne Langer).

In his posthumously published *Notebooks*[41] Lévy-Bruhl abandons his view of primitives as prelogical, though not as mystical: primitives remain different from moderns. He does not, like Evans-Pritchard, say that the Bororo, in deeming Trumai tribesmen fish, are merely comparing the Trumai with fish. He does, however, say that the Trumai are fish supernaturally, not physically. Their "fishness" complements, not contradicts, their ordinary, physical humanness. Primitives thus recognize, not miss, at least the distinction between the supernatural and the natural. Still, the theoretical issue Lévy-Bruhl first raised remains: how *would* one interpret seemingly irrational beliefs and practices?

REFERENCES

BENEDICT, RUTH
1934   *Patterns of Culture*. Boston: Houghton Mifflin.

BENN, S. I., AND G. W. MORTIMORE, EDS.
1976   *Rationality and the Social Sciences*. London and Boston: Routledge & Kegan Paul.

BIDNEY, DAVID
1953a   *Theoretical Anthropology*. First ed. New York: Columbia University Press.

1953b   "The Concept of Value in Modern Anthropology." In *Anthropology Today*, ed. A. L. Kroeber, pp. 682-99. Chicago: University of Chicago Press.

1968   "Cultural Relativism." In *International Encyclopedia of the Social Sciences* 3:543-47.

BORGER, ROBERT, AND FRANK CIOFFI, EDS.
1970   *Explanation in the Behavioural Sciences*. Cambridge, Eng.: Cambridge University Press.

CAZENEUVE, JEAN
1972   *Lucien Lévy-Bruhl*. Tr. Peter Rivière. Oxford: Blackwell.

[41]See Lévy-Bruhl (1975:5-12, 19-22, 38-42, 45-50, 125-29, 136-38). As Horton says: "Thus, although his final picture of primitive thought allows a good deal of common sense in alongside the mystical, ... his characterization of the mystical remains unrepentantly the same" (257-58).

DALLMAYR, FRED R., AND THOMAS A. MCCARTHY, EDS.
1977   *Understanding and Social Inquiry.* Notre Dame, Ind.: University of Notre Dame Press.

DOUGLAS, MARY
1970a   *Purity and Danger.* Baltimore: Penguin Books. Original publ.: London: Routledge & Kegan Paul, 1966.

1970b   "Introduction: Thirty Years after *Witchcraft, Oracles and Magic.*" In *Witchcraft Confessions & Accusations,* ed. Douglas, pp. xiii-xxxvii. London: Tavistock.

1973   *Natural Symbols.* Second ed. New York: Vintage Books. Original publ. of first ed.: New York: Pantheon, 1970.

1975   *Implicit Meanings.* London and Boston: Routledge & Kegan Paul.

1979   "World View and the Core." In *Philosophical Disputes in the Social Sciences,* ed. S. C. Brown, pp. 177-87. Sussex, Eng.: Harvester Press; Atlantic Highlands, N.J.: Humanities Press.

1980   *Evans-Pritchard.* Sussex, Eng.: Harvester Press.

1982   *In the Active Voice.* London and Boston: Routledge & Kegan Paul.

DURKHEIM, ÉMILE
1965   *The Elementary Forms of the Religious Life.* Tr. Joseph Ward Swain. New York: Free Press. Original publ. of tr.: London: Allen & Unwin, 1915.

1975   Review of Lévy-Bruhl, *How Natives Think,* and Durkheim, *The Elementary Forms of the Religious Life.* In *Durkheim on Religion,* ed. W. S. F. Pickering and trs. Jacqueline Redding and Pickering, pp. 169-73. London and Boston: Routledge & Kegan Paul.

DURKHEIM, ÉMILE, AND MARCEL MAUSS
1963   *Primitive Classification.* Ed. and tr. Rodney Needham. Chicago: University of Chicago Press.

EVANS-PRITCHARD, E. E.
1934   "Lévy-Bruhl's Theory of Primitive Mentality." *University of Egypt Bulletin of the Faculty of Arts* 2 (May):1-41.

1937   *Witchcraft, Oracles and Magic among the Azande.* Oxford: Clarendon Press.

1956   *Nuer Religion.* Oxford: Clarendon Press.

FRAZER, JAMES G.
1922   *The Golden Bough.* One-vol. abridgment. London: Macmillan.

GEERTZ, CLIFFORD
1968   *Islam Observed.* New Haven, Conn.: Yale University Press.

1973   *The Interpretation of Cultures.* New York: Basic Books.

1983   *Local Knowledge*. New York: Basic Books.

1984   "Anti Anti-Relativism." *American Anthropologist* 86 (June):263-78.

HERSKOVITS, MELVILLE J.
1948   *Man and His Works*. New York: Knopf.

HOLLIS, MARTIN, AND STEVEN LUKES, EDS.
1982   *Rationality and Relativism*. Cambridge, Mass.: MIT Press.

HORTON, ROBIN
1973   "Lévy-Bruhl, Durkheim and the Scientific Revolution." In Horton and Finnegan (249-305).

HORTON, ROBIN, AND RUTH FINNEGAN, EDS.
1973   *Modes of Thought*. London: Faber & Faber.

KLUCKHOHN, CLYDE
1949   *Mirror for Man*. New York: Whittlesey House.

1962   *Culture and Behavior*. Ed. Richard Kluckhohn. New York: Free Press.

LÉVI-STRAUSS, CLAUDE
1955   "The Structural Study of Myth." *Journal of American Folklore* 68 (October-December):428-44.

1966   *The Savage Mind*. Tr. not given. Chicago: University of Chicago Press.

1970   *The Raw and the Cooked. Introduction to a Science of Mythology*, vol. I. Trs. John and Doreen Weightman. New York: Harper Torchbooks.

1978   *Myth and Meaning*. Toronto: University of Toronto Press.

LÉVY-BRUHL, LUCIEN
1923   *Primitive Mentality*. Tr. Lilian A. Clare. London: Allen & Unwin.

1928   *The "Soul" of the Primitive*. Tr. Lilian A. Clare. London: Allen & Unwin.

1935   *Primitives and the Supernatural*. Tr. Lilian A. Clare. London: Allen & Unwin.

1938   *L' Expérience mystique et les symboles chez les primitifs*. Paris: Alcan.

1952   "A Letter to E. E. Evans-Pritchard." Tr. Donald G. MacRae. *British Journal of Sociology* 3 (June):117-23.

1975   *The Notebooks on Primitive Mentality*. Tr. Peter Rivière. New York: Harper.

1983   *Primitive Mythology*. Tr. Brian Elliott. St. Lucia: University of Queensland Press.

1985   *How Natives Think*. Tr. Lilian A. Clare. Intro. C. Scott Littleton. Princeton, N.J.: Princeton University Press. Original publ. of tr.: London: Allen & Unwin, 1926.

LINTON, RALPH
1952   "Universal Ethical Principles: An Anthropological View." In *Moral Principles of Action*, ed. Ruth Nanda Anshen, pp. 645-60. New York: Harper.

LUKES, STEVEN
1971   "Some Problems about Rationality." In Wilson (194-213).

1973   "On the Social Determination of Truth." In Horton and Finnegan (230-48).

RADIN, PAUL
1933   *Social Anthropology*. New York: McGraw-Hill.

SEGAL, ROBERT A.
1980   "In Defense of Mythology: The History of Modern Theories of Myth." *Annals of Scholarship* 1 (Winter):3-49.

1984   "The Application of Symbolic Anthropology to Religions of the Greco-Roman World." *Religious Studies Review* 10 (July):216-23. Reprinted in revised form in the present book as ch. 12.

1986   "Response to Blasi and Nelson." *Journal for the Scientific Study of Religion* 25 (September):369-72. Reprinted in revised form in the present book as ch. 6.

forth-   "Comment on Steven Kepnes' 'Bridging the Gap Between Understanding
coming₁   and Explanation Approaches to the Study of Religion'." *Journal for the Scientific Study of Religion*.

forth-   "Interpreting and Explaining Religion: Geertz and Durkheim."
coming₂   *Soundings*.

SPIRO, MELFORD E.
1978   "Culture and Human Nature." In *The Making of Psychological Anthropology*, ed. George D. Spindler, pp. 330-60. Berkeley: University of California Press.

1982   *Oedipus in the Trobriands*. Chicago: University of Chicago Press.

1984   "Some reflections on cultural determinism and relativism with special reference to emotion and reason." In *Culture theory*, eds. Richard A. Shweder and Robert A. LeVine, pp. 323-46. Cambridge, Eng.: Cambridge University Press.

1986   "Cultural Relativism and the Future of Anthropology." *Cultural Anthropology* 1 (August):259-86.

TURNER, VICTOR W.
1967   *The Forest of Symbols*. Ithaca, N.Y.: Cornell University Press.

TYLOR, EDWARD B.
1958   *Primitive Culture*. 2 vols. New York: Harper Torchbooks. Vol. I is retitled *The Origins of Culture* and vol. II retitled *Religion in Primitive Culture*. Original publ. of first ed.: London: Murray, 1871.

WILSON, BRYAN R., ED.
1971   *Rationality*. New York: Harper Torchbooks.

WINCH, PETER
1958   *The Idea of a Social Science and Its Relation to Philosophy*. London: Routledge & Kegan Paul.

1964   "Understanding a Primitive Society." *American Philosophical Quarterly* 1 (October):307-24.

Index

Agassi, Joseph 175

Alston, William P. 82

anima 91-92

anthropology, anthropologist 1, 3, 13, 16, 17, 54, 110, 119, 137, 147, 149, 167-168, 174

Aphrodite 155, 160-163

Augustine 93

Beattie, John 176

Bellah, Robert N. 2, 14, 17, 57, 60-61, 63, 67, 68, 110, 123, 126-130

Benedict, Ruth 167, 175

Berger, Peter L. 2, 14, 17, 57-61, 67, 68, 78, 79-80, 82, 83, 90, 100, 110, 123-126, 128-129, 131

Blasi, Anthony J. 58, 67-71

Bleeker, C. Jouco 19

Boas, Franz 167, 175

Braithwaite, R. B. 18, 27

Brown, Norman O. 60, 127

Buber, Martin 60, 127

Bultmann, Rudolf 21-22, 91, 128

Burridge, Kenelm 54

cargo cults 47, 52-54

cause 14-15, 25, 43-44, 52, 58, 67-71, 75-83, 87-94, 95, 100-104, 111, 113, 118, 141, 173

Christianity 47, 63, 91-93, 101, 102, 113, 155, 156-158

civil religion 61, 129

classification 61, 130-131, 150, 151, 171-172

collective representations 169-171

Collingwood, R. G. 15-17, 22, 68-69

comparative method 13-14, 15, 16, 19, 20

comparative religion 19

consequential reductionism 60, 127-129

creed 112, 115, 122, 125, 126, 137, 155

cult 48, 113, 116-118, 120

cultural system 60, 120-121, 123

Demeter 163

de-sociologizing 109-132

dietary laws 61, 130, 156-158, 159

Dilthey, Wilhelm 15, 22

division of labor 113

Douglas, Mary 2, 3, 57, 61, 67, 68, 90, 110, 123, 129-131, 137, 138, 149-158, 160-161, 171-172, 175, 176

Dray, William H. 15, 16, 68

Durkheim, Émile 57, 60, 61, 83, 99, 100, 104-105, 110-116, 117, 118, 119, 122, 125, 127-130, 137, 138, 143, 148, 149, 154, 155, 171, 174, 175